Friendship for Virtue

Friendship for Virtue

KRISTJÁN KRISTJÁNSSON

OXFORD
UNIVERSITY PRESS

Great Clarendon Street, Oxford, OX2 6DP,
United Kingdom

Oxford University Press is a department of the University of Oxford.
It furthers the University's objective of excellence in research, scholarship,
and education by publishing worldwide. Oxford is a registered trade mark of
Oxford University Press in the UK and in certain other countries

© Kristján Kristjánsson 2022

The moral rights of the author have been asserted

First Edition published in 2022

Impression: 1

Published in the United States of America by Oxford University Press
198 Madison Avenue, New York, NY 10016, United States of America

British Library Cataloguing in Publication Data

Data available

Library of Congress Control Number: 2022936575

ISBN 978–0–19–286426–0

DOI: 10.1093/oso/9780192864260.001.0001

Printed and bound by
CPI Group (UK) Ltd, Croydon, CR0 4YY

Table of Contents

Acknowledgements

I began work on this book during a few weeks' lay-off from work in August 2018 because of a sudden illness, the details of which I recount in the Preface. I finished the manuscript much earlier than I had anticipated when the lockdown during the coronavirus crisis in 2020–2022 gave those academics who did not have young children to take care of at home an unprecedented opportunity to work on their own research. So these two clouds both had silver linings for me personally.

I am grateful to my current and past colleagues at the Jubilee Centre for their advice, support and comments on earlier drafts of many of the following chapters. I would especially like to single out David Carr, Randall Curren, Robert C. Roberts, Candace Vogler and—obviously—the Centre's director James Arthur. Various other scholars have offered constructive comments on sections of the present book. I am particularly grateful to Blaine Fowers who offered extensive feedback on parts of Chapters 1 and 2 and Talbot Brewer who advised on Chapter 2. I am indebted to the John Templeton Foundation for funding the work of the Jubilee Centre. Peter Momtchiloff at OUP deserves thanks for being unreservedly supportive of the book project throughout its gestation. Two anonymous reviewers provided generously extended feedback, which was much appreciated. I am in particular indebted to 'Adviser A' who provided no less than three rounds of the most thorough, suggestive but yet sympathetic comments that I have ever received on any manuscript. Dr Matthew Collins in the Jubilee Centre provided invaluable editorial assistance and also gave me some invaluable tips about literacy sources. Dr Kristian Guttesen conscientiously helped me compile the index.

I thankfully acknowledge permissions to recycle material from the following articles: 'Ten Un-Aristotelian Reasons for the Instability of Aristotelian Character Friendships', *Journal for the Theory of Social Behaviour*, 49(1), 2019; 'Filtering Friendship through *Phronesis*: "One Thought too Many"?', *Philosophy*, 95(1) 2020; 'Aristotelian Character Friendship as a "Method" of Moral Education', *Studies in Philosophy and Education*, 39(4), 2020; 'Grounding Deep Friendships: Reconciling the Moralized and Aestheticized Views', *Journal of Philosophical Research*, 45(1), 2020; 'Learning from Friends and Terminating Friendships: Retrieving Friendship as a Moral Educational Concept', *Educational Theory*, 70(2), 2020; 'The Moral Value of Aristotelian Friendships for Utility, with an Online Example', *Amity: The Journal of Friendship Studies*, 7(1), 2021; 'Online Aristotelian Character Friendship as an Augmented Form of Penpalship', *Philosophy & Technology*, 34(2), 2021.

Preface: Motivation, Four Aims and a Roadmap

This book aims for a characterological and educational retrieval of the virtue of friendship, as seen through the lens of updated and applied Aristotelianism. It takes readers on a journey, through scholarship old and new, that will hopefully be enlightening and thought-provoking—albeit not necessarily always reassuring or therapeutic.

It is difficult to write about friendship without taking academic sides; and this opening paragraph already contained at least two potentially controversial assumptions: that there is something distinctively 'characterological' about friendship and that it is a 'virtue'. All I can do at this point is to promise readers that these and other controversial assumption will be gradually justified in the course of the following chapters.

'Oh, no, not one more book about friendship', some people are bound to grumble when they read the blurb. They would seem to have a point. The self-help shelves in bookstores are stacked with books about friendship; *PsycInfo* registers up to 500 psychological research articles per year with friendship as an index term; and the philosophical output on friendship—within which the present work will be earmarked—is also copious. What is more, some of the philosophical writings about the subject are rare treats, both in terms of passion and presentation (see e.g. Sherman, 1987; Brewer, 2005; Nehamas, 2016). The topic of friendship seems to bring out the best in philosophers, at least in terms of style and gusto.

I will be arguing in what follows that the current literatures contain some salient lacunae that stand in need of amelioration. However, that is what writers always say in order to carve out a niche for their own work and to ramp up interest among readers. So rather than elaborating upon my academic aims here at the outset, let me say something first about my personal motivation, as well as offering some initial, rhapsodic observations about the book's subject matter and approach.

I began work on this project in August 2018. That was not a coincidence. In that month I suddenly lost, irrevocably overnight, most of the hearing in my left ear through a nasty viral attack. Losing hearing in one ear may not sound like such a traumatic event, at least not as long as the other ear remains intact. However, loss of this kind has some nasty side-effects regarding physical and psychological balance, because the brain gets very confused for a long time when one of its standard sources of stimuli is thwarted. My life was in many ways turned upside down, significantly enough—lo and behold—for me to have to rely heavily on my network of friends to keep my head above water. To my surprise, the greatest support in this case was not garnered from my closest friends, their valuable contribution notwithstanding, but rather from new and less personal friends that I acquired by joining online support groups of sudden-sensorineural-hearing-loss sufferers. These 'utility friends', as Aristotle would have called them, gave me the inspiration and strength to 'hang in there'; and after gradually regaining my psycho-physical balance, I have been able to pay some of that debt back by helping new sufferers.

I say more about those experiences and elicit some of their academic implications in Chapter 6. Suffice it to say here that soon after my hearing-loss event, I decided to write a book about friendship from the perspective that I know best: virtue ethics. I quickly realised that although much has been written about friendship from that perspective, mostly under the stellar guidance of Aristotle, not everything has been said that needs to be said; hence the perceived lacunae that I mentioned above. I also decided to write a book that would, at least in part, be 'practical' as well as what philosophers call 'alethic'. Those who have read any of my previous work will know that I am not the most patient and dedicated recluse in the ivory tower of pure philosophy. Furthermore, there seems to be something totally unnecessary—if not simply perverse—about pitching a virtue ethical treatise on friendship solely at a charmed circle of fellow philosophers, when even the most minimal concerns with readability and practical application can make it accessible to a larger audience. At the same time, such a practical turn requires paying attention to a wider variety of sources than simply the products of philosophical doyens, mostly long gone. I therefore draw on a variety of contemporary social scientific and literary sources also and attempt, in particular, to attend to the educational ramifications of friendship, in line with my interest in the philosophy of education and how it can impact upon school practice. In a nutshell, I hope that this book will be read not only by philosophers but also by social scientists and educators interested in friendship and, indeed, by intellectually minded readers without any academic commitments to friendship as a research topic but simply keen to understand better this complex human relationship.

All that said, I do not pretend to have written, or even tried to write, a popular self-help book about friendship. I would not know how to write such a book even if I wanted to. Working on this project helped me get to grips with my own views on friendship and its value, and also to identify my limitations as a friend, of which I had been vaguely aware before but had not been able to analyse sufficiently. Although I use myself as a 'case study' at a few junctures in what follows, in what could perhaps be called a self-therapeutic way, and readers may similarly be able to see themselves in clearer light through some of what will be said, these factors do not license the book for inclusion on self-help shelves. After reading through some popular work of that kind, however, during the course of my research (see e.g. Vernon, 2010; Barnard, 2011; Grayling, 2013—all insightful in different ways), my previously negative view of this genre has softened. Moral philosophers tend to throw off, with the most presumptuous and unnerving hauteur, all their usual fair-mindedness when it comes to the self-help literature, and they might be tempted here to mention Dale Carnegie's notorious guide on *How to Win Friends and Influence People* (1936) as a case in point. Nevertheless, there is a sense in which, say, Aristotle's *Nicomachean Ethics* is closer in style and remit to some of the best contemporary self-help sources available on living well and choosing wisely than to the standard obscure monograph written by a latter-day academic philosopher.

One thing on which all the academic and popular sources on friendship tend to agree is that friendship is a good—if perhaps not an unalloyed good. This may be put either solemnly and seriously in terms of the 'things learned and shared' with friends, 'of the burdens halved', 'the sorrows comforted' and 'the laughter enjoyed' (Grayling, 2013, p. 2); or sarcastically and light-heartedly in terms of all 'the precious time you'll squander on someone else's calamities and fuck-ups' (Barnard, 2011, p. 12; citing a character from a Richard Ford novel). We encounter in Chapter 1 Aristotle's rosy-eyed view of friendship as the greatest external good and an important reinforcer of other values also (although not in itself an overriding value), as well as Cicero's further gilding of the lily by seeing friendship as trumping all other values. To be sure, in the background lurk concerns, from within both philosophy and religion, about friendship's potentially subversive role with regard to demands of impartiality and proper perspective on 'the great scheme of things' in the world (e.g. undue favouring of 'buddies'; cronyism; violations of equity concerns); and psychologists sometimes refer to the sense of ambiguity that friendships may engender. Nevertheless, foes of friendship—even modest friendship sceptics—are few and far between, and the argumentative onus is clearly on those who wish to unseat the generally positive view of this unique human relationship.

The old saw that the Western philosophical tradition consists in little more than a series of footnotes to Plato and Aristotle makes its presence felt with considerable force in philosophical writings about friendship. Those almost invariably take Aristotle's extensive analysis as their starting point—either for commendation or critique—to the extreme point, sometimes, of seeming to be cluttered by his baggage. Mitias is not exaggerating, therefore, when he says that Aristotle's analysis of friendship has become 'the fountain' from which all subsequent discussions derive their inspiration (Mitias, 2012, p. 77). Even those accounts that seem to depart most radically from Aristotle's, for example by replacing his search for morally virtuous qualities in a friend with that of aesthetically appealing qualities (Nehamas, 2016), tend to share certain structural similarities with Aristotle's that allow for potential reconciliations (as I argue in Chapter 4).

When discussing the ancient Greek 'baggage' in contemporary accounts of friendship, it is *de rigueur* to dwell briefly on the difference between *philia* (translated as 'love' or 'friendship') and current notions of 'friendship'. In ancient Greek, *philia* could be used for any form of non-erotic love, including parental affection (although the Greeks also had a more specific word for that: *storge*). In some modern languages, the equation of 'love' and 'friendship' will sound alien. In my own native language, Icelandic, the locution 'loving a friend' ('*að elska vin*') would, for example, sound mawkish or erotically laden. However, given the increasingly bloated use of the word 'love' in current English, where the locution 'loving a friend' seems to have no odd connotations, the semantic differences between English and ancient Greek should perhaps be the least of our worries in what follows. In any case, I simply assume, for convenience of exposition, that the term *philia* is correctly understood by present readers, and I try to pursue my line of argument without special pleading with respect to Aristotle's use of language. For instance, I explain in Chapter 1 why, for most present purposes, readers can substitute Aristotle's special concept of a 'character friend' by simply a 'close' or 'best friend' and may thus reflect on the pros and cons of Aristotle's argument without buying into all his specialised conceptual repertoire. This book is definitely not aimed at Aristotelian aficionados only, nor written as an exercise in ancient Greek scholarship.

The vagaries of language aside, deeper worries about the historical incommensurability of ideas may obtrude. Stern-Gillet (1995, p. 4) thus warns readers against the 'shock' they will experience when reading about Aristotle's views, as alien as they may seem from modern concerns. Konstan (1997, pp. 2–5) disagrees completely and argues that the largely independent value that the ancients placed on friendship will resonate much better with us moderns than it would have with our medieval counterparts, steeped in an overbearing religious tradition. This is notably the same Konstan who has elsewhere, in my view, been overly accepting of the socio-linguistic uniqueness of the ancient world (2006, criticised in Kristjánsson, 2018)—which gives us further impetus for taking his view seriously here.

I do not wish, however, to brush all concerns about historical relativity aside. Talbot Brewer (in personal correspondence) has kindly helped me to think through some of the differences between contemporary Western society and Aristotle's Athens regarding the formation and sustaining of friendships. One complication in our era is the modernist obsession with 'authenticity' as a life quest: a quest that encourages continuous self-reinventions which may be inimical to stable, life-long friendships. The demands of authenticity may induce me, for instance, to leave behind old friends if they do fit neatly anymore into the niche that I am carving out for myself in line with 'who I really am now'. We might also want to attend to contemporary sociological work on the variety of roles we are pressed into playing on a daily basis in our lives, and the way these change over time as we take on new tasks. We would need to think about role identities and their place in modern life, about precariousness in the workplace, contemporary immigration and geographic mobility, and about how these experiences change our sense of what does and does not count as a sensible life trajectory with respect to the nature of our friendships. These would be topics large enough for another book project. I simply register them here in anticipation of the objection that the following discussions of some of the perceived strengths and weaknesses of Aristotle's account are suspiciously ahistorical.

There is a tendency, especially in the popular literature on friendship, to draw copiously on literary sources. I follow suit in Chapters 5 and 8, for instance. Given the depth of intimacy that a good novel or a profound poem can convey, and given that friendship is all about intimacy of a certain type, one might be forgiven for assuming that the greatest illumination about the intricacies of friendship will be gained by a close study of world literature. To my surprise—astonishment even—two of the most astute writers about friendship in modernity, the author C. S. Lewis and the philosopher Alexander Nehamas, both make the point, however, that novels and poems typically do not, or even cannot, capture the essence of friendship. Lewis (1960, p. 87) claims that he 'cannot remember' any recent poem or 'any novel' celebrating friendship. Nehamas makes what he himself characterises as a 'radical' and 'sweeping' claim that there is hardly 'a novel of the first rank that takes friendship as its central subject' (2016, pp. 83–7). He mentions just one true counter-example, Flaubert's *Bouvard and Pécuchet*, but that happens to be a novel that takes a bleak view of friendships.

In contrast to the view of these two thinkers, I would venture to make the equally radical and sweeping claim that, in addition to erotic love, strife and the pains of growing up, friendship constitutes nothing less than one of the major themes of world literature, exemplified in such gems, for instance, as the *Icelandic Sagas*, *Adventures of Huckleberry Finn*, *Of Mice and Men*, *Lord of the Rings* and the *Harry Potter* series. Some fictional friendships, such as that between Sherlock Holmes and Doctor Watson, have even become so famous as to overshadow any real-life friendships in terms of popular and academic attention being paid to them. A leitmotif in many of the Icelandic Sagas is the inner conflict of the hero who has to choose between the strict duties of kinship, in a society without a centralised executive power, and attachments to a close friend, often a blood-brother. This agonising psycho-moral disunification, which speaks so starkly against Alasdair MacIntyre's misguided interpretation of Saga morality in *After Virtue* (1981, chap. 10) as depicting socially conditioned protagonists without hidden moral depths, touches the value of friendship on the raw.

My own favourite example of friendship from the Sagas is that of Arinbjörn with Egill in *Egil's Saga*, made more vivid and memorable by the fact that the hero (and in some ways the anti-hero) Egill was not an easy person to befriend. While, on the one hand, a profound poet and cartographer of human frailties, he was, on the other hand, a vulgar ruffian. Arinbjörn's ingenuous efforts in persuading Egill to compose his poem 'Head Ransom' to, literally, save his head from the wrath of the king Erik Bloodaxe, constitute the prototype of true acts of friendship. In *The Lord of the Rings*, few readers will be left untouched by the friendship between the hobbits Frodo Baggins and Samwise Gamgee. They are not warrior heroes and never display more than a superficial intellectual understanding of the momentous task assigned to them, but their friendship meets all the criteria of close friendship (Juričková, 2021). They are completely dedicated to each other and love each other dearly for who they are deep down. I could go on and on with literary examples. In addition to novels, there is the famous Viking poem of *Hávamál*, which many people consider to enshrine the ethical code of the Viking Age. I return to that in Chapter 8.

At all events, when the views of as eminent thinkers as Lewis and Nehamas seem so counter-intuitive, one is tempted to proffer some kind of reinterpretation. Perhaps the key to their understanding lies in Nehamas's observation that where novels and poems fail is in not being very good at depicting in interesting ways the mundane and repetitive modes of conduct that characterise true friendships (2016, p. 98). Think of all the meaningful silences and the long, meandering walks that friends often engage in. Or just helping each other paint a shed. That is not the stuff that novels and poems are typically made of. This is why Nehamas considers drama and films (such as *Thelma and Louise* that he spends a long time analysing) better vehicles for artistic insights about friendship.

I understand this point and I agree that the events crystallising the friendship between Arinbjörn and Egill or Bilbo and Sam are perhaps not the sort of events that represent and reinforce most people's friendships. However, art has always cast light on human affairs and vicissitudes by exaggerating them and thus bringing them into sharper relief. For the mundane acts of friendship, a film may perhaps project a better mirror than a novel. But friendship sometimes requires majestic efforts. In novels and poems, friends often move mountains for one another. In my view, we need the awe-inspiring and exceptional, as well as the mundane and repetitive, to comprehend fully as complex a phenomenon as friendship.

This book has *four main academic aims*. I explain those briefly below as well as offering a roadmap of all the following chapters. Call them spoilers if you like.

As already mentioned, Aristotelianism is in vogue at the moment. Voluminous bodies of literature continue to be published on Aristotelian and Aristotle-inspired virtue ethics, not only within mainstream moral philosophy but also within various practical fields of moral psychology, applied professional ethics and moral/character education. That said, these literatures are highly selective and some of the less palatable parts of Aristotle's moral teachings, by today's standards, tend to be conveniently overlooked. Indeed, the greatest portion of these literatures is reconstructive (or 'neo-Aristotelian' in some sense) rather than exegetical. This book is also reconstructive rather than exegetical *vis-à-vis* Aristotle's own voice: respectful but not deferential. For example, I do not shirk engagement with various often overlooked shortcomings of his friendship writings.

Notably, no less than two of the ten books of the *Nicomachean Ethics* and nearly a third of the *Eudemian Ethics* are devoted to the topic of friendship. Aristotle thus dedicates more space to friendship than to any other virtue. While these analyses tend to be acknowledged as a cardinal element of Aristotelian virtue ethics as a whole, they have not excited as lively an interest in philosophical circles as one might have expected. In other words, a lingering sense remains that the space devoted to the subject of friendship—in particular in its most developed and virtue ethically relevant kind referred to by Aristotle as friendship for character or virtue—is not proportionate to the importance accorded to it in Aristotle's own moral theory.

This concern may seem misplaced given that reams of scholarship have been written about the concept of friendship in Aristotle, stretching back into the early days of virtue ethics (see e.g. Cooper, 1977), and given that his famous tripartite substantive and normative classification of friendships (into those for utility, pleasure and character/virtue; see Section 1.1) has set the terms of most philosophical friendship discourses for 2,300 years. However, what stands out is that the philosophical debate about Aristotelian friendships is often uncharacteristically narrow and textual. Whereas other key virtue concepts in Aristotle tend to be reconstructed quite liberally by neo-Aristotelians in order to be more relatable to modern concerns—and typically brought to bear on the general aim of the good life as *eudaimonia* (Kristjánsson, 2020)—the discussion of friendship has remained mostly interpretative and domain-specific. Even when the aim of the proposed inquiry is moral rather than historical, large questions about the relative weight of friendship in the good life tend to be elided. For example, there is a real scarcity of papers on friendship and *phronesis*, offering clues about how Aristotle's intellectual meta-virtue of *phronesis* (practical wisdom) ideally adjudicates the value of friendship *vis-à-vis* other Aristotelian values and virtues, especially in cases of conflict within different friendships or between friendship and competing virtues (as explained further in Chapter 3; yet see Salkever, 2008, on the role of friendship in 'the *prohairetic* life': the life of overall wise choices).

The *first aim* of the present book is to give the virtue of friendship the pride of place it deserves in contemporary Aristotle-inspired virtue ethics. While most of the discussion will centre on Aristotle's 'complete' type of friendship (namely, friendship for character or virtue), I also argue, in Chapter 6, for the role of 'incomplete' utility friendships in the good life. In Chapter 4, I contrast Aristotle's moralised view of the best type of friendship with Montaigne's and Alexander Nehamas's aestheticised view, according to which one is drawn towards friends for reasons that have to do with aesthetic rather than moral appreciation, but point out how Aristotle's individuality-adjusted view of virtue can help accommodate some of the insights of an aestheticised view. Given Aristotle's own (arguably) aestheticised view of the ethical as aiming for the noble or beautiful (*kalon*), and his lack of a modern concept of 'the moral', this distinction may seem to be misplaced here; but I explain in Chapter 4 why it is not.

I also relate the discussion of complete friendships, in Chapter 7, to much-debated online forms of friendships. That chapter adds ammunition to recent arguments for the possibility of online character friendships in the Aristotelian sense. It does so, first, by examining recent arguments for and against online friendships as virtue enhancing and finding the latter arguments wanting. It does so, secondly, by exploring sustained email correspondence or *epalship* as a potential venue for the creation, development and maintaining of character friendships, and by drawing an analogy with a historically famous example of *penpalship*: that forged between Voltaire and Catherine the Great. I argue in Chapter 7 that epalships allow for various technological extensions in today's cyberworld that were not available to Voltaire and Catherine, and that augmented with those extensions there is even more reason for considering epalships, rather than traditional penpalships, to potentially make the grade as character friendships.

The current state of play (or rather lack of a serious state of play) regarding friendship in current substantive moral discourse is not unique to Aristotelian ethics. Friendship has had a precarious moral status in modernity that is historically well-documented and has to do with the dominance of a Christian world-view during the medieval period and well beyond Enlightenment times: a trajectory that I chart briefly in Section 1.4. While the great medieval thinkers retrieved, accommodated and 'infused' most of Plato's and Aristotle's basic tenets about the virtues, they remained sceptical of any insights that implied elitism, favouritism or differential treatment based on people's allegedly unequal claims to moral worth. Christianity is, after all, at its core an egalitarian moral system, within which one is meant to love all one's 'neighbours' equally through *agape* rather than through the favouritism-tainted lens of *philia*. This assumption was then subsumed within the great secular systems of morality that developed during the Enlightenment and have held sway until the present day: Kantian deontology and utilitarian consequentialism. Although *agape* fell by the wayside as an isolated Christian virtue, what remained was the requirement of *impartiality*: of treating all people equally as ends in themselves or at least as equally worthy of moral consideration.

Now, a worry hovering over both Kantianism and consequentialism from the very beginning was their lack of 'minimal psychological realism' (Flanagan, 1991): of not being feasibly attainable for beings like us. This worry was eventually crystallised in Bernard Williams's integrity objection (1981), whereby he suggested that consequentialists (and deontologists, *mutatis mutandis*, through their reliance on the categorical imperative) were doomed to having 'one thought too many', by being forced, in times of moral conflict, to subject the obvious natural choice to prioritise the needs of a close friend, over those of a stranger, to a theoretical decision procedure before coming up with the 'right' answer. Such requirements of cold-blooded calculation rob us, according to Williams, of psycho-moral reasons by which to live at all. It is standardly assumed that virtue ethics is somehow immune to this objection. Chapter 3 explores this assumption and finds it wanting in various respects. Virtue ethics filters friendship through *phronesis* and thus inserts an extra thought into the mechanism in question. To escape Williams's curse, the only way is to argue that the extra thought required by virtue ethics is not 'one thought too many'. This is precisely what I argue in Chapter 3. The presumed advantage of virtue ethics must lie in the content of its filter of critical decision making (namely, here, *phronesis*) rather than the filter's non-existence.

One of the reasons virtue ethics is typically considered to be better placed than Kantianism and consequentialism to counter William's integrity objection is that it adopts psychological realism in Flanagan's above sense (or, more specifically, empirically friendly naturalism) about what makes people flourish or wilt. Yet virtue ethicists who have written about friendship have rarely tried to integrate their theories with actual contemporary social-science work on friendship. This has partly to do with how the psychological friendship literature within social science has developed in anti-Aristotelian directions. As we see in Section 1.5, this literature remains mired in a genre that overall renounces the normative and embraces the descriptive, and one that has scant understanding of the notion of intrinsic (as opposed to extrinsic or even just instrumental) value. The standard ploy in friendship research in psychology is, for instance, to offer some generic characterisation of friendship, such as that friendship is a reciprocal relationship where there is mutual liking and enjoyment spent in each other's company. People's own specifications of their close or best friendships, then, tend to be taken at face value and the question becomes not what grounds them morally, but rather what 'provisions' such friendships offer and how those provisions are correlated with significant psycho-social variables.

These significant differences from an Aristotelian approach notwithstanding, it is incumbent on Aristotelians—because of Aristotle's empirically friendly naturalism, as an incarnation of psychological realism (see Section 1.3)—to try to find an accommodation between psychological findings and philosophical theory, through some sort of a reflective equilibrium. The *second aim* of the present work is therefore to delve into the social-science literature and explore to what extent it can augment and update Aristotle's theory (or possibly refute parts of it), starting with a concise overview of current psychological research in Section 1.5. For example, what Aristotle says (or rather does not say) about conflicts between eros and friendship requires some serious updating. This book is, therefore, to be seen as an exercise in practical or applied (empirically informed) philosophy, first and foremost, although it does not shun theoretical debates and some modest textual exegesis where needed.

One of the claims that Aristotle makes repeatedly in his account of friendship is that friendship of the highest kind— 'character friendship' or friendship for virtue—is stable and enduring. Apart from a limitation that he mentions on the number of character friends, Aristotle is surprisingly cavalier about he formation and sustaining of character friendship, as if those are relatively unproblematic from psycho-moral and psycho-social perspectives. In contrast to the rest of the *Nicomachean Ethics*, where Aristotle is keenly aware that he is venturing over the terrain of an inexact science, mined with various counter-examples and dilemmas—for which he is eager to 'offer help' (1985, p. 36 [1104a10–11])—the exploration of character friendships is strangely devoid of examples of cases that may debar, stunt and ultimately dissolve such friendships, and how such cases should be tackled. Moreover, here for once, where Aristotle himself may need to be put right, philosophical watchdogs have mostly failed to bark.

While a number of scholars have noted problems with specific aspects of Aristotle's account of character friendships, no one has to the best of my knowledge offered a sustained and systematic meditation on the various difficulties that may mar or even destroy such friendships. This area of Aristotelian scholarship continues to constitute what Nehamas calls 'an isolated area of calm in philosophy's roiling waters' (2016, p. 14). One gets the feeling that 'friendship for virtue' has almost illimitable justificatory dominion over the discursive area, and seems to be considered beyond reproach, at least among neo-and-quasi-Aristotelians. The *third aim* of the present work is to repair the dearth of attention paid to the difficulties in question: to explore to what extent they threaten the viability of Aristotelian friendship theory and to what extent they can be ameliorated. I begin with an overview of those difficulties in Chapter 2 and continue to discuss them throughout, in particular (for educational contexts) in Chapter 5.

More specifically, in Chapter 2, I address five potential problems attached to character friendships between 'equals' (of substitutability; self-verification; mismatched developmental levels; divergent developmental paths; initiation and trust) and five problems between 'unequals' (of proportionality; the mentee's conflicting motivations; the mentor's conflicting motivations; paternalism; role inertia). I pay special attention to potential eros–*philia* conflicts, by drawing both on popular sources, such as the film *When Harry Met Sally,* and on recent psychological findings on the perils of cross-sex friendships. My conclusion is that despite the attractiveness of much of what Aristotle says, and all the positives that emerge in Section 1.1, his account of character friendships cannot be endorsed without various caveats and qualifications and even, in some cases, more radical departures.

Friendship is, astoundingly, not one of the twenty-four character strengths identified in the widely used VIA classificatory schema within current positive-psychology-inspired moral education—although love is (Peterson & Seligman, 2004). This fact illuminates an even more surprising aspect of a friendship lacuna in current accounts of moral education: namely, its absence in most of the recent character-education literature. Typically understood as the practical application of virtue ethics, which in turn is largely driven by Aristotelian or quasi-Aristotelian considerations (Kristjánsson, 2015), contemporary character educators are in tireless pursuit of ways in which to apply Aristotelian conceptualisations and craft Aristotle-based interventions for school practices: for instance by using habituation (via service learning), stories and music or role modelling. A large discourse already exists on the last-mentioned strategy, also known (in Aristotelian language) as the emulation of moral exemplars (see e.g. a special issue of *Journal of Moral Education*, ed. by Campodonico, Croce & Vaccarezza, 2019). Notably, however, Aristotle himself devotes much more space to friendship as a source of character education than to the emulation of glorified exemplars. Why does no one seem to pick up that fact and run with it?

The only sustained discussion of this issue that I have come across is in a paper by Hoyos-Valdés (2018), who asks in exasperation why Aristotelian character educators prioritise role-modelling so much over friendships. However, tellingly, that paper was published neither in an education journal nor in a pure philosophy one. Mainstream philosophers have written insightful papers on Aristotelian friendship, even foregrounding its educational element (e.g. Cooper, 1977, and Brewer, 2005), but those papers tend to be written with exegetical or moral theoretical aims in mind rather than as contributions to an essentially educational discourse.

To cut a long story short, the *fourth and final aim* of the present work is to retrieve friendship as a moral educational concept: to explain how moral educational goals ground and sustain deep friendships, and how the thorny issue of when friendships should be terminated is best understood in terms of considerations as to whether the friendships have exhausted their educational potential. By arguing that education is the *raison d'être* of close friendship, I want to show how friendship is developmentally constituted and, in its most complete form at least, educationally oriented. This is not only needed to elicit the educational implications of Aristotle's friendship theory and to bring it to bear on contemporary concerns about people's online friendships (as I do in Chapter 7), although those are important goals. More significantly, for present purposes, there is simply no way to make sense of the philosophical content of Aristotle's friendship theory without foregrounding the relevant connotations of the word 'for' in the title of this book: Friendship *for* Virtue. I couch most of my discussion of the educational value of friendship in terms of 'moral education'. Although there is no such term in Aristotle—because he did not operate with a modern concept of 'the moral'—I decided to talk about 'moral education' rather than simply 'character education' throughout, because much of what counts as 'character education' nowadays is exclusively instrumental, individualistic and inimical to Aristotle's conception of such education (as critiqued in Kristjánsson, 2015). Talk of 'moral education' will thus appeal to a wider contemporary audience of educationists and educators.

The reason why friendship occupies such a central place in Aristotle's virtue theory is precisely because of its developmental value in helping us become virtuous—*phronetic*—agents, by mirroring our self-conceptions in the eyes of our friends and using their feedback to enhance our self-cultivation (and vice versa). After all, our best friends are our 'other selves', as Aristotle repeatedly puts it. Thus, an Aristotle-defined type of close friendships may have a unique role to play in facilitating moral growth, above and beyond other developmental learning mechanisms. The choice of book's title is not fortuitous. I consider the fourth aim the most novel and hopefully most enlightening of all the themes pursued in what follows.

In a nutshell, then, this book works through the *puzzles* of Aristotle's friendship theory, explores its *pitfalls* and elicits its moral and educational *potentials*. The only chapter I have not given a spoiler for in this section yet is the final one. Chapter 8 offers an overview of the main findings and conclusions of the previous seven chapters and adds some further reflections, for instance about practical applications. The chapter also presents a laundry list of ideas for further research for philosophers, psychologists and educationists.

List of Tables

1

Setting the Scene

Friendship from Aristotle to Contemporary Psychology

1.1 The Concept of Friendship and Aristotle's Typology

To understand the concept of friendship, we need to follow the scent back to Aristotle. While not meant as a panegyric to Aristotle, the present section will act as a reference point for much of what I have to say in following chapters: in all my forthcoming 'footnotes' to Aristotle, if you like. This section mostly follows and expands upon standard interpretations of Aristotle's texts, although there are places where interpretations differ, and I cannot avoid stirring controversy. I leave complaints and corrections mostly to the subsequent discussion, however. This is more like the match programme to be read before the actual football match starts. I do not aim for an exhaustive overview; I will be priming readers only on those general issues that are relevant to discussions in subsequent chapters and that offer some maps through the various labyrinths.

Yet, even before turning to Aristotle, it helps to offer some musings on the very concept of friendship to be explored. I talked in the Preface about a 'bloated' concept at work in common parlance. The term 'friendship' has an everyday use nowadays that is very permissive and accommodates all sorts of acquaintances, mates, work colleagues, accomplices, Facebook friends and friendly neighbours that you say 'hi' to on the way to work, in addition to what I would call 'true friends' in a narrower understanding. The broad concept at stake here is what philosophers would call a *family-resemblance* or *cluster concept* (such as the concept of game, in Wittgenstein's famous example), without a common core. Cluster concepts do not, by their nature, lend themselves well to conceptual analysis. As 'resembling' or 'being related to' are not transitive relations, two games such as football and chess may have nothing in common except their relation or resemblance to a third game, tennis, which is like football played with a ball and like chess played by two persons. Similarly, two instances of friendship in this broad sense would not, *ex hypothesi*, need to have anything else in common other than some resemblance with a third instance, perhaps commanding a wider measure of assent as an example of friendship.

However, most lay speakers—if pressed—would probably agree that within this cluster concept, there is a narrower concept of a 'real' or 'true' friend. It is that

Friendship for Virtue. Kristján Kristjánsson, Oxford University Press. © Kristján Kristjánsson 2022.
DOI: 10.1093/oso/9780192864260.003.0001

concept that I happen to be interested in here, as was Aristotle. It has, I maintain, a common core which can be identified with sufficient specificity to constitute a single concept, although disagreements will linger on about its margins. In other words, this presumed narrow concept remains contestable. Some would say that it is 'essentially contestable' (see e.g. Smith, 2019). However, I happen to have a problem with the notion of 'essentially contestable concepts' (Gallie, 1955–1956) in general, because I consider the notion paradoxical. Either the presumed core of those concepts is itself contestable or not. If it is contestable, then the concept does not really have a common core; it is simply a cluster concept or an umbrella concept covering two or more discrete concepts. If, on the other hand, the core is not contestable, then it is hard to see why different conceptions of the concept should be essentially contestable either since the best conception could, at least in principle, be picked out by comparison with the proper non-contestable core (Kristjánsson, 1996, chap. 7).

In the case of a concept such as friendship, based on the narrower understanding on which I rely here and henceforth, a better way to describe its nature is through the label of *open-texture*. The concept has a common core that we may not completely agree upon but that we can at least argue about constructively (i.e. without talking at cross purposes), by providing good reasons and engaging in critical conceptual analysis via naturalistic revisions: revisions in light of empirical evidence and with as much respect as possible for ordinary language use and common intuitions. Yet, because the concept is open-textured, no fixed set of necessary and sufficient conditions can be given for the inclusion of an item under the concept; disagreements may continue about various marginal cases.

When theorists complain about the concept of friendship being too kaleidoscopic to analyse properly, or like a greased pig, difficult to get hold of, I think they may be mixing up the broad and the narrow concepts, or over-exaggerating the disagreements that hold in relation to the referents of the latter which, although contestable, are not 'essentially' so, at least not on Gallie's (1955–1956) understanding. For example, before this chapter closes, we will have seen that while Aristotelians and contemporary friendship theorists within psychology approach the concept very differently, considerable consensus would obtain between them about what sort of relationships count as falling under the concept. This is why, as I stress repeatedly in this work, there is no urgent need to buy into Aristotle's entire surrounding conceptual and theoretical repertoire to appreciate the things he says about the nature of close friendships.

What complicates matters slightly is Aristotle's division of true friendships into three different types. However, while that typology is not standardly replicated in contemporary psychology, at any rate not for research purposes, my own experience of explaining it to ordinary language users is that it resonates well with them. Although each generation must appropriate this typology anew and relate it to their own context, my interlocutors—both young and old—tend to find it as least reasonable and worthy of consideration. It is salutary to see how Aristotle grounds it, given that he considers only one of the types 'complete', as I explain below. He argues that to confine the use of the term to the complete form of friendship alone 'is to do violence to observed facts and compels one to talk paradoxes' (1935, p. 375 [1236b22–23]). This is the standard sort of argument seen in critical natural- istic revisions as a method of conceptual analysis (Kristjánsson, 1996, chap. 7). One argues, as does Aristotle here, that to try to define the concept more nar- rowly (or more broadly) than the proposed definition 'does violence' to observed facts; facts having to do with standard language use or the way the world actually operates: physically, socially, psychologically etc. One then turns the 'difficulties and contradictions' in the current language use and locutions and tries to 'solve' those (1935, p. 365 [1235b14–16]) through a sort of two-way traffic: a reflective equilibrium between the theoretical construct and the apparently aberrant usage. Indeed, this is Aristotelian naturalism at its best (see further in Section 1.3), applied to conceptual studies.

I have so far just focused on the form of the concept of friendship but let us now turn to its substance. Aristotle understands friendship as 'a virtue' or a rela- tion between people that 'involves virtue' (1985, p. 207 [1155a1–2]). While the conceptualisation of friendship as a relation may resonate better with modern sensibilities than that of friendship as a virtue, it is easy to see how the latter des- ignation can fit into Aristotle's architectonic of virtue as a personal trait of charac- ter. The capacity to give and receive (a particular kind of) love regularly and in the right way (by both loving and being loved, see 1985, p. 222 [1159a27–29]) would thus constitute a trait-like personal quality, potentially representing a virtue. Some of the things Aristotle says later about friendship trajectories may indicate that insofar as friendship can be understood in the virtue sense, it actually incorp- orates two distinct virtues: one being the virtue to find and make proper friends easily; the other to sustain virtuous friendships. However, as Aristotle does not make this distinction explicitly, I do not wish to muddy the conceptual waters by insisting on it here. Cooper (1977, pp. 629–30 [n. 11]) explains well how friend- ship as a potential virtue satisfies one of the standard conditions of Aristotelian virtue: of including an emotional component—a virtuous emotion (cf. Kristjánsson, 2018). However, Aristotle does not provide the standard description of friendship *qua* virtue in terms of a golden mean between two extreme forms of excess and deficiency—like, for instance, in his standard example of bravery as a medial state of character flanked by the extremes of cowardice and rashness.

Aristotle's reference to friendship as a virtue *or* a relation that involves virtue may give the impression that there is something unique about friendship as a vir- tue: namely its being necessarily *relational*. At first sight this may not be easy to conceptualise. All moral virtues seem to be relational and have a triadic structure. They are directed from the (1) self (the benefactor, the possessor of the moral quality) towards (2) a person or an event, and they take place within (3) a certain characteristic domain. For example, pride involves a self–self relationship in the domain of self-evaluations of worth; compassion involves a self–other-person relationship in the domain of undeserved bad fortune; courage involves a self–event relationship in the domain of fearful episodes, say a war. Once bitten, twice shy with respect to his mentor Plato's idealism, Aristotle notably ignored the fourth potential type of relational moral virtues, involving a self–abstract-ideal relationship. There is thus no moral virtue of *awe* in Aristotle, directed at ideals of truth, beauty or goodness. While I have complained elsewhere about this elision and tried to 'update' Aristotle (Kristjánsson, 2018; 2020; cf. also Jordan & Kristjánsson, 2017, about a missing virtue of harmony with nature), this is not a relevant worry for present purposes.

In an important recent paper, Sungwoo Um (2021a) has argued, however, that some virtues are relational in a stronger sense than others and deserve to be categorised as forming a subcategory of virtue. He explores the example of filial piety in particular but also mentions friendship and love. According to Um, the person who possesses a relational virtue has proper sensitivity to the normative demands of the relevant relationship and appropriate modes of responsiveness to them. At first glance, this does not seem to pick out a unique feature of a virtue like friendship. In compassion, say, the compassionate person also needs to have proper sensitivity to the normative demands of the relationship with the beneficiary of the compassion. The glories of Um's paper, however, consist in his being aware of all the relevant doubts and counter-arguments and offering clever rejoinders. First of all, he is talking about other-regarding virtues, ruling out self–self and self–event types of virtues. However, this is ultimately not a very informative distinction. He then further excludes unilateral self–other virtues. There has to be a certain reciprocity, as well as intimacy and dependency, involved. This condition leads him into some difficulties regarding filial piety because Confucian ethics, for example, demands that children exhibit filial piety even towards undeserving and unloving parents. Um explores this potential counter-argument in detail and explains how a relational virtue needs to involve a reasonable degree of forbearance, such as that although parents fail partly in their duties and act as less than 'perfectly parental', the justificatory force of the virtue still persists. Um is, however, forced to concede that, in extreme cases, where the parents turn out to be serial killers, for example, the grounds for filial piety may be undermined because of the complete disintegration of reciprocity.

I cannot help observing that Um's argument would have worked better in the case of friendship than filial piety. There is a sense in which common moral intuitions tell us that children should never completely abandon an affectionate bond with their parents (or vice versa) even if the other party turns irrevocably bad and does not requite the affection in the slightest. It is much easier to argue for a necessary condition of persisting reciprocity in the case of friendship, and indeed this is exactly what Aristotle does. So, by his lights, friendship distinguishes itself from (most other) other-regarding virtues in that it requires the other person to requite the feelings: be a friend also. Aristotle first explains here that one cannot be a friend to soulless things, such as one's prized bottle of wine. Furthermore, friendship must be reciprocated and both parties must be 'aware of' this reciprocation (1985, p. 210 [1155b28–1156a4]).

Section 1.5 below reveals that some young people in the contemporary era do not share this conceptual intuition; they consider themselves to be friends of people who do not perceive themselves in the same way and, in extreme cases, of people who do not even know them. One could perhaps most charitably reject those views on grounds of youthful ignorance; these young people simply do not understand the concept of friendship correctly, just as they might not understand what the virtue of gratitude truly means, and perhaps confuse 'friend' with a 'role model'. A trickier counter-example to Aristotle's thesis about reciprocity is if A considers and treats B as a friend and B reciprocates the friendship in practice but still does not consider herself A's friend. Does being mutually 'aware' of the friendship require defining oneself as a friend or just behaving as one (and I am not talking about intentionally feigned friendships here, but simply people who do not conceptualise the relationship as friendship although they do the things a friend would normally do)? And what about self-deceptions, which contemporary psychologists are obviously more *au fait* with as a concept than Aristotle was? Suppose B does not only reciprocate A's affection in practice but also harbours strong feelings of goodwill towards A deep down, yet is unaware of those in her conscious mind because of wilful or unwilful self-deceptions (or just simple lack of self-transparency): can the bond between A and B still be appropriately conceptualised as friendship?

Let us leave these conceptual puzzles about the conditions of the relational virtue of friendship in Aristotle behind us for now (cf. Romero-Iribas & Smith, 2018, for some more) to focus on a more consensual feature. All virtue ethicists will agree that for something to count as a virtue it has to be conducive to, and indeed constitutive of, a person's flourishing (see further in Section 1.2). Here, Aristotle's view would, arguably, command almost universal consent, well outside the circles of virtue ethics. For Aristotle, friendship is intrinsically valuable (indeed invaluable) and noble as a constituent of the good life. I take it this is because certain 'virtuous relational activities' (using Um's 2021b formulation, although he does not ascribe this view to Aristotle in particular)—namely, the activities of virtues required in intimate relationships such as close friendships—happen to be *constitutive of* human flourishing. However, in addition to its constitutive value, friendship is also 'the greatest external good', *conducive to* flourishing (1985, pp. 208; 257 [1155a29; 1169b9–10], cf. p. 258 [1169b20–23]). Aristotle's voice is magisterial on this point: *qua* virtue, friendship 'is most necessary for our life', for 'no one would choose to live without friends even if he had all the other goods'. Moreover, contrary to most other virtues, whose proper role depends on social position, friendship is as necessary a refuge—and manifests itself similarly—among rich and poor (1985, p. 207 [1155a1–12]). Aristotle later modifies this claim, however, when explaining the difference between equal and unequal friendships, as I explain later.

Notice what Aristotle is saying here but also what he is not saying. He is saying that, in addition to its own intrinsic value, friendship adds value to other goods, so much so that having them *without* friends is vastly inferior to having them *with* friends. Indeed, the former option is not only lacking in value; it is not even choiceworthy. Friendship augments other goods (such as knowledge, creativity, beauty): imbues them with additional value. More specifically, as Sherman explains, friendship creates a context or arena for the expression of other virtues (1987, p. 595). In this sense, friendship is not so much *uniquely* human (for aliens might also be able to make friends) as *essentially* human (cf. Kreft, 2019): part of what being human means. Aristotle is not saying, however, that friendship is a master virtue that trumps all other virtues and values. It is still an open question what to do in case friendship conflicts with other values: a point I elaborate upon in Chapter 3.

When I say that few would want to dissent from Aristotle on the value of friendship, I am simply referring to the received wisdom, noted in the Preface, that friendship is generally considered a good. Reverting to literature again, Dostoevsky is particularly poignant in teaching us through his characters how not being able to love or enjoy friendship is nothing less than hell on earth; and I am sure many readers will share my experience of having had nightmares as a child projecting myself into Robinson Crusoe's predicament on that desert island, having no soul to speak to or relieve him through a meeting of minds. The thought of friendlessness may be just a variation of the fear of loneliness. However, it takes it to a different level, for as the German proverb has it, 'loneliness with another person is the worst kind of loneliness'. We do not just want *any* person with us on that desert island, perhaps someone we cannot relate to at all. We want a friend.

Let us now return in more detail to the conceptual conditions of true friendships. Those need first to be distinguished from various kinds of 'friendships' on a broader understanding, in particular a virtue Aristotle dubs 'friendliness in social intercourse' as a mean (medial state) between being ingratiating and cantankerous when meeting other people through casual encounters. Aristotle seems to be faced with exactly the same linguistic problem as we moderns in that there was no distinct name for this virtue in ancient Greek to distinguish it from 'friendship', so he just coins one, but he says it 'differs from friendship in not requiring any special feeling or any fondness for the people we meet' (1985, pp. 107–09 [1126b11–1127a11]). This is an important concession, for with most other virtues, Aristotle identifies a discrete emotional component: a 'virtuous emotion' (Kristjánsson, 2018). To be friendly in social intercourse, however, one just needs to go through the motions of being agreeable and tactful. This virtue is one of social glue and convenience rather than personal attachments: about manners more than morals (Kristjánsson, 2007, chap. 10).

In contrast to mere friendliness and acquaintanceship, according to Aristotle, all types of *true* friendship involve reciprocated goodwill and the loving of friends for their own sake (1985, p. 210 [1155b31–32]). Such true friendships assume three main types, where the first two—loving friends for their own sake but with the love still grounded in the *pleasure* or *utility* they bring—are 'incomplete' because of their essentially extrinsically valuable and transitory natures. The most developed type, however, namely character friendship—in which the love is grounded in the friend's *virtuous character*—is 'complete' because of its unique intrinsically valuable and enduring nature (1985, pp. 211ff [1156a6ff]). Most of us will have friends whose company we simply enjoy because they are funny and nice, and also friends who help us out when we need to have things fixed (and vice versa)—yet without these friendships ever developing towards mutual deep love of each other's character. Nevertheless, the two inferior types are not mere *ersatz* versions of character friendship that can be disposed of like sucked oranges once they have served their purpose—so this is a not a case of the good, the bad and the ugly. Pleasure and utility friendships have clear uses and are necessary for smooth human association. While 'base' people can actualise them, but not the complete type, 'good' (namely virtuous) people enjoy all three types in different contexts but most specifically the complete type (1985, pp. 212 and 216 [1156b6–8 and 1157b1–4]). Because of their extreme closeness, the number of character friends will be limited (1985, pp. 262–3 [1170b29–1171a21]). This claim, as well as the one about the enduring nature of those friendships, allows us to consider Aristotle's view as a view of the nature of what contemporary psychologists would call 'deep', 'close' or 'best' friendships (see Section 1.5 below).

Curzer (2012, p. 248) has drawn together all the things that Aristotle says about the characteristics of 'true' friendships (comprising the three subtypes) in different places, including the *Rhetoric*. In addition to the three above conditions of (a) reciprocating the affection and being aware of it: namely, perceiving oneself as a friend, (b) having goodwill for each other (*qua* positive evaluative attitude and kindly feeling: *eunoia*) and (c) wishing each other to exist and live well for each other's sake, Aristotle also mentions that friends (d) are glad of each other, (e) try to do good things for each other, and share with each other (f) tastes and values, (g) time and activities, and (h) joys and sorrows. Since conditions (d)–(h) are fairly uncontroversial, in the sense that someone who rejected them would seem to miss the very point of the concept of friendship, I will not say more about them here. I have already discussed condition (a) briefly and explained that although it seems reasonable, it is not one that all contemporary language users agree upon; and it imports a complication having to do with one's self-definition as a friend versus simply behaving as one (cf. also Pangle, 2003, p. 39). However, the real concerns and controversies revolve around conditions (b) and (c).

The inconvenient truth is that Aristotle waffles and fudges, at best, or flatly contradicts himself, at worst, on these conditions. He begins by making it an explicit necessary conceptual condition of *all* the three (true) types of friendship that to 'a friend […] you must wish good for his own sake' (1985, p. 210 [1155b31–32])—which seems to indicate that you must not only value the friend as a means to an end, and which distinguishes true friendship from mere friendliness, camaraderie or acquaintanceship. Shortly later he says, however, that those 'who love each other for utility love the other not in himself, but in so far as they gain some good for themselves from him' (1985, p. 211 [1156a11–12]), and that such friendships can be easily dissolved once the benefit has been depleted (1985, p. 243 [1165b1–2]), indicating that only character friendships make the grade as true friendships. In the *Eudemian Ethics*, Aristotle espouses the first of those views with his claim that the 'kindly feeling' of goodwill is just the 'beginning of friendship', but not true friendship because the clause of it being for the sake of the other is missing (1935, p. 409 [1241a8–15]).

As it was not Aristotle's wont to indulge in self-contradictions, exegetes have tried to save his face. It could be pointed out that Aristotle introduces the view that (in all friendships) you must wish good for the friend's own sake simply as the received view without endorsing it explicitly; perhaps he wanted to overrule or revise it? However, unless he notes otherwise, Aristotle is usually in the business of 'saving the appearance' (*endoxa*), namely rescuing somehow the views of 'the many'. I take him to be doing exactly that here. I am therefore in broad agreement with Cooper's contention that Aristotle must be focusing on different parts of the utility-friendship trajectory with his apparently inconsistent remarks: its necessary instrumental formation versus its more noble development and maintenance. More precisely, Cooper takes Aristotle to be making the psychological claim that those who 'have been mutually benefited through their common association will, as a result of the benefits […] tend to wish for and be willing to act in the interest of the other person's good, independently of considerations of their *own* welfare' (1977, pp. 633–4). Whiting (2006, p. 286) bolsters this interpretation with the general observation that 'we cannot move immediately from the claim that a relationship *comes to be* for the sake of some end to the conclusion that the relationship *continues to exist* for the sake of that end'. I take it, then, that friendships for utility (and pleasure) are true types of friendship although only character friendship is 'complete' and intrinsically valuable (but for the opposite view, see Brewer, 2005, pp. 730–1; cf. also Hursthouse's, 2007, pithy and poignant response to Brewer).

I say more, in Chapter 6, about why utility friendships tend to be undervalued in the relevant literatures. Suffice it to say here that it is common practice to conceptualise the distinction between the complete type of friendship and the two incomplete types as that between '*noninstrumental* or *end* friendships' versus '*instrumental* and *means* friendships' (e.g. Badhwar, 1991, p. 483; cf. also

Brewer, 2005, p. 731). While there is some truth to this distinction, we miss something important by repeating it too often. Indeed, I argue in Chapter 6 that the distinction between intrinsic and extrinsic value is not the same distinction as between non-instrumental and instrumental value and that a type of friendship can, for example, be (merely) extrinsically valuable but (still) non-instrumentally so. This distinction has the additional benefit of helping to save Aristotle's face with regard to the apparent contradiction above, although it is not a distinction that he himself makes, explicitly at least.

Let us now turn from true friendship in general to the only 'complete' form: character friendship. Bear in mind here that, in Aristotle, as distinct from contemporary psychology, no clear distinction is drawn between the descriptive and the evaluative; his criteria place normative constraints upon what can properly be called an example of the highest form of friendship—however the individuals themselves may choose to describe their relationship or claim to feel about it. Bear in mind also that character friends continue to derive pleasure from their friendships, and those friendships are also useful for them, but the pleasure takes on a different form from that experienced in mere friendship *for* pleasure. It becomes the sort of unique Aristotelian pleasure in unimpeded activity that typically crowns the display of a virtue once it succeeds. Similarly, the utility becomes a happy side-effect of the intrinsic value of the relationship.

Now, celebrations of close friendships between 'soulmates' and 'kindred spirits' are obviously as old as the hills, predating Aristotle. However, Aristotle's account of the highest type of *philia* has some unerring marks that make it stand out—collectively—as unique. Apart from the characteristics they share with the incomplete types, character friendships present some discrete features of their own: for example, (a) loving the friend for her own sake in the special meaning of loving her moral character (as her set of virtues), (b) soulmateship in the strong sense of being 'related to his friend as he is to himself, since the friend is another himself' (1985, p. 246 [1166a30–33]; cf. pp. 260 and 265 [1170b6–7; 1172a32–34]) and (c) viewing the friendship as intrinsically valuable to the extent of seeing the friend as irreplaceable, not only painfully replaceable as in the more developed forms of utility friendships. Moreover, it stands to reason that even in the case of the characteristics they share with the two other types of true friendships, such as (d) spending time together in shared activities and (e) sharing joys and sorrows, those will assume new extended features in character friendship because of its closeness, devotion and intimacy. While pleasure friends may go fishing together and utility friends may seek comfort in one another after a trauma, character friends will share activities as a way of enjoying each other's virtues and they will confide in each other about joys and sorrows out of intrinsic interest in each other's psyches—with hearts laid bare and no holds barred. That said, in the case of character friendship, we are obviously still dealing with an open-textured concept, so variables may admit of differing interpretations. For example, the precise referent of the notion of 'shared activities' becomes a significant apple of discord in the debate about online friendships as putative character friendships (as I explain in Chapter 7).

The condition about the friend as 'another self' or *alter ego* is problematic. It is not entirely clear whether Aristotle is (a) speaking *metaphorically*, (b) making a *moral* point about the essential substantive sharing of affection, direction and purpose (what he calls in the *Eudemian Ethics* 'mutual reciprocity of affection and purpose', 1935, p. 373 [1236b2–3]) and the eventual rational unity of choice between two full *phronimoi* (Stern-Gillet, 1995, chap. 1)—or (c) making an *ontological* point about the inherently relational nature of selfhood. Sherman interprets Aristotle's claim ontologically as presupposing 'some notion of an extended self, or a self enlarged through attachments' (1987, p. 600). I am sceptical of this strong interpretation as Aristotle did not have at his disposal a selfhood theory in the modern sense (Kristjánsson, 2010; cf. Stern-Gillet, 1995, pp. 18, 24) which would allow for such ontological acrobatics. Moreover, it becomes mysterious how friends are loved for their own sake if they are seen as literal extensions of myself; and why is Aristotle then so concerned to stress that the individual friend is also a 'separate self' (*autos diairetos*; see 1935, p. 443 [1245a35])?

I will be returning to this puzzling 'another-self' thesis at various junctures in what follows, culminating in an 'educational' interpretation of it in Chapter 5. However, whichever interpretation one favours, all speak against the objection commonly lodged by proponents of 'care ethics' (see e.g. Noddings, 1999) that Aristotelian virtue ethics somehow fails to take account of the relational nature of human wellbeing.

Aristotle makes an initial comment about complete (namely, character-based) friendships (1985, p. 212 [1156b6–8]) that has often been interpreted to mean that such friendships are possible only between two people who are not only, as he says, 'similar in virtue' but also equal in social standing, and even already both of perfect virtue (namely what he calls fully fledged *phronimoi* or we could call 'moral heroes'). Yet a careful reading of Aristotle's texts reveals that almost nothing in his account, apart from the initial comment, supports the assumption that such friendships are limited to people of *perfect* virtue, and much militates against it. While perfectly *phronesis*-guided character friendship is clearly his ideal instantiation, Aristotle spends considerable space in the following discussion delineating friendships that are complete while not perfect: namely, 'imperfect' but genuine character friendships among people who are unequal in various ways and/or on the path towards full *phronesis* rather than *phronimoi* graduates already (see below). As Cooper adamantly puts it, 'it is clear that Aristotle is willing to countenance a virtue-friendship where *both* parties are quite deficient with respect to their appropriate excellences' (1977, p. 628; see also Sherman, 1987, p. 610).

More specifically, Aristotle seems to take it for granted that inequality in social standing involves some sort of inequality in virtue, although equality in social standing does not guarantee equality in virtue (see further in Chapter 2). Given his penchant (the Platonic legacy, if you like) for defining things with reference to their most fully realised instances, Aristotle is admittedly tempted to draw upon descriptions of character friendships not only between social and virtuous equals but between equals of 'perfect' virtue: the fully developed *phronimoi*. The main purpose of their friendship is the mutual appreciation and affirmation of each other's ethical outlooks, along with the unique pleasure that this mutuality of purpose and outlook brings (cf. Brewer, 2005). Importantly, however, Aristotle allows for three exceptions to the view of 'complete' friendships being 'perfect' in this sense: namely, variants of complete character friendships in which the friends are either not *phronimoi* or not of equal virtue. The first one involves friends of unequal social standing and at unequal levels of virtue. The second involves friends of equal social standing and equal levels of virtue, but where the level they share is not one of perfect virtue. The third also involves friends of equal social standing but where their levels of virtue are unequal. I flesh out those options with examples in Chapter 5. Suffice it to say here that the second and third categories represent potentially edifying character friendships that can serve as a school of virtue for two budding *phronomoi* who, having been habituated into virtue in their early years, have yet to infuse it fully with *phronesis*. They need mutual guidance to further steer their 'natural' (habituated but not yet *phronetic*) developing virtue, and this need serves as the binding force drawing them into each other's fold. Eventually, it turns out that the fundamental *raison d'être* of character friendships is not only moral and emotional (loving each other's virtue) but also educational. The aim of such friendships is not loving moral character per se, but loving it in the service of mutual character development (see Chapter 5 below).

Although one would have wanted Aristotle to elaborate more on this developmental-cum-educational theme, what he says—even if brief—is explicit enough to elevate this theme to a major strand in an updated and reconstructed neo-Aristotelian account of friendship, as I propose to do in this book. Indeed, from a moral educational perspective, Aristotle's account of character friendship can be seen as a treasure trove precisely because of the developmental element that reigns supreme in it.

The insensitivity to the pathologies of friendship—and the causes which malform and compromise it—is the place where Aristotle seems most clearly to go off the scent in his pursuit of understanding this complex human relationship, as I rued already in the Preface. Uncharacteristically, he is here, as Schoeman puts it, 'almost frivolous in the face of troublesome questions' (1985, p. 269). Why Aristotle 'tended to turn away from friendship's darker, more painful, and more compromising sides' (Nehamas, 2016, p. 5) is a question for a more dedicated Aristotelian exegete than the present author. Perhaps it has to do with Aristotle's own psychology; perhaps his intended readership (of well brought-up budding young statesmen); perhaps his overestimation of the unity and tranquillity of virtue in general. What matters for present purposes is not so much to identify the roots of his mistakes as to correct them—and the aim of Chapter 2 will be to address that task head-on.

At the close of this fairly long section, readers may have started to wonder whether I have reneged on my promise not to write a work of predominantly Aristotelian exegesis. However, there are a couple of reasons why I have devoted so much space to the nuts and bolts of his friendship theory. First, since my aim is to secure a more prominent place for friendship within virtue ethics, it is worth exploring in detail the virtue ethical account that seems, at first glance at least, best suited to the task: looking for resources to exploit and shortcomings that stand in need of amelioration. In that sense, Aristotle's friendship theory fascinates and frustrates in equal measure. Second, it just so happens that no philosopher has, to the present day, written as detailed and perspicuous account of friendship—as shown by the already-noted fact that all subsequent friendship theories in philosophy seem to serve as responses to Aristotle's. Fidelity to Aristotle does not grant an account of friendship any academic immunity, but avoidance of engagement with him consigns it to the niche of oblivion.

1.2 The Background Theory of Virtue, Flourishing and Education for Character

Section 1.1 made abundant use of a number of concepts from the Aristotelian arsenal, such as 'flourishing' (*eudaimonia*), 'character', 'virtue', '*phronesis*', 'virtue ethics' and 'character education'. I also rehearsed various findings derived from Aristotle's 'naturalistic' method of exploring friendship, but without offering any elaboration of what that method is. This is not good philosophical practice. I explained in the Preface that I aimed my work at both philosophers and non-philosophers interested in friendship. However, my failure so far to fill in the background picture threatens to do disservice to both groups of readers. The non-philosophers may not fully grasp what all those Aristotelian background concepts are meant to capture, and the philosophers may feel cheated by not knowing more about my take on various controversial exegetical and theoretical issues on which interpretations of Aristotle's theory (and other forms of virtue ethics) differ.

To make amends, the present section and the following Section 1.3 (on method) aim to fill in the background information needed to set Aristotle's friendship theory in the proper theoretical context. I realise I may say too much for the non-philosophers and too little for the philosophers, but I refuse to bow to the common view in academia that crossover work of this kind is bound to fall between two stools. After all, we have shining examples of books that seem to do justice to 'both stools', such as Julia Annas's (2011) incredibly lucid and accessible, if by no means uncontroversial, introduction to Aristotelian virtue ethics, and Nehamas's (2016) book on friendship which has been praised by philosophers and general readers alike. For those with scant interest in theory and method and eager to crack on with making sense of friendship as a discrete topic of study, I recommend skipping Sections 1.2 and 1.3 and moving straight on to Section 1.4. For the rest of readers, I suggest fastening the seatbelts and waiting for take-off.

Whatever their differences, most philosophical accounts of friendship post-Aristotle seem to take as gospel his insistence that friendship is at once conducive to and constitutive of human flourishing. This testament to the enduring vibrancy of Aristotle's writings is heaven-sent for a neo-Aristotelian philosopher such as myself. Various forms of Aristotelianism and neo-Aristotelianism have become cutting edge within contemporary virtue ethics (Annas, 2011; Wright, Warren & Snow, 2021), as well as within its educational incarnation as character education (Kristjánsson, 2015), psychological studies of character and virtue (Peterson & Seligman, 2004; Fowers et al., 2021), current theories of wellbeing as flourishing or *eudaimonia* (Kristjánsson, 2020) and psycho-moral theories of emotion (Kristjánsson, 2018). As I have contributed to all those discursive fields before, I attempt in this book to bring my arguments about friendship to bear on various other issues in surrounding areas where Aristotelianism is blooming. Hence, for instance, my prospective focus on the character-educational aspects of friendship in Chapter 5. However, I need to sketch out a way first through this complex conceptual parish.

The foundational concept in Aristotelian virtue ethics, as well as in its educational incarnation as character education, is actually neither virtue nor character, but rather *flourishing*, or what modern social scientists understand as objective wellbeing. Aristotle's concept of flourishing (as *eudaimonia*) rests on one fundamental argument: the so-called *ergon* (function) argument, according to which human beings have a natural function, just as an oak tree or a tiger: a function that can be elicited by looking at what humans are best at (1985, p. 15 [1197b25]). The function peculiar to human beings, according to Aristotle, 'is the soul's activity and actions that express reason'. As 'each function is completed well when its completion expresses the proper virtue', the human good 'turns out to be the soul's activity that expresses virtue'—infused with reason (1985, p. 17 [1198a12–16]). What is 'proper to each thing's nature' (here, reason-infused virtue), is 'supremely best and pleasantest for it' (1985, p. 287 [1178a5–7]). Hence, to flourish or live well in the distinctive human way will give human beings a kind of pleasure as an ornament: a kind nowadays referred to as 'flow'. It is part of human psychology to enjoy the exercise of our realised human capabilities; and each kind of virtue constitutive of flourishing happens to come with its unique kind of flow-like pleasure. That includes friendship—although the specific pleasure of 'friendship for pleasure' is not of that flow-like kind, as actualising such friendships is not a virtue in itself.

Aristotle makes so many references to flourishing, not only in the *Nicomachean Ethics* but throughout his corpus, that fleshing out a full-blown account of Aristotelian flourishing requires a book-length study rather than a brief section. I have tried elsewhere to do justice to the various nuts and bolts of Aristotle's concept by defining it such: *Human flourishing* is the (relatively) unencumbered, freely chosen and developmentally progressive activity of a meaningful (subjectively purposeful and objectively valuable) life that actualises satisfactorily an individual human being's natural capacities in areas of species-specific existential tasks at which human beings (as rational, social, moral and emotional agents) can most successfully excel (Kristjánsson, 2020, chap. 1). This may read like the small letters in an insurance contract, as a critic pointed out to me. But it simply indicates how nuanced and detailed Aristotle's account is.

Complicating this matter philosophically is a long-standing debate about whether or not Aristotle's account of flourishing as the ultimate aim of human life constitutes a form of *rational egoism* (or a weaker but still basically egoistic form of *psychological self-directed eudaimonism*), or whether it can count as an *altruistic* account (Schuh, 2020; for the latest contributions to this debate in the context of friendship, see Kim, 2021; 2022). I do not want to enter the rabbit hole of that debate except by registering my agreement with Whiting (2006, pp. 277, 302; cf. Kraut, 1989) that not only is it clear that an individual's flourishing incorporates other people as her *alter egos* (recall Section 1.1), Aristotle nowhere says that it is the agent's own flourishing that is or should be the ultimate end of all her actions, as distinct from the flourishing of other people. His virtue ethics is not, on my reading, a form of rational egoism according to which one does or should do everything, ultimately, just for the sake of one's own *eudaimonia*. Not being a utilitarian, Aristotle does not require ordinary *phronetic* people to synchronise their decisions with the *eudaimonia* of all human beings in mind, but simply the people most immediately affected by the decision. Indeed, the very idea of maximisation is out of place in Aristotelian moral theory (as I go on to explain in some detail in Chapter 3 and 4). Notably, however, all this changes once you become a ruler in charge of people; then decision making becomes about the common interest or the common good. In their decision making, the rulers need to take into account what is good for all their citizens (1985, p. 154 [1140b7–11]).

Generally speaking, however, the very idea of a strict distinction between egoism and altruism assumes a theory of independent personal selfhood that may have been foreign to Aristotle as well as to most, if not all, ancient Greek thinkers. That said, Aristotle clearly does believe that without the capacity to love oneself, one cannot learn to love others (e.g. friends)—an idea that I flesh out in Chapter 4. To further complicate matters, Aristotle's thesis about the ultimate end of actions is not couched primarily, as it would in modernity, in normative terms (about what the end *should* be) but is typically rendered in descriptive terms, about what actually *does* motivate the *phronetic* agent. Unaware of Hume's later 'is–ought'

dichotomy, Aristotle simply takes it for granted that the best evidence for something being a desirable motivation is that it is actually desired by the *phronimoi*.

Although actualising the virtues is the chief mode of living well, Aristotle has
nothing but scorn for the Socratic view (also attributed to Buddha, Confucius
and the Stoics) that nothing can harm the virtuous person. Flourishing 'also
needs external goods', Aristotle says; those who maintain that we can flourish
'when we are broken on the wheel, or fall into terrible misfortunes, provided that
we are good [...] are *talking nonsense*' (1985, pp. 21 and 203 [1099a32 and
1153b19–21]; my italics). What are the resources or goods of fortune that we need
in order to so much as stand a chance of flourishing? Aristotle provides extended
lists of those, but for present purposes the one that stands out is friendship, This is
why Aristotle talks about friendship being both conducive to (as an external
good) and constitutive of (as an internal good) of flourishing. But what if friendship apparently requires one to sacrifice one's flourishing, for example if one is
being 'broken on the wheel' because of one's motivation to protect a close friend?
Is the tortured person than engaged in a flourishing activity or not? Aristotle does
not really answer that question, but his famous claim that the ultimate judgement
about a person's flourishing cannot be passed until the person is dead may seem
to indicate that suffering as a result of virtue may be part—an inevitable part
even—of an overall flourishing life (e.g. sacrificing oneself on the battlefield as the
ultimate act of bravery). However, this does not mean that the virtuous person
cannot be harmed. It is always better if an activity inimical to flourishing can be
avoided. However, if it cannot be avoided as part of an overall flourishing life,
then it is better (more flourishing-enhancing overall) to take it on the chin than
to avoid it in a cowardly way.

Character in Aristotelian theory refers to one's make-up of virtues and vices
(and other intermediate states of being and doing in the ethical sphere). His
understanding tallies with the modern conception of character as the reason-
responsive, morally evaluable and educable subset of personality—although
Aristotle did not have at his disposal a discrete concept of non-moral personality,
as I explain at later junctures in this book. Good character, on an Aristotelian
view, involves the cultivation and execution of *virtues* as specific human excellences. What sort of capacities are the virtues? Unfortunately, most of the general
terms that can been used to describe them carry unfortunate connotations in
modernity. The closest answer is perhaps 'traits', but in psychology the term 'trait'
typically refers to attributes that are (at least partly) inherited. The virtues, however—or so the Aristotelian story goes—are acquired, first through upbringing
(esp. habituation and role modelling), and later through one's own repeated
choices, coalescing into stable patterns. At all events, let us say here that the
virtues constitute stable dispositional clusters concerned with praiseworthy functioning in a number of significant and distinctive spheres of human life. Each
virtue is typically seen to comprise a unique set of *components*: of perception/

recognition, emotion, desire, motivation, behaviour and comportment or style, applicable in the relevant sphere, where none of the component (not even 'correct' behaviour) can be evaluated in isolation from the others. The person possessing the virtue of compassion, for example, notices easily and attends to situations in which the situation of others has been undeservedly compromised, feels for the needs of those who have suffered this undeserved misfortune, desires that their misfortune be reversed, acts (if humanly possible) for the relevant (ethical) reasons in ways conducive to that goal and exudes an outward aura of empathy and care. The virtues Aristotle talks about are ethical, political and intellectual. This corresponds reasonably well to a typical modern taxonomy of virtues as moral, civic and intellectual, although a fourth category extolled in modernity, that of performative virtues, would have been designated by Aristotle not as a set of virtues but of useful skills (*techné*). One of the intellectual virtues, *phronesis*, serves a unique metacognitive function in Aristotle's system and I return to it at the end of this section.

Anyone vaguely familiar with the history of ethical theorising will know how *virtue ethics*, harking back to Aristotle, has since Anscombe's landmark paper on modern moral philosophy (1958) become the third alternative, alongside Kantian deontology and consequentialist theories, as a theory of choice both for moral philosophers and applied professional ethicists. According to virtue ethics, an action is right not because it is required as one's duty in accordance with a formalistic principle (as in Kantianism) or because it has desirable overall consequences (as in consequentialism) but because it exhibits good character. In contrast to other moral theories, the concept of good character is thus what is foundational in virtue ethics, rather than the concepts of duties or consequences; and what defines acting well is derivative or a matter of what is consistent with good character. However, the term 'virtue ethics' needs to be understood quite permissively, as it has been ascribed to philosophers as distinct as Plato, the natural-law Stoics and Nietzsche. For present purposes, the sort of virtue ethics that need concern us is exclusively of the Aristotelian kind, according to which an action is right when it enhances virtue and contributes to a flourishing (*eudaimonic*) life, or simply 'living well'—as opposed to a languishing or floundering one. Here, the focus is not so much on the correctness of individual actions as on their role in the well-rounded life and their roots in the 'inner world' of the agent: in stable states of character that incorporate motivational and emotional elements. What matters in the end for moral evaluation is not merely observable behaviour, but the emotions with which an action is performed, the motivation behind it and the manner in which it is performed.

As with other ethical theories, virtue ethics imports a lot of difficulties and controversies, not least if understood as permissively as suggested above. Even if confined to the Aristotelian variety, textbooks account of it tend to trade in over-simplifications. In addition to disputes about motivations (egoistic versus altruistic interpretations), already mentioned above, various thorny questions arise about the relationship of virtue ethics to the other two theoretical alternatives. In short, textbooks tend to exaggerate the differences between them, by focusing on far-fetched situations in which their action-guidance would differ. However, in most ordinary problematic cases, all three theories will give one more or less the same advice about what to do (although not for exactly the same reasons). Moreover, virtue ethics of the Aristotelian kind does seem to incorporate quite a few ethical principles within its repertoire (for example that adultery and patricide are always wrong), and it cannot avoid cost-benefit analysis of the consequentialist kind altogether, especially if you are a ruler in a state (see above). Specifically, in the case of friendship, the uniqueness of Aristotelian virtue ethics in being able to account unproblematically for acts of spontaneous friendship, without importing 'one thought too many' like the other two theories, has been celebrated far beyond good measure, as I explain in Chapter 3.

Aristotelian *character education*, as this term is used nowadays (Kristjánsson, 2015), refers to a form of holistic moral education focusing on the systematic development of virtues as stable traits of character, with the aim of promoting human flourishing and founded on Aristotle's virtue theory. On this understanding, character education forms a specific subset of moral education which, in turn, forms a subset of general values education. Character education has had a chequered and tumultuous history and continues to accommodate fairly different theoretical, disciplinary and practical perspectives. If we focus on the Aristotelian version only, it may be an understatement to say that it is 'founded on' Aristotle's virtue theory. As I explain in Section 1.3, Aristotle did not define his enterprise in the 'sandwich' treatises of the *Nicomachean Ethics* and *Politics* as that of an exercise in ethical theorising. Rather, their purpose is fundamentally *educational*. What both treatises aim at is arguing for and furthering the cause of character development at the individual (*Nicomachean Ethics*) and collective/state (*Politics*) levels. The primacy of educational concerns in Aristotle's extensive analysis of friendship will be foregrounded in Chapter 5. In the meantime, what we can say with good reason is that the two concepts of what is nowadays referred to as 'virtue ethics' on the one hand and 'character education' on the other cannot be easily separated in Aristotle's work.

The final construct that I need to elucidate briefly in this overview section is that of *phronesis*. The intellectual meta-virtue of practical wisdom (*phronesis*), operating in the sphere of *praxis* (decision and action), is about 'doing' as distinct from 'making'. Although Aristotle likes to compare *phronesis* to a skill, such as playing the flute, in particular regarding how it is picked up (namely experientially) and internalised (through repeated practice), he remains clear on the distinctions between the two. One key difference is that the excellence of *techné* lies in the product or outcome of actions, but the excellence of *phronesis* lies in the process of thinking and acting. To complicate matters, Aristotle describes *phronesis* as a sub-species of a more general cognitive capacity that he calls 'cleverness' or 'calculation' (*deinotes*): the intellectual virtue of being able to figure out the proper actions 'that tend to promote whatever goal is assumed and to achieve it. If, then, the goal is fine, cleverness is praiseworthy, and if the goal is base, cleverness is unscrupulousness; hence both [*phronetic*] and unscrupulous people are called clever' (1985, p. 169 [1144a23–28]). As distinct from general *deinotes*, *phronesis* only concerns issues that fall under the sphere of ethical character (see further in Kristjánsson et al., 2021).

Aristotle writes a lot about *phronesis*, both in the *Nicomachean Ethics* and the *Politics*, but none of it is very systematic. To 'operationalise' the construct in the service of empirical interventions and measurements, we need to reconstruct from bits and pieces in Aristotle's corpus a more holistic account. In doing so, my colleagues and I have come up with a construct of *phronesis* via a four-componential model (Darnell et al., 2019), based on four functions that I delineate below.

(i) Constitutive function. This is the ability, and eventually cognitive excellence, which enables an agent to perceive what the salient features of a given situation are from an ethical perspective, and to see what is required in a given situation as reason(s) for responding in certain ways. *(ii) Integrative function.* This component involves integrating different components of a good life, especially in dilemmatic situations where different ethically salient considerations or virtues appear to be in conflict. This function is highly situation-specific, which means that traditional wisdom research, which homes in on more global capacities, is mostly irrelevant to the derivation of a *phronesis* construct. *(iii) Blueprint function.* Phronetic persons possess a general conception of the good life (*eudaimonia*) and adjust their moral identity to that blueprint, thus furnishing it with motivational force. This does not mean that each ordinary person needs to have the same sophisticated comprehension of the 'grand end' of human life as a philosopher or an experienced statesperson might have in order to count as possessing *phronesis*. Rather a blueprint of the aims of human life informing (and informed by) *phronesis* is within the grasp of the ordinary, well-brought-up individual and reflected in ordinary acts. It draws upon the person's standpoint of life as a whole and determines the place that different goods occupy in the larger context and how they interact with other goods. This blueprint is ideally 'on call' in every situation of action. *(iv) Emotional regulation function.* Phronesis requires, and contributes to, the agent's emotions being in line with her construal of a given situation, moral judgement and decision, thereby also offering motivation for the appropriate response. Notice that emotional regulation must not be understood here in terms of emotional suppression or policing, but rather as the infusion of emotion with reason—reason which calibrates the emotion in line with the morally and rationally warranted medial state of feeling—and the subsequent harmony between the two.

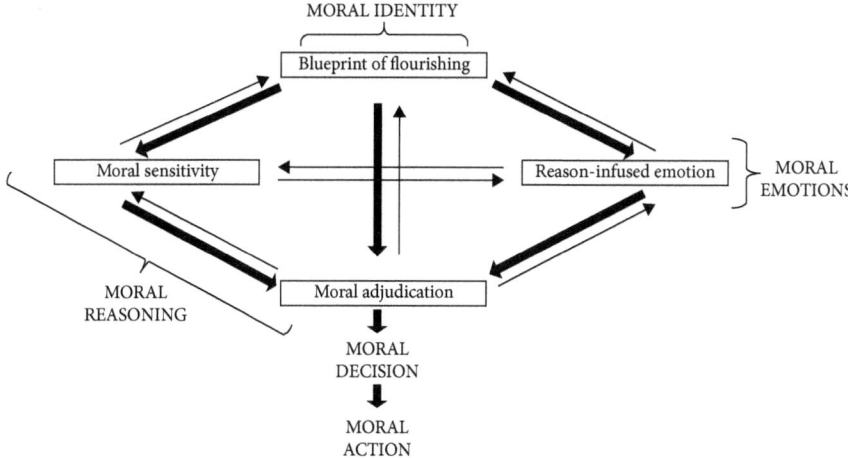

Figure 1.1   A Neo-Aristotelian model of wise (*phronetic*) moral decision making

Figure 1 (Kristjánsson et al., 2021) illustrates this overall conceptualisation of *phronesis*. Notice that I try to couch the components there in a language that will be more familiar to psychologists (entirely capitalised words) than the names of the four 'functions'. Notice also that (as can be seen in Figure 1) the components do not refer to psycho-moral capacities that are completely independent of one another and can be turned 'up' or 'down' in isolation. For example, the cultivation of moral sensitivity is likely to impact in various ways upon the capacity for moral reasoning about the situations identified with greater sensitivity.

As with other virtues, the question of what constitutes proper friendship and how friendship needs to be adjudicated upon, should it come into conflict with other virtues, falls under the jurisdiction of *phronesis*. I say much more about *phronesis* as a meta-virtue and specifically its role with respect to friendship in Chapter 3.

1.3 Aristotle's Naturalism

One of the reasons why Aristotelianism seems to strike a chord with practically minded academics outside of philosophy, which has led to its modest domestications into some areas of social science (see e.g. Fowers & Anderson, 2018, on friendship), is Aristotle's naturalistic method, which seems to entail that all moral theorising needs to be answerable to findings from empirical science. Beginning with Section 1.5 below, and throughout this book, I draw upon empirical work on friendship in ways that most (non-Aristotelian) philosophers would not. By way of explanation and justification of this interdisciplinary approach, some observations about Aristotle's method, as well as my own, are in order.

It is almost a platitude to say that Aristotle was an ethical naturalist and more interested in the practical applications of his ethical inquiry than its theoretical contribution. After all, the purpose of such inquiry 'is not to know what virtue is, but to become good, since otherwise the inquiry would be of no benefit to us' (1985, p. 35 [1103b27–29]). Naturalism of this kind is often taken to imply what Flanagan (1991) calls 'minimal psychological realism': the thesis (already anticipated in my Preface) that all recommendations posited by moral theory must be 'attainable for creatures like us'. Moreover, Aristotle's naturalism is typically understood—in the contemporary academic climate—as a clarion call for more interdisciplinary research on morality and for supporting theoretical positions by use of social scientific methods, both quantitative and qualitative. While all this is warranted up to a point, it is only half the story and not even the more interesting half.

The first thing to note is that Aristotle never describes himself as conducting ethical theorising. He refers to the subject matter of both the *Nicomachean Ethics* and *Politics* as 'political science' (1985, p. 2 [1094a27–28]), which in ancient Greek literally meant the science about the state (*polis*). Elsewhere he names this subject matter 'the philosophy of human affairs' (1985, p. 298 [1181b15]). The important takeaway lesson is that he does not refer to his inquiry anywhere as 'ethics' or 'ethical philosophy' although both terms were available to him. The most felicitous modern denotation of the kind of study Aristotle claims to be pursuing is simply 'social science'; hence, he would probably find it puzzling that his theory about friendship from the *Nicomachean Ethics* is nowadays almost exclusively studied in philosophy departments, not social-science ones, and that virtue ethics is considered a branch of moral philosophy, not a social scientific theory.

Now, if Aristotle is basically conducting social science, what precisely is the naturalistic method that he is applying? Here I want to aver that very few people seem to have grasped how radically different his method is from those that are typically applied in contemporary social science, and what a tall order it would be to persuade most current social scientists of its credibility. Everyone knows about the competing, but sometimes synergic, paradigms of quantitative versus qualitative studies in social science. The former aim for width and comprehensiveness, and the identification of causal (or at least correlational) links, while the latter aim for greater depth and understanding by probing the meaning that agents ascribe to events and activities and interpreting them through a discursive lens.

Although the quantitative–qualitative dichotomy was not available to Aristotle, at least not in the terms in which it is couched nowadays, one could argue that he captures the essence of these two different sources of information/knowledge through his frequent allusions to eliciting the views of both the 'many' and the 'wise'. However, he would find the notion odd that agents can be considered ultimate authorities about the meaning they ascribe to facets of their lives. Even if the researcher understands the agent's words correctly, that is surely not the end of the story. People lack self-transparency; hence, they can be systematically mistaken about what is truly meaningful. For instance, someone who is really worthy of great things can think herself unworthy of great things: a vice that Aristotle called 'pusillanimity' (1985, p. 98 [1123b10–13]) but would probably be called a 'lack of self-esteem' by moderns. In such cases, the task of the social scientist will be to correct the self-deception and identify the relevant objective truth of the matter. More generally speaking, there is no meaningful social-science method that does not criticise and offer guidance. The true aim of social science must be the improvement of socio-political discussion and socio-political activity (cf. Salkever, 2005, p. 48), not just the systematic gathering of information. Aristotle would probably acknowledge that there can be social scientists who are mainly in the business of collecting data. However, if that data gathering is not to be written off as completely haphazard and otiose, it must be done in the light of some hypothesis which itself is evaluative, critical and aims at offering guidance. Normativity will thus enter any proper social scientific study at some juncture.

The unique feature that sets Aristotle's social-science method apart can perhaps most felicitously be called *axiological teleology*. It contains two assumptions that would both be rejected by (most) post-Weberian social scientists. The axiological assumption is that social science is an inherently normative enterprise, in the sense of applying (assuming, making, identifying and creating new) value judgements. Aristotle thus completely rejects the Humean fact–value distinction or, perhaps better put, he has no sense of this distinction and writes as if it does not exist. For Aristotle, evaluative judgements are just a sub-category of factual judgements that describe an objective world of evaluations, rather than merely evaluating subjectively an independent objective world of description. This means that the question that a modern philosopher might ask about my method in this book of repeatedly citing social scientific findings about friendship in order to make philosophical points—namely, the question of whether this enterprise reduces the moral to the non-moral—would sound bizarre to Aristotle. As I explain in more detail at a later juncture, there is no special realm of 'the moral' in Aristotle's theory: all we have are evaluative and non-evaluative facts about the natural world, and the former do not stand in need of any reduction to the latter. They are simply facts of a certain kind that need to be tested for accuracy.

The whole *raison d'être* of social science (or what Aristotle calls 'political science') is to study human flourishing (*eudaimonia*, i.e. how to live well, recall the preceding section), and in such a study, the truth of evaluative judgements (e.g. about physical incapacitation, humiliation, callousness and loneliness being bad for people; but health, virtue and friendship good) is simply taken as given. For what academic purpose would be served by second-guessing the unanimous verdict of both the many and the wise about these features of human existence? What the student of social science needs is a deep experiential understanding of how those features play out in different contexts and different individuals, just as a doctor assesses the health of an individual patient rather than some average patient (Aristotle, 1985, p. 297 [1181b3–5]). What the student does not need, however, is anti-realism or cynicism about the nature of goodness as such. If one refuses to accept the experientially grounded claim that a human being's happiest life, both as an individual and as a citizen, is a life of virtue, shared with close friends and accompanied with those enjoyments which virtue usually procures, one would, by Aristotle's lights, not just be a moral cynic but a bad social scientist.

This axiology of goodness is not only grounded in simple empirical observations about human affairs but in a much deeper probing into the different 'causes' steering the existence and development of all well-ordered natural beings. One of those is the final cause (the *telos*)—the ideal realisation to which the being is naturally drawn. So, for example, a plant seed has a nature inherent to it, and this nature determines its teleological ends. The plant is a good plant insofar as it reaches these ends and bad insofar as it does not. The general idea here is that goodness is thought of in terms of fulfilment, and this fulfilment is one of inherent potential reaching its teleological end, its best manifestation. The *telos* of the human person is an active state of moral maturity, health and happiness, just as the *telos* of the human group is a well-ordered state. This is, for Aristotle, not an esoteric metaphysical claim but simply a naturalist one, derived from observing how two natural entities (a human person and a human group) best develop and reach a mature, homeostatic condition. He would probably have found Enlightenment anti-teleological catechisms challenging theoretically but, in a practical sense, totally beside the point. A doctor who does not operate with a clear sense of the *telos* of human health, or a teacher who has no vision of the *telos* of good education, are simply bad professionals, unable to do their jobs well; the same, *mutatis mutandis*, applies to the social scientist who refuses to acknowledge an objective sense of the human good.

Social scientists often complain about philosophers being mute about their methods. I have now explained what I call Aristotle's naturalistic method, and which I endorse. However, I need to add a few additional observations about my own method by acknowledging that certain 'terms and conditions apply'. Those terms and conditions have to do with the fact that I happen to be representative of a group that Owen Flanagan (2017) calls 'WEIRD' (Western, educated, industrialised, rich and democratic)—and one could add male and middle-aged to the present equation. Notably, although only 12 per cent of humankind live in WEIRD societies, 96 per cent of psychology studies published in top journals involve WEIRD participants only (Heinrich, Heine & Norenzayan, 2010). I draw unabashedly on my personal experiences in what follows, and those may not be representative of the majority of human cultures and historical contexts, for example those of Aristotle's Athens. As already announced, I will be drawing upon various current empirical sources in my exploration and hence not waxing entirely personal or anecdotal. However, surprisingly little of the social-science literature carries any direct significance with respect the notion of Aristotelian character friendship. For example, no longitudinal studies seem to have been carried out on the development of his friendship types. It could even be argued, as Fowers and Anderson (2018) do, that certain assumptions in much of the social-science literature (instrumentalism, individualism and the equation of the good life with that of subjective wellbeing) are directly inimical to any study or understanding of friendships on an Aristotelian account.

In any case, the methodological point I wish to make here is that, although this book is meant to constitute more than mere philosophical analysis, the scarcity of social scientific sources directly relevant to a characterological exploration of friendship means that my empirical claims will have to make do with considerable input from armchair psychology, based on context-dependent and personal experiences—by someone who happens to have found character friendships difficult to form and sustain.

1.4 The History of Friendship from Aristotle Onwards

Sections 1.2 and 1.3 served the purpose of explaining some of the background assumptions and methodological considerations without which we cannot make sense of Aristotle's friendship theory. The time has now come to pick up again the historical thread from Aristotle's theory, fleshed out in Section 1.1, and follow it towards the contemporary empirical research to be sketched in Section 1.5.

This book is not a historical treatise on friendship. Nevertheless, it is worth visiting some of the stepping stones in the development from Aristotle's theory to present-day concerns, if only to understand why friendship gradually took a backseat in anything that could be usually categorised as moral theorising—a position from which the topic has never fully recovered despite the interest it arouses in contemporary social science and popular literature. I need to warn readers, however, that this will be very much history in tabloid format. Just as I have left out Aristotle's predecessor, Plato, so far (although he becomes part of the plot later), I have no space to expand here upon a number of historically important writers on friendship, such as Lucretius, Seneca and Bacon.

The major landmark writing after Aristotle is probably Cicero's work on how to be a friend (2018, written in 44BCE). The 2018 edition touts this as 'arguably the best book ever written on the subject' (pp. viii–ix). While clearly a work that it is difficult not to love, I would take exception to this pitch. First, while written as a dialogue, the stylistic advantages of that format are not utilised anywhere near as cleverly as in Plato's dialogues. Second, if submitted as a student essay, it would probably not make it through a standard plagiarism app such as *Turnitin*. It shamelessly plunders Aristotle's texts for ideas, without acknowledgement, sometimes doing no more than paraphrasing whole sections of the *Nicomachean*

Ethics. For example, Cicero says unblushingly, without a nod to Aristotle: 'A friend is, quite simply, another self' (2018, p. 119). However, we must bear in mind that authors in the Roman period were nowhere as sensitive to issues of copyright and authorship as we moderns are, and there were no APA or Harvard-system protocols to fall back on. Moreover, the reigning philosophy of the day, Stoicism, had strong practical aspirations, which by today's standards would probably count as therapeutic (Sherman, 2021), more so than aspirations to original philosophising. It is no coincidence that one of the most popular and effective treatment options in today's clinical psychology, namely cognitive behavioural therapy, has explicit Stoic roots (Robertson, 2010).

What is most to admire in Cicero's work is his lucid and eloquent style of writing that draws readers in. If only current self-help writing were as gloriously presented! Other than that, familiar themes from Aristotle are presented in rapid succession: different types of friendship, its intrinsic value, how only good people can become complete friends, how life without friends in futile, etc. Here is an example of the panache of Cicero's writing on the merits of friendship:

> Wherever you turn, there it is. No door shuts it out, no time is wrong for it, and never is it in the way. We need friendship in every part of our life as much as we need the proverbial water and fire, the two necessities of life.   (2018, p. 45)

For those who like artistic embellishments of philosophical ideas, Cicero on friendship is a good bet. For those who like rigorous philosophising, which takes counter-positions seriously and engages with them, Aristotle will count as the preferred option.

There is only one point at which Cicero's guide to true friendship signals a radical departure from Aristotle. Cicero does not hesitate to count friendship as the greatest value—or a master virtue, if you like—trumping other values. He thus claims that 'you should place friendship above all other human concerns', that it 'exceeds other virtues by far' and that it is, simply, 'the greatest thing we can find in life' (2018, pp. 35, 45, 177). Because Cicero presents those claims as articulations of faith rather than arguments in an ongoing academic debate, it is unclear whether or not he saw them as the significant departures that they really are from Aristotle's more modest claims about the value of friendship, or just as natural extensions of the high premium that Aristotle placed on friendship. However, if the latter was his view, Cicero was certainly wrong. There is no true moral master virtue in Aristotle, either friendship or anything else, as for instance justice is in Plato (although *megalopsychia*, or great-mindedness, comes close to it for a particular group of wealthy philanthropists, see Kristjánsson, 2020, chap. 4). Instead, we are furnished with the intellectual meta-virtue of *phronesis*, which adjust the demands of each particular moral virtue to the nuanced situational contexts of the relevant decision making. Given what Aristotle says about friendship, especially friendship for character or virtue, *phronesis* may give greater overall weight to friendship than to many other virtues, but friendship is not automatically overriding in any context. If it were, the core function of *phronesis*, that of adjudication or arbitration (Darnell et al., 2019), would scarcely be needed any more. So Cicero's departure does have significant theoretical implications, bringing him closer than Aristotle to contemporary accounts that claim one should prioritise the needs of friends—simply because they are *their* needs—without hesitation (see e.g. Koltonski, 2016). However, Cicero's cop-out from the problematic implications of this position—that one may need to resort to wicked ways to help wicked friends—is to rely on the assumption that true friends are, *ex hypothesi*, not vicious: 'Nature gave us friendship as an aide to virtue, not as a companion to vice' (2018, p. 143).

All in all, then, a few centuries after Aristotle's death, we had reached a time when friendship was accorded the highest moral acclaim by the leading philosopher of the day: seen as a virtue responding to a deep psycho-moral and social, if not an ontological, need for soulmateship (depending on how one interprets the 'another-self' thesis). Given this historical fact, it is even more stunning to consider the vicissitudes that the ideal of friendship was to undergo in the following centuries, within the emerging dominant Christian paradigm, from Augustine to Kierkegaard. However, it only requires a smattering of understanding of Christian doctrine to understand the profound suspicion that the Greek concept of *philia* was to evoke during medieval times and into modernity and how it came to be seen as a noxious historical residue from the ancient heathens that deserved nothing less than full doctrinal dismemberment (see Mitias, 2012, for a comprehensive historical overview; cf. Lewis, 1960, chap 6; Nehamas, 2016, pp. 30–5).

First, the high regard in which friendship was held by Aristotle, and even more so by Cicero, smacks—by Christian lights in a God-centred world—of idolatry. We have one true friend in Christ; to elevate mere mortals to the same level of intimacy is to idolise them in an anti-Christian way. As Albert Midlane's hymn has it, 'There is a Friend for little children / Above the bright blue sky. / A friend who never changes, / Whose love will never die' (cited in Barnard, 2011, p. 249).

Second, we are all created equal in the eyes of God, and before him, we are all sinners. Adopting due humility, we should see each other as neighbours, as brothers and sisters in Christ, like the Good Samaritan did. To give unequal consideration to individuals, based on presumed merit, desert or level of attachment, is to reject the Christian emotion of *agape* or *caritas* (all-inclusive universal love or charity) and replace it with the pagan ideal of *philia*, which we hubristically consider ourselves capable of attaching to individuals of our own choice, tainted by partiality: overruling the equal value emanating from divine love of all human beings created in the image of the Lord.

Lurking in the background of the Christian denigration of friendship is also a deep worry about the fecundity of happiness that Aristotle and Cicero ascribe to the fruits of successful friendships. After all, any real happiness is to be achieved in the afterlife. While solidarity among human beings in our current valley of tears is to be commended, insofar as it is motivated by a Christian spirit of neighbourliness, once we begin to enjoy the interaction with our friends to the extent of seeing it as intrinsically valuable, we have succumbed to a conflation of the ephemeral and the eternal, losing sight of the wood for the trees. This is one more reason why the ideal of friendship fell into eclipse in the Christian world from Augustine onwards. Indeed, the timing of this eclipse coincides more or less with that of Augustine's own conversion, which more than anything else can be seen as encapsulating a shift from a lover of personal friends (such as Nebridius, whose death overwhelmed him) and worldly pleasures to a lover of God and all humanity as created by God. In contrast, Jesus himself seems to have been slightly more accommodating of personal friendships: witness his love of individual disciples, although he does make some pretty uncompromising demands on those who come to him about needing to learn to 'hate' loved ones first (*Luke*, XIV, 26).

Notably, although I am only telling the Western story here, a similar—if less radical—trajectory can be seen in China, as the secular ethics of Confucius was replaced, or at least supplemented, by Buddhism's command for universal benevolence, which extends even further than Christianity to all sentient beings. This is another example of what C. S Lewis refers to as a transition from our congenital preferences for 'safe investments and limited liabilities' (1960, p. 168) to a truly universalist ethics which does not allow any preferential treatment.

The culmination and entrenchment of Christian thinking about friendship can be seen in the writings of the Danish philosopher Kierkegaard (esp. 1991, originally published 1846–1847). A message that was, during medieval times, often dressed up in fairly general and abstract theological language is pitched more vociferously in existentialist terms by a philosopher who did not believe in taking any prisoners. Thus, Kierkegaard explains in no uncertain terms how Christianity has thrust friendship (along with erotic love), 'the love rooted in mood and inclination, preferential love' from the throne, 'in order to establish spiritual love' (1991, p. 235). What he dislikes most about the pagan (Aristotelian) view is that love of friends is grounded somehow in one's capacity for *self-love*: a veritable Christian vice (along with Aristotle's virtue, but Christian vice, of 'proper pride'). Scorning Aristotle's idea of the friend as another self, Kierkegaard does not see that thesis as being about self-extension but rather self-enhancement. It is not about a union of me and another but rather about my selfish choice of deciding to incorporate another person in my own self-identity, hence making what Murdoch was later to call my 'fat, relentless ego' (2001, p. 51) bigger—and, by selfishly excluding others, creating the conditions for yet another Christian vice: jealousy. In sum, Kierkegaard does not only express scepticism of common-sense notions of friendship; he rejects them altogether as totally un-Christian. This hatchet job turns out to be part of his personal grand project of renouncing Hegel's presumed synthesis of the 'best' in pagan and Christian thought about the human spirit and turning it somehow into a universal system.

Now, there are various twists and turns to this story of the Christian rejection of Aristotelian friendship that I cannot go into in detail. Suffice it to mention here briefly that there has always been a strand of Catholic thought that is more accommodating of Aristotle's ideas about this matter. St. Thomas, reluctant as ever to denounce completely any view argued for by 'the Philosopher', tried to reinterpret Aristotle on friendship by focusing on the altruistic strand in the virtue and how it may be psychologically true that the palace of universal love (*agape*) can only be entered through the courtyard of partial love (as *philia*). The same idea was vividly expressed by the Victorian cleric John Henry Newman (the author of the famous *Idea of a University*), whose influence on Catholic thought, at least in the UK, is still profound. Pedagogically minded as ever, Newman asks us to think of friendship, *qua* Christian ideal, as a school of virtue and to consider the possibility that 'the best preparation for loving the world at large [...] is to cultivate an intimate friendship and affection towards those who are immediately about us' (cited in Vernon, 2010, p. 146). In a similar vein, Pope John Paul II idealised Aristotle's virtue friendships, both in theory and in his own life (Wojtyla, 2013).

This potential modification of Christian thought notwithstanding, it is more about the development of universal love through friendship than it is about the wholesale accommodation of the latter into Christian doctrine. Thus, St. Thomas's reluctance to let go completely of the Aristotelian heritage does not change the fact that the Christian era marked a true paradigm shift in thinking about friendship. It is naïve to see this shift only in terms of a change in a religious world-view, however; it needs to be understood against the context of various other simultaneous developments in the history of ideas, especially as the medieval world morphed gradually into the modern one. Protestantism, individualism, capitalism, technicism, rationalism, professionalism and increased mobility all contributed in different ways to the demise of relationships based on intimacy with 'other selves' (cf. Konstan, 1997, p. 18). Philosophers who one would normally have expected to say something substantial about friendship, from Hobbes to Mill and Kant, mostly remained mute or lukewarm, even overtly critical (see e.g. Slomp, 2019, on Hobbes). Moreover, as already hinted at in the Preface, the Christian heritage created the conditions for the sluggish uptake of friendship as a moral value in both Kantian deontology and utilitarian consequentialism. The main barrier was the requirement of *impartial altruism* in both those large ethical theories: of giving all human persons (friends or non-friends) equal weight as equally worthy of moral consideration.

The funeral oration had not been sung over the corpse of the friendship ideal. But what began to replace the Aristotelian one was an ideal with a completely different sort of rationale. In 1580, the French Renaissance thinker Michel de Montaigne published a short essay on friendship in the memory of his dear friend, the humanist poet Étienne de La Boétie, whom he had only known for four years but of whom he had grown immeasurably fond. Whereas Augustine had used a religious conversion almost like a defence mechanism to react to the death of his best friend Nebridius, motivating him to move away from friendship exceptionalism, Montaigne turned the tragic untimely departure of La Boétie into the representation of a new heightened form of friendship exceptionalism and particularism, according to which deep friendships are grounded, arationally and amorally, in the uniquely aesthetically attractive and non-fungible qualities of a friend. A new friendship ideal was born: a genuine and formidable competitor to the Aristotelian one.

Montaigne's essay (2015) was to influence most subsequent writers on friendship, including Nietzsche, although not all of them fully grasped the radical implications of Montaigne's view. After all, the depth of the attachment to the friend and the idealisation of their interactions, as described by Montaigne, are quite reminiscent in many ways of the picture painted by Aristotle. The difference lies not much so in the psychological 'symptoms' of the friendship, so to speak, but rather the way in which those are seen to be grounded. Montaigne is thus deeply disillusioned with the treatments of friendship 'left to us by antiquity'. Those seem to him 'flat and poor, in comparison of the sense I have of it'. The main mistake he identifies among the ancients is to think of the close friend in terms of all-round virtue. Just as we do not care if our footman is chaste or the good cook a swearer, we prefer beauty before goodness in bed; wit before wisdom at the dinner table. So, in life, there are horses for courses. In the case of our closest friend, we look for that ineffable attraction which cannot be reduced to any rationally definable qualities, partly because we are not looking for the done deal in the friend's self but rather for a self that allows for mutual self-fashioning as the two friends strive towards 'absolute concurrence of affections'. There is thus an educational ideal at work here also, just as in Aristotle's account, but it is grounded in a very different moral psychology, of what would be referred to nowadays as 'anti-self-realism' (i.e. the denial of any objective selfhood, as explained in Kristjánsson, 2010), and in a different pedagogy, which in many ways anticipates modern postmodern pedagogies of growth as crystallisation—atheoretical and unpredictable in advance (Gergen, 1991)—although the postmodern idea of the essential shallowness of all human bonds would obviously have been anathema to Montaigne.

Alexander Nehamas's (2016) book does a great job of resurrecting Montaigne's view for the present day and contrasting it with Aristotle's vision. Moreover, Nehamas achieves the almost impossible, of writing a 'trade book' on friendship that is as strong on academic gravitas as on readability: coming as close to a philosophical page-turner as you can get. Because I will be using Nehamas's account and the original Montaigne essay to represent what I call the 'the aesthetised view' of the grounding of friendship—comparing and contrasting it with Aristotle's 'moralised view'—in Chapter 4, I leave Montaigne out of further consideration here except to recommend his essay to readers as an unmissable, tersely worded and briskly placed but incisive reading on the mysteries of deep friendship.

To what extent Montaigne influenced Nietzsche is moot, although the idea of friendship as an aesthetic ideal permeates various aphorism from Nietzsche's middle period where he mentions friendship. But, then, Nietzsche had his own way of aestheticising most ideals that other philosophers had moralised. The most original insight about friendship is perhaps this following aphorism which is worth reproducing in full:

> Two types are distinguished amongst people who have a special faculty for friendship. The one is ever on the ascent, and for every phase of his development he finds a friend exactly suited to him. The series of friends which he thus acquires is seldom a consistent one, and is sometimes at variance and in contradiction, entirely in accordance with the fact that the later phases of his development neutralise or prejudice the earlier phases. Such a man may jestingly be called *a ladder*. The other type is represented by him who exercises an attractive influence on very different characters and endowments, so that he wins a whole circle of friends; these, however, are thereby brought voluntarily into friendly relations with one another in spite of all differences. Such a man may be called *a circle*, for this homogeneousness of such different temperaments and natures must somehow be typified in him. Furthermore, the faculty for having good friends is greater in many people than the faculty for being a good friend.
>
> (Nietzsche, 2020, §368)

Nietzsche here offers a different typology of friendship from Aristotle's, based on two different personality types, and how those seek out different types of friendship. It stands to reason that he considered himself to fall into the 'ladder-type' and also as one whose faculty for initiating friendships was greater than remaining a good friend. His tense and tumultuous friendship with Richard Wagner is a case in point (see Vernon, 2010, pp. 73–7, for a quick overview). Nietzsche is perhaps the first philosopher to turn the ditching of a friend into a virtue, or at least a developmental asset. For 'ladder' types, such as Nietzsche, manufacturing a break with a friend becomes a psychological necessity once the friend has served her purpose, in order to be able to continue with one's personal 'ascent' in the most profitable way. This may sound very much like a self-serving instrumentalisation of friendship. However, as I explain in Chapter 6, utility friendships can have value that goes beyond instrumentalisation, while they last. Being non-intrinsically valuable is not tantamount to being only instrumentally valuable. The unusually solemn tone of many of Nietzsche's aphorisms about friendship and the depth of the friendship that he was able to cultivate himself with people like the philosopher Paul Rée do not indicate that Nietzsche's view of friendship was that of a value parasite. However, his service to the friendship discourse is to direct attention, in his unique way, to the different kinds of friendship trajectories and endings (cf. Verkerk, 2019).

The final philosopher I want to mention here is Ralph Waldo Emerson (2020). In 1841 he wrote a beautiful essay on friendship. While scarcely rising to the level of deep philosophy, and not taking a direct stand on the issue that, for example, divides Aristotle and Montaigne, Emerson's measured tribute to friendship is, however, the source of some profound observations about this virtue as it plays out in people's everyday lives. The argumentative sketchiness and the meandering chattiness of Emerson's text are more than made up for by his practical insights and semi-poetic reflections on the ambiguities of friendship. He muses, for example, about the nature of letter writing to a friend and how that practice often generates 'troops of gentle thoughts', surpassing in quality those of any scholarly inquiry. Yet, he is keenly aware of the ebbs and flows of friendship, and how even the best of friendships are, like erotic love, laden with 'shades of suspicion and unbelief'. Emerson also has much more interest than Aristotle in friendship beginnings. He expresses surprise at how friends tend to come to one 'unsought', without conscious effort. They are 'self-elected': one recognises them rather than finds them. Soon, they become part of one's identity, such that I 'feel pride in my friend's accomplishments as if they were mine,—and a property in his virtues'. Moreover, a friend 'is a person with whom I may be sincere. Before him I may think aloud'. The first element of friendship is thus truth; the second tenderness. Together they make up the 'essence of friendship' which is 'entireness: a total magnanimity and trust'.

Emerson speaks in headlines: 'I hate the prostitution of the name of friendship to signify modish and worldly alliances. I much prefer the company of plough-boys and tin-peddlers' to 'silken and perfumed amity'. To his merit, Emerson simultaneously embellishes the philosophical discourse on friendship and brings it down to earth. Again, Emerson's short essay is a must-read for all students of friendship, although they will be searching for wool in a goat house if they expect to extract a *theory* of friendship from it.

We may seem to have come a long way from Aristotle now. The philosophical discourse on friendship has, through the centuries, become ever more circuitous and treacherous. I will be exploring some of the most treacherous issues in subsequent chapters. It has admittedly become more and more difficult to find anything singular in the prodigious plurality of philosophical (and religious) views on friendship. Yet one rarely gets the impression that theorists are talking at cross purposes about different concepts. There is clearly an everyday concept of friendship that forms the crux of all the inquiries and enables us to categorise them as inquiries about the same thing. The same is, fortunately, true of social scientific studies also, in modernity, although those may seem to be plotting quite a different path to the philosophical ones. The social scientists are, in short, interested in understanding friendship for the same reason as Aristotle or Montaigne—although their methodology is different. Let us now try to cross the fence between the disciplines.

1.5 Contemporary Psychological Research on Friendship

Aristotle himself notes that, regarding friendship, some of the 'puzzles' surrounding it are 'more proper to natural science' than to philosophy (1985, p. 209 [1155b1–10]). Obviously, social science did not exist as an independent category in Aristotle's time. Yet he could in some ways count as its progenitor, while in others (namely with respect to the Weberian idea of a 'value-free' social science) as its archvillain. In any case, the sort of science that has devoted itself in recent times to the 'puzzles' that Aristotle alluded to is, of course, psychology: the discipline to which I now turn. Generally speaking, my own neo-Aristotelian view is that a rapprochement between philosophy and psychology is a force for the good—as long as it does not obscure important demarcating lines (Kristjánsson, 2018, chap. 10).

What are these 'demarcating lines' in the case of friendship? It is difficult to summarise those without succumbing to undue generalisations. Yet let me try. *First*, most psychologists will either refuse to understand or at least to accommodate talk about the potential intrinsic value of friendship. The term 'intrinsic value' is simply not part of their vocabulary. For those who acknowledge some 'ungrounded grounder' of human strivings, that grounder is almost invariably considered to be subjective wellbeing. Instrumentalism with respect to all values, down to the bottom ground of subjectively experienced wellbeing (which is understood as somehow being 'value-free'), counts as psychology's stock in trade, with only a handful of exceptions of psychologists who pursue objective accounts (Fowers, 2010). However, this seems to make all values (including friendship), apart from subjective wellbeing, essentially replaceable (Fowers & Anderson, 2018). *Second*, this instrumentalist orientation links up with psychology's fear of normativity: its insistence to remain value-free. Normativity is here taken to encompass both evaluations and prescriptions in equal measure, both to be thrown overboard except insofar as psychologists are interested in studying what people actually value, without passing any qualitative judgements about those value choices (critiqued in Kristjánsson, 2013). That said, many psychologists have developed a knack for clandestinely helping themselves to the benefits of normative inquiry while renouncing it in principle (see e.g. Peterson & Seligman, 2004). *Third*, psychologists tend to have a scant interest in conceptual inquires as such, let alone in posing as 'the wise', revising the usage of 'the many'. For instance, within relationship studies, their sole conceptual concern is with what ordinary people actually take words such as 'friendship' to mean and how they use them to express their views, feelings and preferences. Sensing this, many philosophers see 'conceptual work' in psychology as lax or lazy. Conversely, psychologists will complain about the Procrustean attitude of philosophers, superimposing their preferred assumptions on a given concept in the name of conceptual rigour. Psychologists tend to find such 'conceptual fetishism' quirky or mildly amusing (see further in Kristjánsson, 2018, chap. 10). *Fourth*, while philosophers consider the understanding of a concept, value or virtue to have worth in itself, psychologists are looking for practical applications. This is indicative of the *predictivism* that animates social science in general. The psychologist's Eldorado is to find a trait of personality or temperament (say, the trait of finding it easy to make friends) that predicts significant life outcomes—most importantly subjective wellbeing—beyond the predictions provided by, say, the ubiquitous Big-Five Model (Kristjánsson, 2018, chap. 10). *Fifth*, psychologists are concerned with 'operationalising' friendship in order to study it empirically, and these operationalisations do not usually 'test for' friendship as philosophers understand it.

As already hinted at in the Preface, this means that what we tend to see in psychological studies of friendship are fairly permissive conceptual specifications (as inclusive of different lay views as possible), where friendship is, for example, characterised as a reciprocal relationship in which there is mutual liking and enjoyment spent in each other's company (Majors, 2012). As people's self-reported specifications of friendships thus tend to be taken at face value, the question becomes not what does—let alone what should ideally—ground them morally or otherwise, but rather what 'provisions' such alliances between self-described friends offer (e.g. companionship, intimacy, reliable assistance, self-validation, emotional security) and how those provisions are correlated with psycho-social variables, most notably either subjective wellbeing or a positive self-concept (understood as socially constructed 'identity', rather than morally grounded character). Normatively grounded distinctions, such as Aristotle's tripartite typology, are eschewed, that is unless those turn out to be firmly rooted in everyday discourse (Murstein & Spitz, 1974; cf. Anderson & Fowers, 2020). The normatively most advanced kind of friendship in Aristotle, namely character friendship, is replaced by what people themselves happen to describe as the most advanced kind, in terms of their 'closest', 'deepest' or 'best' friendships. Finally, 'moral' concerns about friendship are replaced by 'prosocial' ones which are meant to be descriptive rather than normative (as questioned by Walker, Curren & Jones, 2016, pp. 286–7).

With only a few exceptions (see e.g. Anderson & Fowers, 2020), characterising the standard methodological approach to friendship research in psychology is therefore a unidimensional, instrumentalist and amoral understanding, where friendship will vary quantitatively with respect to a number of variables but is not taken to assume normatively different types. One further general point to note is that in most studies in psychology of established associations between friendship and other variables, the associations are correlational rather than causal

(Perlman, 2017, pp. 293–4). For example, when an association is found between friendship and health, we cannot infer that friendship *leads to* better health. It could also be that healthy people are simply more apt at establishing and maintaining friendships, or that a third variable (say, a given personality trait) might be conducive to both friendship formations and health. Some existing research does indicate bidirectional causality, however (Bryan, Puckett & Newman, 2013). Notably, most of the studies in question are conducted on fairly uniform cohorts, which tend to be predominantly WEIRD (recall Section 1.3) and often comprise university (mostly psychology) students who are within easy reach.

I am not listing all these caveats and considerations to detract from the merits of psychological research on friendship. I am just noting that it is limited and has certain questionable assumptions built into it, just as philosophical research does—witness some of the Aristotelian assumptions that I cast doubt on in Section 1.1. I do not agree, therefore, with the sociologist Fred Pahl that friendship has 'eluded the grasp' of psychology (cited in Nehamas, 2016, p. 103). Psychologists have grasped it, but exclusively so on their own distinctive terms. To what extent those are considered to be the 'right' terms depends on one's view of the methods and assumptions of contemporary psychology in general rather than any specific misgivings about its approach to friendship. To be sure, some of the reported findings may seem to replicate only what any intelligent person would think is obvious (Fowers & Anderson, 2018), or dress up quasi-conceptual truths as empirical results. However, confirming received wisdoms and truths, by identifying actual antecedents, dynamics and consequences (Perlman, 2017, p. 283), has always been one of the services provided by experimental psychology.

The final general caveat is that since I am aiming solely here for a broad overview of psychological findings, in order to juxtapose those with all the armchair theorising otherwise characterising this work, I rely mostly on secondary sources: namely, works that have aimed to collate and generalise from primary research. If readers are interested in the primary sources, they may have to do some further spadework to identify the original findings.

To begin this brief empirical overview by revisiting the definitional issue, psychologists studying friendship are aware of the considerable conceptual disarray in the field. However, they see it as an unavoidable implication of relying on research participants' own definitions and self-reports (Monsour, 2017, pp. 60–2). The standard recourse is then to bring together under the 'friendship' umbrella those features that are most commonly mentioned by respondents, such as voluntariness (free choice), liking (affection) and reciprocity (mutuality)—and try to distinguish those from features associated with other nearby umbrella terms, such as acquaintanceship (Morrison & Cooper-Thomas, 2017, p. 125). The end product will be 'a fuzzy set', where some of the contours and outskirts may differ between theorists (Perlman, 2017, p. 286), but psychologists are generally comfortable with such variance for the same reason as philosophers have learned to live with open-textured concepts. The difference is that the psychologists generally stop (or at least claim to stop) at the same place as the respondents, whereas the philosophers will want to proceed further and at least get rid of blatantly contradictory or otherwise anomalous intuitions through conceptual revisions.

I cited earlier a fairly bland definition from Majors (2012) of friendship, as representative of the field. Despite the acknowledged fuzziness, the variables that show up in different definitions are fairly homogeneous and seem to single out a concept fairly similar to what Aristotle meant by true friendship (including utility, pleasure and character friendships), whereas his narrower 'character friendship' would resemble most what psychologists call 'best' friendships. True friendship, from the point of view of psychology, is a reliable and mostly positively valenced relationship characterised by the features of voluntarily established reciprocal affection and companionship/involvement, mutual psycho-social aid/provisions and enhancements of worth—all in the context of psychological intimacy (Rawlins, 2008, pp. 11–12; Erdley & Day, 2017, pp. 4–5; Perlman, 2017, p. 285). Sometimes it is also posited that friendship does not contain 'open sexuality' (Wrzus et al., 2017, p. 21).

One of the puzzles mentioned but mostly left unanswered by Aristotle is whether people are more drawn towards friends who are similar or different from themselves. The empirical findings indicate that, at least in terms of objective variables, people tend to make friends with individuals similar in age, gender, race, educational attainment, marital and career status and socio-economic level (Rawlins, 2008, p. 274). For example, almost half of white Americans only have white American friends. In that sense, friendships rarely serve the purpose of rocking us out of our social comfort zones. Regarding personality traits and interests, people also seem to be attracted to people who are similar to them in terms of attitudes, values and temperament (Wrzus et al., 2017, p. 26). This does not necessarily undermine the hoary old saying that our *best* friends are often those most different from us—through the psychological synthesis (of thesis and anti-thesis) generated—but at least it shows that, in terms of frequency, birds of a feather tend to flock together.

Research into male and female friendships confirms the stereotypes: the genders seem to be looking for slightly different things in friendships or at least their friendships play out in different ways. Men's friendships are more task-and-action oriented; women's more confidentiality-and-shared-emotion focused (O'Meara, 1989). The same applies to boys and girls from a young age (Poulin & Chan, 2010, p. 261). Women also seem to more demanding about the quality of friendships that deserve to be maintained (Oswald, 2017) and more willing to confront friends about perceived violations of the relationship (Rawlins, 2008, p. 109). This research into genders and friendships has some limitations, however. Women are simply more articulate about the details of their friendships and more explicit about what they get out of them (e.g. encouragement about diet and exercise, raised self-esteem, spiritual guidance: Moremen, 2008), whereas men tend to answer more in generalities and platitudes. However, this does not mean that deep down they may not be looking for the same benefits. Furthermore, some of the historical research in this area looks hackneyed in an age of increasingly fluid gender specifications (Monsour, 2017). Finally, little attention used to be paid, until recently, to cross-sex friendships—a topic I revisit in some detail in Section 2.4 which also includes a separate summary of empirical findings.

One of the objective indicators of the role of an activity in people's lives is the time spent on it. In that respect, friendship scores high. Chicago high school students spend 30 per cent of their time with friends but only 18 per cent with their family. Employed Texas women spend as much time with friends as with their spouses and more than with their children (Perlman, 2017, p. 284). Much of the research on time assigned for friendships is fairly dated, however, and does not account for time spent with online friends. The topic of to what extent those can be called true friends in general, and character or close friends in particular, will be addressed in Chapter 7.

In terms of quantity, by far the largest mountain of psychological literature on friendships revolves around their presumed health benefits (for both mental and physical health, including longevity)—and, conversely, about the health hazards of friendlessness. I mentioned some limitations of this research earlier; one can add here the shortcoming that most studies equate 'health' with 'self-reported health' (Holt-Lundstad, 2017, p. 240). Nonetheless, the results are striking. Majors presents various findings showing how having friends is 'essential to our mental health and well-being and amongst the most significant factors for life quality and enjoyment' (2012, p. 127). Even a single friend can make a huge difference in this regard (Erdley & Day, 2017, p. 14). Friendships, at least of satisfactory quality, lower our blood pressure and reduce stress (Holt-Lundstad, 2017, p. 236). The findings are even more impressive in the field of mental health where friendships are seen as nothing less than a powerful 'vaccine' against mental distress of various kinds (King, Russell & Veith, 2017), building on more general insights and findings about links between rewarding human relationships and mental wellbeing.

The flip side of the coin is that friendlessness or friendship ruptures create loneliness, anxiety and in some cases more dangerous disturbances (Erdley & Day, 2017); even greater risk for early mortality (Holt-Lundstad, 2017, p. 233) through viral infections and heart disease. The sad fact here is that these negative features are stronger predictors than the positive ones of the relevant outcomes (Bagwell et al., 2005). In other words, low-quality or non-existent friendships are a stronger predictor of negative health-and-happiness outcomes than high-quality friendships are of positive outcomes. Somewhat surprisingly, having just what Aristotle would have called an imaginary friend (i.e. a person who one perceives as a friend but not vice versa) is considerably better than having no friend at all (Poulin & Chan, 2010). Given psychologists' penchant for relying on self-reports as evidence that is not to be second-guessed, they seem to face a dilemma here about whether or not to 'correct' young people's reports about their 'friendships' with people who do not reciprocate the affection, or just abandon the conceptual condition of friendship constituting a bilateral relationship.

Research on friendship among co-workers is slightly ambivalent. On the one hand it indicates that workplace friendships are correlated with job satisfaction and job performance, team cohesion, creativity, involvement and commitment; on the other hand it reveals various challenges, ambiguities and complications that can be avoided by not mixing work and friendships (Morrison & Cooper-Thomas, 2017). Interestingly, variables beyond the most immediately obvious ones are affected here. For instance, friendships at work increase employees' satisfaction with their boss by nearly 50 per cent and also increase their perception of being well paid (Vernon, 2010, p. 17). Friendship's influence is thus sometimes quite oblique and materialises in unexpected places. Workplace friendships are the subject of significant research scrutiny at the moment (Beard, 2020, e.g., reviews a trio of new books), perhaps spurred on by the recent lockdown during the 2020–2022 pandemic, which eroded the foundations of many previously taken for granted shared activities in the workplace.

Talking of mountains of research, one of the highest peaks is represented through research into the role of friendships in childhood and adolescence. Some of that research is about young people's identity formation (see e.g. Poulin & Chan, 2010). There are two reasons, however, why that research is not as relevant for those interested in an Aristotelian account of friendship as one could otherwise have expected it to be. First, 'identity' is here typically understood in an anti-self-realist sense as the totality of person's conceptions, beliefs and feelings about themselves (i.e. as self-concept), not as one's deep underlying selfhood that one may be aware of or not, in a realist sense (Kristjánsson, 2010). I return to this distinction and its relevance in Chapter 4. Second, even within the limited purview of identity understood as self-concept only, the focus tends to be on the non-moral aspects of identity. So I have yet to come across a paper that puts the spotlight firmly on the value of friends (as distinct from role models) for moral identity formation (see e.g. Hardy & Carlo, 2011).

That said, the existing research on childhood and teenage friendships is a treasure trove of insights for those interested in the developmental aspects of friendships. I particularly recommend Rawlins's helpful overview of the literature (2008, chapters 2–5) and the stage theory that he extracts from it (pp. 39–40). The names of the stages are already revelatory: 'Momentary physicalistic playmates' (roughly ages 3–7), 'Activity and opportunity' (roughly ages 6–9), 'Equality and reciprocity' (roughly ages 8–12) and 'Mutuality and understanding' (roughly ages 9–14). I will be returning to insights from this literature at various junctures in what follows. Let it suffice to say here that the importance accorded to friendships in the lives of young children by the children themselves and the psychologists researching them unfortunately does not appear to filter down to parents and practitioners, who do not seem to have a full understanding of the importance of affective and connective bonds of peer-friendship relationships at an early age (Brogaard-Clausen & Robson, 2019).

There is a scarcity of psychological research on the characterological aspects of friendship. The explanation lies in factors discussed at the beginning of this section. Character has to do with moral virtues, but most psychologists tend to shy away from research into moral variables in general and virtue constructs in particular, in order to bow to the prohibition on value judgements and for fear of violating normative neutrality. This 'shyness' creates the impression that mainstream psychologists, on the one hand, and neo-Aristotelian philosophers, on the other, are ploughing quite separate furrows, despite the latter's embrace of empirical-research-friendly ethical naturalism.

That impression is partly illusory, however. As readers will probably have realised themselves without needing to be told so, most of the research reported on in this section is relevant in various ways for any normative theory about the value of good friendships, not least an Aristotelian theory. Moreover—somewhat ironically and on a bleaker note—neo-Aristotelians and contemporary psychologists seem to share a reluctance to engage in brutal honesty with some of the dark, vulnerable and tragic sides of friendship (cf. Rawlins, 2008, pp. 278–9; Hojjat, Boon & Lozano, 2017, p. 196). At all events, in order to bring these two traditions into even closer harmony, it would be desirable if more social scientists were willing to countenance the idea of friendship as a characterological concept and conduct research into its moral aspects in particular. I will be reporting later on a study that does so in the case of fairly young children (Walker, Curren & Jones, 2016), and an even more recent paper (Wagner, 2019) presents interesting findings about the character strengths that early adolescents crave for in a friend: in particular honesty, humour, kindness and fairness.

The most sustained effort to rehabilitate Aristotle-based normative conceptions of friendship within mainstream psychology, however, has been made in recent years by Blaine Fowers and Austen Anderson (Fowers & Anderson, 2018; Anderson & Fowers, 2020). Their first paper offers an exercise in theoretical and historical retrieval, while the second one presents findings indicating how different friendship characteristics (namely the 'Aristotelian' ones of pleasure, utility and virtue) are differentially related to conceptions of wellbeing as hedonic or *eudaimonic*. The juiciest finding, from a neo-Aristotelian perspective, is perhaps that respondents rated their perceived best friends differentially in terms of the friend's utility, pleasure and virtue characteristics. Not surprisingly, from that same perspective, virtue-friend characteristics had a significant direct relationship with *eudaimonic* wellbeing. However, pleasure traits failed to correlate with hedonic wellbeing in the way the authors had expected. Utility turned out to be indirectly related to both conceptions of wellbeing, perhaps indicating that utility friendships are closer to character friendships than most Aristotelians tend to assume (see further in Chapter 6). This work is very promising and if, as word has it, Fowers and Anderson are working on a psychology book on friendship from a neo-Aristotelian perspective, one may hope for a gradual change of compass in the research area.

The Aristotelian idea of close (character) friendship as an exercise in mutual character coaching has faded in prominence in contemporary psychology, replaced by a broader notion of mutual psychological support (as lamented by Anderson & Fowers, 2020). There is quite a lot of research highlighting the educational role of friendship, in the sense of showing how good student friendships are associated with strong academic performance and school adjustment (Majors, 2012), but there is little research paving the way towards anything that could helpfully be called a school or classroom 'pedagogy for friendships' (Brogaard-Clausen & Roberts, 2019, p. 356). There, neo-Aristotelian theory has a valuable contribution to make, as I hope this book will demonstrate.

All in all, whatever quarrels one may pick with contemporary psychological research, neo-Aristotelians and other philosophers exploring friendship can only ignore it at their peril. The time has now come for me, however, to pass again on to an academic ground that I am more familiar with, in Chapter 2.

2

Fragile Friendships

Instabilities and Terminations

2.1 Introduction: Clarifications and Deck-Clearing

I have already noted how Aristotle's exploration of character friendships is strangely devoid of examples of cases that may debar, stunt, decimate and ultimately dissolve such friendships, and how to tackle those. As Schoeman puts it, 'Aristotle offers scarcely any reason to suspect that friendship may engender emotional dilemmas, let alone moral dilemmas' (1985, p. 273). Admittedly, there are long sections addressing problems and difficulties in friendships more generally (see esp. 1985, pp. 232–43 [1162b1–1165a35]), but those are almost entirely focused on the two incomplete kinds of friendship (for pleasure and utility), suggesting that once elevated to the complete type of character friendship, these problems will vanish—for such friendship is stable and enduring, once established (see 1985, pp. 213; 223; 238 [1156b17–19; 1159b3–4; 1164a12–13]). This stability-and-endurance assumption does not simply constitute an off-hand remark; it is one of the cornerstones of Aristotle's one-sidedly positive illumination of character friendships as compared to the other types. While character friendships may still have a lot to recommend them even though we modify or relinquish this assumption, there is quite a lot at stake here regarding Aristotle's overall friendship theory.

Aristotle is sensitive to only one significant limitation placed upon character friendships: namely, that, owing to their extreme closeness, devotion and intimacy, they can be actualised only with a small number of people (1985, pp. 218; 262–263 [1158a10–16; 1170b29–1171a21]). More specifically, 'those who have many friends and treat everyone as close to them seem to be friends to no one' (1985, p. 263 [1171a15–17]). Incidentally, this citation seems to be the source of the common misquote from Aristotle, found in Kant, Montaigne, Diogenes Laertius and numerous books of quotations: 'My dear friend, there is no such thing as a friend'—something Aristotle obviously never said. In any case, one could argue that Aristotle is too sensitive to this specific limitation, so that focusing on it, as he does, is itself a limitation of his account. Apart from the fact that modern means of communication have made the conditions of closeness and intimacy easier to satisfy than in Aristotle's time, a case could be made that even before those technological changes, some individuals at least seem to have been

Friendship for Virtue. Kristján Kristjánsson, Oxford University Press. © Kristján Kristjánsson 2022.
DOI: 10.1093/oso/9780192864260.003.0002

able to form 'friendships of the highest kind' with a significant number of people. Another potential counter-argument is that the number limitation is just an implication of Aristotle's overly high bar of what counts as character that is good enough to sustain character friendships. However, in the relevant paragraphs (1985, pp. 218; 262–3 [1158a10–16; 1170b29–1171a21]), Aristotle is not mainly referring to the price of entry into character friendships being high (because there are so few virtuous ones around) but rather to the maintenance costs (the time required for the devotion and intimacy to sustain them) being so high.

I will not pursue these lines of reasoning here but simply accept, for the sake of argument, the claim that the number of one's character friends is bound to be small and that the criteria for inclusion are pretty stringent. By letting Aristotle off this hook, I avoid a potential proliferation of possible reasons for the instability of character friendships. More specifically, I want to argue in this chapter that even if we accept Aristotle's stringent inclusion conditions, character friendship is far from being as stable as he thought.

It could be argued in Aristotle's defence that his exploration is meant to address a limited number only of specific questions about the nature and varieties of friendship rather than offering an exhaustive systematic account. Yet the discussion of friendship is longer than that of any other topic both in the *Nicomachean Ethics* and *Eudemian Ethics*; and elsewhere in those works he is eager to work through conflicting common intuitions and dilemmas; so the puzzle remains. The main aim of this chapter is, precisely, to repair the dearth of attention paid to the difficulties in question by Aristotle himself and his followers. More specifically, after a brief rehearsal of some Aristotelian essentials in the present section, I address five potential problems attached to character friendships between 'equals' in Section 2.2 and five between 'unequals' in Section 2.3. I address potential eros–*philia* conflicts in Section 2.4 and close with some summarising remarks in Section 2.5. Logically speaking, Chapter 2 should come later in the book, after I have spent more time analysing different kinds and complications of friendship, but since I revisit many of the putative character-friendship problems in subsequent chapters, it helps to offer a taxonomy of them at this early stage. Notice that the taxonomy of ten problems on offer in Sections 2.2–2.3 is fairly skeletal and mostly presented there in order to sow initial seeds of doubts in readers about the viability of Aristotle's stability-and-endurance assumption with respect to character friendships. The most serious of those problems will be subjected to further scrutiny and exemplification in Chapters 4 and 5.

Before proceeding further, I need to add some flesh to the sketchy discussion of *equal* versus *unequal* friendships in Section 1.1. Some interpreters (see e.g. Brewer, 2005, p. 725) take Aristotle to be making a distinction between equality and inequality of moral character/virtue only. However, the examples he takes (father–son; man–woman; older–younger person) and the way he describes them as relationships 'of any sort of ruler towards the one he rules' (1985, p. 220 [1158b12–14]) indicate that he is referring more widely to social status and power relations (of natural or institutional superiority–inferiority). While those will also normally, in Aristotle's view, coincide with qualitative differences in moral character/virtue, the possibility is not ruled out that people can be of equal social status but still unequal in virtue, and Aristotle allows for character friendships between such individuals. In short, in what follows I assume, for the sake of argument, that all socially unequal friendships involve unequal virtue but that not all socially equal friendships involve equal virtue (recall Section 1.1). The reason for this (admittedly) controversial assumption is that I wish to question Aristotle's stability claim in the context of his own set of basic assumptions, rather than taking on the more radical (but perhaps somewhat easier) task of questioning those assumptions themselves. In other words, I argue that even given what Aristotle himself professes about equal and unequal friendships, both kinds import difficulties that he circumvents.

The main conclusion of this chapter will be that, despite the plausibility of much of what Aristotle argues, his account of character friendships cannot be taken on board without various qualifications regarding their stability and fecundity. By providing an argumentative counterweight to the singularly positive description of those friendships in the *Nicomachean Ethics*, I am not offering a pessimistic alternative, however. Indeed, I consider many of the claims made by Aristotle here to involve compelling psycho-moral truths. However, by focusing too heavily on the positives, we may be missing something important: namely, the insight that character friendships are fragile and contingently (though not essentially) quite unstable. That they are not essentially unstable is shown by the fact that most of us will either have experienced stable friendships of this kind ourselves or seen such friendships actualised by others in close personal proximity. However, I gather most of us have also experienced the break-down of what appeared to be the most stable of friendships, and any sound theory of friendship owes us an explanation of what has gone wrong in such cases.

As I propose to elicit in the following two sections some of the more *general* psycho-moral and psycho-social problems that may threaten character friendships, and which do not register on Aristotle's radar, I postpone consideration of a number of specific issues that merit lengthy discussions and even whole sections of their own. Let me briefly mention three.

Husband-and-wife character friendships. Aristotle says just enough about this form of friendship to whet readers' appetites. Such friendships, while characterised by inequality, are natural and possible, Aristotle maintains, as long as both parties are 'decent'; for each 'has a proper virtue' (1985, p. 232 [1162a25–26]). This topic is crying out for a fuller account of what in the nature of those family relationships facilitates and what hinders character friendships. I shelve this issue until Section 8.4, where I return to a discussion of friendship within families.

Parent-and-children character friendships. Parental friendships are entirely natural and normal, for Aristotle, and they do not represent a one-way traffic of virtues being picked up by children from parents, but also the other way round, as the parent 'regards his children as his own' (1985, p. 230 [1161b20–4]; unfortunately Aristotle only talks about the father as the parent here). Parents are, in a sense, learning about themselves, and unfolding their own characters, by learning with and from their children. Nothing attests more clearly to the assumption that character friendship does not require fully developed (*phronetic*) virtue than Aristotle's acknowledgements that children are capable of such friendships, for children will obviously not yet have (fully) developed their *phronesis*. Notably, Aristotle did not explore character friendships *between* children. However, speaking against the apparent consensus in the literature that friendships between children are mostly, or even exclusively, of the two lower types (in particular friendship for pleasure) are findings from one of the few empirical studies that have systematically applied Aristotle's taxonomical repertoire (Walker, Curren & Jones, 2016; cf. also Hoyos-Valdés, 2018, who argues against the consensus). Some of the discussion in Chapter 5 will be relevant to the issue of potential friendships between parents and children, but I return to it head-on in Section 8.4 in the context of the exploration there of friendships within the family.

Philia–eros conflicts. Aristotle is crystal clear about the distinction between *philia* and eros. Yet surprisingly, from a modern perspective, he does not discuss cases of conflict between the two, for instance where erotic/romantic attraction gets in the way of character friendship. Meilaender (1993) seems to assume that this conflict is already dealt with by Aristotle as part of the potential conflict between friendship for pleasure and friendship for character. However, arguably, the motives and desires underlying erotic attraction are deeper—and tap into different psychological resources—than the motives behind standard cases of pleasure-driven friendships. The most nuanced recent book-length philosophical study of friendship, namely that of Nehamas (2016), does not attend to this issue in any detail either.

I am not assuming here that there is an inherent incompatibility between romantic attraction and character friendship. However, if popular modern works of literature and film are to be believed, one of the commonest reasons for the non-formation or eventual dissolution of what would be meant to be non-sexual friendships between males and females (or between same-sex friends who are potentially sexually attracted to one another) is a conflict between *philia* and eros in instances where one or both of the friends are already romantically attached to someone else, or where sexual attraction from one of the friends is not reciprocated by the other. This is a topic that deserves a substantial discussion of its own; hence the fairly lengthy Section 2.4 below.

I have mentioned these three issues here as part of a deck-clearing exercise of the various interesting topics that benefit from being shelved for a while until I have got the more general problems out of the way in the following two sections.

2.2 Five Potential Problems Affecting Character Friendships between Equals

I single out below five potential problems affecting character friendships between 'equal' or relatively equal parties: problems that could all lead to a diminution of the fixity and durability that Aristotle attributes to character friendships in general.

Problem of essential substitutability. This is a direct descendant of a well-known problem considered to affect 'Platonic love' (on a true Platonic under-standing, not the popular modern one). In Platonic love—so the standard objection goes—one loves a person to the extent that she instantiates certain admirable universal qualities of goodness, truth and beauty. However, this seems to imply that if another person appeared on one's radar who did an even better job of manifesting those qualities, one's love *would* (and even *should* morally) transfer to that new person. Much tends to be made of Aristotle's escape from Plato's idealism in general and Plato's depersonalised view of *philia* in particular. Aristotelian friendship is meant to represent love of another person *qua* person, and thus not fall prey to the substitutability objection. The argument here would be that the character friend constitutes a unique other self; and that one loves the friend 'because of the friend himself, not coincidentally' (1985, pp. 212–13 [1156b7–12]).

While this signals an escape route from the Platonic *horror mundi* (fear of the real world), it may not suffice to quell entirely all unease. Remember that what motivates character friendships are not specifically amoral relational features that are commonly foregrounded in contemporary social scientific accounts of friend-ship, such as disclosure, reliance, bonding and similarities in personality profiles. Rather, it is essentially the other person's character repertoire: precisely how and to what extent she is virtuous. Aristotle admits freely that character friendships can be actualised only with a limited number of people; hence, one must be highly selective in one's choice of friends. Indeed, the friendship attachment thrives on its exclusiveness (cf. Sherman, 1987, p. 604; Nehamas, 2016, p. 203), and one needs to get the exclusive friendships right.

However, a tension arises here in Aristotle's account between the intrinsic liking of a person who one happens to have befriended and the liking of the virtues in that friend—which one may also like intrinsically, in addition to the benefits they confer upon oneself in helping mould one's character. But liking those virtues is still not the same as liking the person *qua* this individual, warts and all. As Schoeman correctly notes, Aristotle's account runs the risk of becoming 'dangerously Platonic' (1985, p. 278). It is difficult to see why a reasonable choice could not be made between friends on grounds of the admirability of their character profiles only, in which case the one with the greater virtues or better fit of virtues to one's own might be seen to stand in a privileged position.

To give one example, a mentee might decide that she prefers spending quality time with her new mentor friend than with a fellow mentee friend. That would mean privileging a relationship of unequal friendship over an equal one, but there is nothing in Aristotle's own account that defines equal friendships as inherently better than unequal ones, at least not if the unequal friendship satisfies the 'equalising principle' discussed in Section 2.3 below.

I consider the problem of essential substitutability nothing less than the major problem threatening a moralised account of friendship, such as Aristotle's, and I revisit it at length in Chapter 4 when I compare moralised accounts with aestheticised ones. As will become clearer there, while the problem of essential substitutability may leave some character friendships untouched, it will continue to speak against the strong claim that all character friendships, by their very nature, are essentially stable.

Problem of self-verification. Aristotle makes an innocent-looking remark, in his discussion of friendship, about those wanting honour from good people being in the business of 'seeking to confirm their own view of themselves' (1985, p. 222 [1159a21–4]). While this remark does not amount to any psychological theory of self-confirmations, it bespeaks sensitivity to concerns that have been raised and conceptualised in contemporary psychology under the umbrella of 'self-verification theory'.

Psychologist William Swann has conducted a number of experiments which demonstrate that people tend to pay attention to, seek, believe, value and retain feedback that confirms their present self-concept, whether that self-concept is positive or negative. These findings contradict the well-entrenched assumption that people in general are self-enhancement seekers: consumed by an overwhelming desire to think well of themselves and always on the lookout for responses that show them in a positive light. In contrast to this assumption, Swann's studies suggest that once people have incorporated a given characteristic—however negative—firmly into their self-concept, they seek feedback that verifies that characteristic, even if it brings them pain. In other words, we like to seek out others who see us as we see ourselves, and we tend to flee contexts in which such self-verifying evaluations are not forthcoming. Swann refers to this tendency as 'self-traps': stubborn impediments to higher self-esteem. Swann does not reject the view that we also have a desire for positive feedback, but he suggests that people with a negative self-concept are deeply torn and ambivalent emotionally; they want both a favourable and an unfavourable evaluation, and are therefore caught in a self-trap. The underlying motive, Swann hypothesises, is the desire for self-stability and self-cohesion: the desire for a homeostatic self (Swann, 1996, pp. 10–14, 23–5, 51; see further in Kristjánsson, 2010, chap. 10).

Aristotle is obviously a great believer in psychological homeostasis also, especially in terms of the harmony of virtuous emotions, where the task of modifying emotions to bring them into harmony with the golden mean in each case and for each individual is simultaneously a task of modifying individual physiology (Kristjánsson, 2018). Full homeostasis, and the pride and the praise that come with it, can only be accomplished through the attainment of full virtue. However, not being an island, the person on the path to virtue will also care about the praise and encouragement of the character friend and strive to be worthy of it. Brewer explains how this desire is different from being moved to self-reform by the mere wish for another's approval (2005, p. 735). Brewer also describes an ideal trajectory in which the two friends collaborate on 'the ongoing task of talking their own half-formed evaluative commitments into a full-fledged and determinate stance in the world' (2005, p. 735). This all sounds good in theory. However, if Swann is right, the desire for self-verification—say, the desire for the friend's confirming one's own persistent character weakness as endearing—may, for psychological reasons, often trump the desire for self-improvement, even in people who are upwardly mobile morally. This is the reason why social media outlets, such as Facebook, typically turn into echo chambers of the self, as one chooses 'friends' with whom one can live inside a filter bubble of mutual self-verifications. I have seen (budding) character friendships disintegrate precisely when talking through the other's 'half-formed evaluative commitments' is seen as a threat to the other's self-concept instead of verifying it. Aristotle's innocent-looking remark about friends 'seeking to confirm their own view of themselves' may actually suggest the possibility of incipient tensions between friends—when such confirmations are not immediately forthcoming—that can turn into full-scale antagonisms, making the friendships vulnerable and unstable.

Problem of mismatched developmental levels. Interestingly, Aristotle considers it an empirical question, to be settled by natural science, whether similar or dissimilar people make better character friends (1985, pp. 208–9 [1155a32–1155b10]). That said, as I have repeatedly stressed, he does allow for character friendships between people unequal in virtue. In the following section, I explore some problems relating to such friendships between people who are also of unequal power ('ruler' versus 'ruled'), but I am presently focusing on friends of relatively equal natural and social status, yet occupying different levels of character development. Driving the aspirations of the less developed friend may be a certain degree of dissatisfaction with the state of her character (cf. Brewer, 2005, p. 737); she may even see the more developed friend as worthy of emulation. Conversely, the better developed friend may see in the other individual a person upon whom a lot of love can be constructively bestowed.

While 'in friendships of virtue, there are no accusations' (Aristotle, 1985, p. 235 [1163a21–2]), the attitude of the better developed party is not likely to assume a cringing spirit of indiscriminate tolerance towards the particular weaknesses of the less developed friend. This can engender the problem of (lack of) self-verification discussed above. However, more importantly for present purposes, even if the desire for self-improvement trumps the desire for self-verification, well-known problems of moral emulation are likely to kick in. Those include *hero-worship*, where the learner uncritically imitates or mimics a role model, warts and all; *moral inertia*, where moral exemplars are seen as standing so high above the learner that idolising them becomes disempowering rather than uplifting; and *moral over-stretching*, where the learner tries to follow in the footsteps of a role model, but not being as sure-footed, may end up in unfamiliar circumstances where, rather than virtue progressing, vice breaks forth with redoubled ardour because the learner falls to temptations that the advanced role model could overcome (Kristjánsson, 2020, chap. 7). As Hoyos-Valdés (2018) notes, this may be a reason not to over-emphasise a role-model approach to character development in the context of character friendships. It is not difficult to imagine how—*mutatis mutandis*—difficulties in navigating the dual purposes of character emulation and character friendship could take its toll on the latter and gradually enfeeble it by dissipation. I offer a more nuanced discussion of this topic in Chapter 5.

Problem of divergent developmental paths. Even if character friends start at relatively equal levels of virtue and aspire to mould each other's characters in progressive ways, life is complex and has a way of upsetting the best of plans. Thus, events can intervene through which 'friends come to be separated by some wide gap in virtue, vice, wealth, or something else' (1985, p. 221 [1159a33–4]). Indeed, this—along with geographical distance which (obviously prior to modern technological advances) makes the friendship impossible to cultivate—is almost the only qualification which Aristotle himself accepts on the stability-of-character-friendship thesis; for 'then they are friends no more and do not even expect to be' (1985, p. 221 [1159a34–5]). Otherwise, one is led to assume (although Aristotle does not state this explicitly) that character friendships, once formed, typically last for life.

However, it is almost as if Aristotle has second thoughts on this, for later he qualifies the earlier qualification. Even if the friend pursues a radically different developmental path in terms of character (e.g. becoming god-like in virtue, or vicious), the friendship should not be 'dissolved at once'. Moreover, the fact that the friend regresses morally is not a valid reason for the termination of the friendship unless he becomes 'incurably vicious'. 'If someone can be set right, we should try harder to rescue his character than his property'; and even if termination becomes the only option, we should 'accord something to past friends because of the old friendship' in terms of sweet memories and kind thoughts (1985, p. 244 [1165b15–35]).

Aristotle is clearly willing to cut the wayward friend a lot of slack here. That is perhaps understandable in light of the fact that the loss of friendship can engender feelings of loss as strong as those of grief over another's death (cf. Kristjánsson, 2018, chap. 7). Recall here also that given the Aristotelian friend-as-another-self thesis, mourning the loss of friendship may be tantamount to mourning the loss of oneself. While admirable, Aristotle may be placing unreasonably strong psychological restrictions on the dissolution of friendships as a result of the friends following divergent developmental paths. For true character friendship to be sustained, some common sensibilities have to be throbbing in the nerves of the two parties. If the two stop pursuing similar virtues in similar enough contexts, it is likely the mutual interest in each other's destiny will gradually fade—and I would hypothesise that this will happen, in many cases, long before the friend has become 'incurably vicious'. In some cases of divergent paths, the friendship simply reaches its natural summit at some point and then begins to veer slowly in the opposite direction. As Nehamas puts it well, friendship 'leads in new and surprising directions and, for that reason, our understanding of each other and ourselves is, and will always be, provisional, contestable, and incomplete' (2016, p. 206).

In Section 5.4, I revisit the problem of divergent developmental paths through a literary example that illustrates quite the opposite to a trajectory of one of the parties turning towards vice. Both that example and the discussion above cast doubt on Aristotle's argument that only radical departures from a common virtue basis towards incurable vice *can* and *should* (Aristotle does not make a clear distinction between the two) upset the inherent stability of equal character friendships.

Problem of initiation and trust. The problem of friendship beginnings is obviously not a problem of 'stability'. However, equally obviously, for a friendship to become stable, it must get off the ground in the first place. Perhaps it would have been logical to begin the section with this problem, but I consider the four previous problems to cast some retrospective light on the initial difficulties in establishing character friendships. Aristotle blithely ignores these difficulties, apart from a couple of off-hand remarks where he says that 'though the wish for friendship comes quickly, friendship does not' (1985, p. 213 [1156b31–2]), and that we should never try to 'make a friend of someone who is unwilling' (1985, p. 234 [1163a2–4]). Aristotle's discussion here elides the full repertoire of issues that most people, I believe, will have experienced as obtruding when trying to forge new deep friendships. As Cooper puts it, he 'does not, except incidentally, have anything to say about how friendships are formed in the first place' (1977, p. 645).

The first concern is the very fact that, in addition to its intrinsic benefits, friendship is by its nature an 'external good' (1985, p. 257 [1169b10]): namely, a good that requires certain propitious external circumstances to be in place. To put it bluntly, some people simply never come within shouting distance of anyone whom they deem, rightly or wrongly, to be a potential character friend, and some people simply do not see the need for such friendships, full stop. As sensitive as Aristotle normally is to the vagaries of moral luck, one would have expected him to at least address cursorily some of those external-luck issues relating to friendship initiation, but he does not. Yet as Sherman correctly notes, the moral-luck problem hits harder at friendship than other character virtues, especially insofar as we understand *philia* as a relational activity, requiring reciprocity, rather than just an individual state or trait of character (see 1987, p. 602). So identifying the potentially ideal friend is not enough; the other person must be motivated to pursue the friendship also.

The second difficulty concerns the very act of initiation. Analogous concerns apply here as to the initiation of romantic relationships. The more eager party must not seem to be too eager, making a dead set at winning someone else's character friendship by flinging herself at her feet. Too much eagerness may undermine trust and cause the other party to pull up the drawbridge. There is also the danger of the existence or at least suspicion of ulterior motives. Is the person who is approaching me with so much enthusiasm really interested in getting to know me as a person, and growing together with me, *or* is she really looking for some sort of utility friendship, *or* is this eros masquerading as *philia*? Compounding the complexity of those questions is the fact that human beings do not possess self-transparency. Even if we got an honest answer from the other person about her motives, it might not be the true answer. She could be self-estranged. In my experience, many potentially rewarding character friendships never pass through this initial stage and get on a firm footing because of a lack of trust. Some people are simply too fastidious and worried about the possibility of ulterior motives to let anyone get as close to them as character friendships require in terms of psychological intimacy and self-disclosure. Perhaps Aristotle would consider such extreme suspiciousness an evidence of character failings, clouding the person's moral vision. However, much as he discusses forms of excess and deficiency in connection with other virtues, he remains mute about those in the case of friendship.

A more coherent Aristotelian than Aristotle himself would say that the formation of character friendships requires a lot of free-flowing, fluid interactions to begin with, and that the eventual consolidation and coagulation of this fluid is subject to many internal and external constraints. There seems to be little inherent stability about the way character friendships are formed, or how, if at all, they proceed beyond the stage of initiation, through possible barriers of lack of trust, confidence and mutual personal attraction. Someone might point out that we should not over over-emphasise these difficulties as most people somehow manage to make good friends, after all. Nevertheless, given the various psycho-social barriers that can hinder this process, it would have been nice if Aristotle had given this some more thought.

This issue signals one of the few places where Cicero thinks beyond Aristotle. He says that it is 'difficult to determine who has the desirable qualities of a friend without trying them out—and the only way to try them out is by being their friend. Thus friendship runs ahead of judgment and removes the possibility of a trial period' (2018, p. 113).

2.3 Five Potential Problems Affecting Character Friendships between Unequals

To help illuminate problems in character friendships between people of unequal social standing, let us consider cases of relationships between what I shall call 'mentor' and 'mentee' (PhD supervisor–PhD student, and others of a similar ilk), rather than the cases Aristotle foregrounds and that I postponed discussion of in Section 2.1, between parents and children and husbands and wives. Those latter cases are more complex because of the supposed admixture of 'social' and 'natural' superiority. To avoid getting caught up in the quagmire of potential debate about that assumption, let us focus on the purely 'social' cases.

Problem of proportionality. Aristotle implicitly acknowledges the danger of instability in character friendships between unequals by placing a stringent condition on what makes them work. This is his principle of proportionality, or 'equalising principle', according to which, in unequal friendships, the stronger party 'must be loved more than he loves; for when the loving reflects the comparative worth of friends, equality is achieved in a way' (1985, p. 221 [1158b26–9]). So while the weaker party gets 'more profit' (presumably in terms of character growth), the stronger party gets more honour and devotion (1985, pp. 236–7 [1163b1–15]). It is thus 'proportion that equalizes and preserves the friendship' (1985, p. 238 [1163b34]).

This is an astounding principle which can be assailed on many fronts. First, it seems to fly in the face of ordinary human psychology, old and new. Indeed, Aristotle himself seems to be flatly denying his own principle empirically when he says later that 'benefactors seem to love their beneficiaries more than the beneficiaries love them [in return]' just like the craftsman 'likes his own product more than it would like him if it acquired a soul' (1985, pp. 250–1 [1167b16–35]). It does not help much to argue that these are psychological observations about how human beings really are, whereas the equalising principle is a normative principle, for Aristotle is eager throughout to ground his normative theory in actual human psychology: what makes real people tick.

Second, as Aristotle presumes that the stronger party is also superior in terms of virtue, she will be superior in terms of moral sensitivity and perception: what Brewer calls 'unclouded moral vision and deliberation' (2005, p. 747). The mentor will thus, under normal circumstances, be more alert to spotting sprouts of developing virtue in the mentee, which can be nourished, than the mentee will be to fathom the depth of the mentor's character strengths—not least because young people tend to 'think they know everything' already (Aristotle, 2007, p. 150 [1389b5–7]). Even if the mentee realises she has more to gain from the friendship, she may appreciate the mentor more in terms of utility friendship than character friendship (see further below). This makes the relationship uncomfortably instrumental and transactional.

Third, the mentor is likely to be older than the mentee, and it is—anecdotally at least—more common for an older person to have 'a crush' on a younger person than vice versa, at least if the older person is male. I would hypothesise that the same applies for both erotic and intellectual stimulation. Again, this would impede the equalising principle.

All in all, the equalising principle leaves uncomfortable residues. It seems neither psychologically nor morally plausible. If 'proportionality' in terms of this principle is a necessary condition for the successful development of unequal character friendships, it is likely to make them extremely difficult to form and even more difficult to sustain.

Problem of the mentee's conflicting motivations. The strict condition of the non-instrumentally motivated nature of character friendships places heavy psycho-moral burdens on the mentee seeking (an unequal) friendship with a mentor. On the one hand, the mentee (e.g. a student approaching a famous professor) knows how much potential utility she can gain from forming a lasting bond with the mentor. Aristotle reminds us that the type of friendship 'that seems to arise most from contraries is friendship for utility', for example of 'ignorant to knowledgeable; for we aim at whatever we find we lack' (1985, p. 223 [1159b12–15]). On the other hand, however, the mentee is not allowed to aim at the friendship solely as a means to an end—even as a means to her own self-improvement (cf. Brewer, 2005, p. 723 [footnote 3])—if it is to constitute a potential character friendship. Aristotle does not say explicitly that character friends cannot be motivated at all by instrumentalist concerns. However, at least they must not be motivated by such concerns only. As 'all or most people wish for what is fine, but decide to do what is beneficial' (1985, p. 234 [1162b35]), the mentee may become internally torn regarding her motivations.

The mentee may run the risk of having 'one thought too many' about the prospective friendship (Williams, 1981). In trying to suppress the thought of the potential benefits of the friendship with the mentor, and by focusing on its intrinsic benefits, the mentee may end up being (or at least appearing) duplicitous to herself and others. The mentor, who will have had many experiences of such approaches, will most likely be acutely sensitive to possible mixed motives. This can lead to serious conflicts and disruptions, for—as Aristotle says—'friends are most at odds when they are not friends in the way they think they are', and he likens these situations to finding out that a currency is debased (1985, p. 243 [1165b5–11]). We see the same tendency in lay conceptions of friendship today: namely, to consider any break-down of friendship to indicate that what had appeared to be 'real friendship' was in fact all along something 'lower', such as masked selfishness (see Nehamas, 2016, p. 23).

This problem of conflicting or conflicted motivations suggests less a failure of Aristotle's account of the potential value of unequal friendships, for both parties, than it speaks to the psycho-moral challenges posed by being allowed to aim at the good of self-improvement, in a potential relationship with a friend, only obliquely. I have seen friendships break-down for those reasons. Once again, Aristotle's lack of attention to this problem bespeaks insensitivity to some of the small leaks that may sink great friendships. He might point out correctly, in response, that the reasons we embark on a project need not be our reasons to continue to engage with it. So the student who approaches the famous professor originally for the 'wrong' reasons may actually develop true character friendship with her later. Thus, the problem of the mentee's conflicting motivations will often sort itself out in due course. That said, the threat of the 'debased currency' may resurface if the mentor finds out about the original motivation.

Problem of the mentor's conflicting motivations. Analogously to the problem of the mentee's conflicting motivations, Aristotle's specification of true character friendships places significant burdens on the motivational make-up of the mentor. We know that, for Aristotle, pleasure supervenes upon and crowns successfully completed virtuous activities. However, the pleasures of friendship cannot be aimed at directly in the case of character friendship, any more than the substance of the virtues in general can be short-circuited to get straight to the benefits. However much the mentor may enjoy the mentee's company and admiration, the mentor must love the mentee for the latter's own sake; not for the sake of any present or future pleasures. Otherwise, of course, the friendship is simply relegated to the 'for-pleasure' type.

Aristotle sweetens this pill with his remark that 'good people are pleasant both unconditionally and for each other' (1985, p. 213 [1156b14–16]). I take that as a reminder that there is nothing wrong (but indeed everything right) with character friends reaping pleasure from each other's company as long as the friendship is not sought solely for the sake of the pleasures. It is also worth mentioning that nothing in Aristotle's account excludes the possibility that different types of friendship relations can be pursued with the same person simultaneously or in tandem. So the mentor and the mentee may enjoy playing squash together, just for the pleasure of the sport, without paying any attention in those moments to the deeper layers of the friendship. Sherman takes a good example of a friend developing a love for Georgian houses, picked up from a character friend, having had no interest in them earlier (1987, p. 599). This new interest may then motivate the person to seek pleasure in this new pastime independent of the character friendship which originally occasioned it.

I would hypothesise that, in some contexts at least, the motivations of friendship for pleasure and friendship for character are more difficult to separate psychologically than the motivations underlying utility versus character friendships. Both friendships for pleasure and character require an easy spontaneity rather than an arm's-length, calculating stance. Precisely because of that psychological fact, and the fact of our own essential non-self-transparency, the mentor may experience role conflicts and blind spots in his love of the mentee: shortcomings that may in the end stultify the friendship relation (by instrumentalising it through depriving it of unconditionality) rather than keeping it enduring and refreshed.

On the bright side, however, as Grayling points out, there may be less danger of jealousies ruining the friendships between unequals than equals: 'There will in reality always be some reserve, some shadow of fear between equals, which in the friendship of unequals, if happily assorted, can find no place' (2013, p. 110). Thus, a professor is more likely to be jealous of the success of her equal-friendship peer—perceived of as a competitor—who publishes in a top journal than that of an unequal-friendship junior scholar who hits the jackpot and unexpectedly gets a paper accepted in the same journal.

Problem of paternalism. Talbot Brewer (2005) has written a tightly argued and beautifully turned article about character friendships as the mutual affirmation of evaluative outlooks. He explains how character friends progress through appreciatively attending to good character, progressively unveiled in the other person. Rather than constituting a 'static and complacent mutual admiration society', the friendship relation involves an evolving bond within which 'friends draw each other out and participate in the fine-toothed articulation of each other's character' (2005, p. 726), 'so as increasingly to approximate a standard of shareability' (2005, p. 722). The question which assails us here, however, is to what extent the friends need to affirm each other's evaluative outlooks 'unreservedly and unconditionally' (2005, p. 730) and to what extent the 'collaboration' of 'two jointly produced sensibilities' (2005, p. 758) can include critical and potentially painful challenges to the other's outlook.

What matters here, however, is the nature of the revision process that takes place between the aspirations for what Brewer calls 'self-affirmability' (2005, p. 728) and the eventual mutually affirmed outlooks. It is an Aristotelian commonplace that *phronetic* virtue does not have any ethical value unless it is self-chosen in a strong sense (i.e. autonomously from 'a firm and unchanging state' of character: 1985, p. 40 [1105a30–2]): indeed, otherwise it does not even deserve the name *phronetic* virtue. Fully virtuous persons are not only 'in concord with themselves' but also with their character friends 'since they are practically of the same mind' (1985, p. 250 [1167b5–7]). This does not mean that two character friends will always act in the same way, because their choice of actions will always be relative to personal temperament and circumstance (including social roles), but each will have an understanding and appreciation of the rationale behind the other's decision making, as it is all guided by the same intellectual virtue of *phronesis*.

Before friends, as Sherman notes, we 'bare ourselves and acknowledge the foibles and weaknesses we hide from others' (1987, p. 611, cf. Aristotle, 2007, p. 135 [1384b22–3]). It is easy enough to understand how this process works in friendships characterised by equality. Equality of social standing will often correspond to (approximate) equality of character development, and roughly similarly developed friends will—at least ideally—cherish the mutual self-disclosures and self-corrections that aim towards the goal of self-affirmability and growth in virtue. However, things may not be that simple in unequal friendships. For as Aristotle himself puts it, it is proper for good people 'not to permit [error] in their friends' (1985, p. 223 [1159b7–8]). Now, being told about the error of your ways by a friend of similar standing, and prone to errors of similar magnitude, is one thing; being told the same by someone superior to you may smack of condescending paternalism—although one could argue that everything will depend here on the openness of the mentee to correction, and the gentleness and sensitivity of the mentor in correcting her.

What I have seen in many unequal friendships is one or two of the following extremes: either the mentor dissolves all the faults of the mentee in the *aqua regia* of his affection—hence depriving the protégé of the opportunity to learn and grow—or the mentor becomes too eager to help the mentee, ending up (to use a famous Confucian metaphor) by pulling the shoots upwards with too much force, thus uprooting them. It is the latter option that smacks of paternalism, and such paternalism not only is unfortunate for all the well-known general reasons but is specifically bad from an Aristotelian standpoint as it prevents the mentee from developing a *phronetic* mind of her own.

Schoeman (1985) offers enlightening thoughts on this potential problem of paternalism that may jeopardise the best of unequal character friendships. He senses in Aristotle's account a lack of healthy tolerance (when the friend fails to live up to expectations), as well as a lack of respect for the independence of the other. Interestingly, Schoeman sees in this tendency not only an over-zealous aspiration to correct the other but also unwillingness to expose the vulnerability of oneself to the independence of the other (1985, p. 282—although this is a fairly uncharitable reading of Aristotle). Of course, if one accepts Sherman's (1987) strong ontological interpretation of Aristotle's 'another-self' thesis, mentioned in Section 1.1, little breathing room seems to remain for the notion of two autonomous selves.

Whatever the exact psychological mechanisms at work here, the problem of paternalism is, in my experience, a danger that menacingly threatens unequal character friendships. In Grayling's words, 'it has to be part of the voluntary obligations attached to being a good friend to accept the differences between oneself and one's friend—which involves giving one's friend space to have some interests and tastes different from one's own, and agree to disagree about some things' (2013, p. 35). I return to the problem of paternalism in the context of formal education in Section 5.4.

Problem of role inertia. This problem is basically a warped mirror image of the above problem of divergent developmental paths. We could even paraphrase this problem as that of converging developmental paths. In an ideal situation, the mentee gradually catches up with the mentor in terms of character development: their paths converge. However, the two typically remain stuck in the roles in which they first met. Whole undergraduate courses in sociology and social psychology are basically about this very issue of social roles and social-role inertia. This is, for example, what makes student reunions so awkward when the old teachers are present also. The students almost automatically lower themselves to a level at which they were long ago so as not to challenge the authority of the teachers.

The problem of role inertia does not mean that the mentor and the mentee cannot remain friends, even character friends. In fact, is does not pose a direct challenge to Aristotle's stability assumption as such. The problem lies rather in the form that the friendship takes. It risks becoming inauthentic, even phoney, if its stability is secured via a connection of continuing unequal friendship when the two parties have, in fact, progressed to a level where it should have assumed the nature of equal friendship.

2.4 Where Eros and *Philia* Clash

Perhaps the greatest specific oversight—at least from a modern perspective—in Aristotle's account of friendship is not to delve into potential conflicts between friendship (*philia*) and eros. As initial reading on the topic, I recommend a paper by Gilbert Meilaender (1993) that draws on a host of relevant sources and discusses the topic in ways redolent of Aristotle (or, more precisely, of what an imagined Aristotle might have said about the topic in a contemporary context). While written from an overtly Christian perspective, Meilaender subtly analyses the faint undercurrent of excitement often floating close to the surface in friendships between the genders and how this undercurrent may gradually plunge any budding character friendship into a maelstrom of misunderstandings, jealousies and conflicts. He is also keenly sensitive to the hidden motives and secret desires that may be at work in the subterranean regions of the minds of such friends, while not entirely transparent to themselves.

This problem deserves a lengthy section, and I cannot avoid some engagement here with Plato as well as Aristotle—not to mention some modern psychological sources. I begin by highlighting certain modern assumptions that the ancients did not share. I then explore Plato's and Aristotle's views on eros and friendship, respectively. I finally take a modern turn by examining what current research on cross-sex friendships can tell us about potential eros–friendship conflicts.

Let me begin, then, by positing three assumptions about eros, friendship and flourishing that arguably figure prominently in the modern consciousness as 'received wisdoms', being endorsed both by those whom Aristotle would have called 'the many' and at least a considerable number of 'the wise':

Assumption (1): The satisfaction of the need for erotic love is essential—at least for most human beings—to their leading flourishing lives.

Assumption (2): The most perfect sort of erotic love is intermingled with deep friendship and ideally actualised within the institution of marriage or a stable partnership, through a synthesis of psychological and physical need-satisfaction. This is crystallised in the almost platitudinous exclamation that 'my spouse in my best friend' and in the neologism 'flovers': (best) friends and lovers. Notably, the very words 'boy*friend*' and 'girl*friend*' did not emerge until the 19th century.

Assumption (3): Because deep friendships are possible with more than one person (although not too many), but erotic love normally only with one, eros often gets in the way of such friendships, leading in particular to the non-initiation or eventual disintegration of cross-sex friendships.

What is most striking about these three assumptions is that Plato and Aristotle either rejected them or simply circumvented them in their analyses of love and friendship. This is perhaps not all that strange in the case of Assumption (1). It is very much a modern construction which hardly makes sense outside of the context of Freudianism, the Kinsey Report, the sexual revolution of the 1960s and other uniquely 20th-century developments in scientific research and public mores. There is, therefore, not much use in trying to enter into a 'dialogue' with the ancients about the adequacy of this assumption; one either simply has to take it or leave it as a piece of scientific evidence, at least insofar as current studies of human flourishing can be considered scientific as well as normative.

Suffice it to make two quick observations here. One is that the idea of celibacy, say for monks, nuns and priests, being potentially harmful for them, psychologically and even physically, would have sounded quite bizarre to most pre-moderns. The other is that, contrary to popular conceptions, it is not so much that moderns are more cavalier and frivolous about sex; quite the contrary, we are more seriously hung-up about the health ramifications of insufficient or dissatisfying sex than our forebears were. The general attitude among ancient and medieval writers towards sex, outside of purely religious writings, was one of humorous ridicule, as one may treat any academically lightweight but slightly embarrassing subject (Lewis, 1960, p. 139).

The same cannot, however, be said about Assumptions (2) and (3). Apart from the reference to marriage as the ideal site for 'flovers' in (2)—which would have sounded odd in times when marriage was very much seen as an institution of social convenience rather than the institutionally sanctioned culmination of synthesised eros and *phila*—Assumptions (2) and (3) seem to speak to the very human condition rather than to any particular historical period. Consider some of the greatest love stories through ancient and medieval times, from the Greek tragedies, to Tristan and Isolde, Laxdæla Saga and Romeo and Juliet, and one sees a depiction of erotic lovers who are also best friends, alongside numerous complicating sub-plots where the exclusive bond of the 'flovers' is threatened by friendships by one or both of them outside of the dyad, evoking jealousies and misunderstandings. As Meilaender (1993) puts it, the 'difficulties of combining eros and *philia* are the stuff of our daily life'; and 'our' is here best seen as a non-time-or-culture-bound term.

It is somewhat surprising, therefore, that neither Plato nor Aristotle took Assumption (2) seriously nor gave any sustained thought to Assumption (3). I am interested in exploring the reasons for those elisions. Subsequently, however, my attention turns exclusively to Assumption (3), the reason being that whereas Assumption (2) is primarily a normative one, about an *ideal* eros-friendship combo, Assumption (3) is empirical and easier to substantiate: about whether eros does in fact have a tendency to subvert important friendships between the sexes and why. I return briefly to Assumption (2) in Section 8.4, however.

Before proceeding with this task, some conceptual and linguistic clarifications are needed for scene-setting and deck-clearing. First, a disclaimer about potentially insensitive language. For reasons of space and simplicity only, I discuss the Assumptions in question in terms of the relationships between the two sexes. There is no intention to marginalise LGBT people here. 'Cross-sex' issues can be read, *mutatis mutandis*, as 'inter-sex' or 'inter-gender' issues for people attracted to those of the same sex. I simply cannot explain all the possible permutations in each case and, moreover, most of the relevant current academic literature is still couched in terms of 'cross-sex' friendship in a literal sense (perhaps because most of it was written before the current era of 'wokeness').

Second, unpicking the exact meaning of 'eros' and 'erotic' can be tricky. I have referred to it above as either romantic or sexual—to distinguish it from *philia*—but both terms import difficulties. 'Romantic' has connotations that date back no further than to the 'knightly' literature of the Middle Ages and even just back to 19th-century Romanticism. Equating all 'erotic love' with 'romantic love' is therefore anachronistic. 'Sexual love' may seem less fraught with difficulties, but that is a chimera. There are a considerable number of people who consider themselves asexual; that is, not aroused by sexual stimuli (Asexuality Visibility and Education Network, 2020). Those people would find it deeply offensive, however, if they were just denigrated as 'frigid' or considered incapable of erotic love, confined to being 'just friends' to their partners. Their erotic desires are simply not sexual desires. But what are they then? Is there a difference between subjective and objective physical desires?

These questions evoke an even deeper one about the characterisation of eros versus friendship. Somewhat paradoxically, the everyday distinction between eros and friendship does not have any entrenched academic taxonomy to undergird it. The psychological attraction and intimacy characterising friendship is typically considered to be replaced (or even better augmented) in erotic love through physical attraction and intimacy—although it is moot what that means in the case of asexual people, given the fact that 'just friends' often give each other hugs and warm embraces also. C. S. Lewis famously tried to offer a more symbolic distinction, about how eros and *philia* are separated via distinct behaviour patterns and gestures, as seen is artistic expressions of those two relationships: 'we picture lovers face to face but Friends side by side; their eyes look ahead' (1960, p. 98).

What Lewis seems to have in mind is that whereas friendship is outside-facing and involves side-by-side engagement in common projects, usually accompanied by verbal exchanges, the basic 'project' that lovers engage in is themselves, in an inward-facing way, often characterised by 'meaningful silences' aimed at complete psycho-physical union: of being welded into one another. Vernon says that whereas friendship is 'calm, reasonable, harmonise and sober', erotic love is 'spontaneous, irrational, wild and orgiastic' (2010, p. 50). Yet various counter-examples threaten this neat taxonomy: of friendships that are tumultuous and of erotic love that is deep but fairly tame and apparently prosaically rational.

So academic accounts seem to fall desperately short of establishing necessary and sufficient conditions of erotic love and friendship, respectively, which would somehow drive a conceptual wedge between them. That said, pragmatically speaking, the proof of the pudding lies in the eating, and I think most readers will have some intuitive grasp of where the dividing line between the two is. I will therefore leave these conceptual problematics by the side here and rely on readers' intuitions about there being a distinction between even the deepest of friendships versus erotic love, and how those two relationships—as significant as both purportedly are for human *eudaimonia*—may come into conflict in various scenarios and require considerable *phronesis* for adjudication.

Now, so much has been written about eros in Plato (esp. in his *Symposium*) and his notion of what is often described, albeit somewhat misleadingly, as 'Platonic love' that it would amount to the carrying of coals to Newcastle to add to the exegesis here. So I simply want to draw attention to a few features that are relevant for an assessment of Assumptions (2) and (3) above.

On a literal reading of what Plato (or rather his mouthpiece Socrates) says about eros, he may seem like an ardent supporter of Assumption (2). Eros is said to be an indispensable part of a flourishing life, and the erotic impulse also drives us towards values such as friendship and wisdom. If anything, Plato may seem to over-prioritise eros, in sharp contrast to his mentee Aristotle's deprioritisation that we witness later. However, this apparent over-prioritisation of eros actually denudes it of its carnal element and its exclusive focus on a beloved person. By reconfiguring eros—turning it into an undifferentiated attraction towards the 'form' of the good, true and beautiful—Plato essentially sublimates it and deprives it of any serious connection to ordinary-language uses of the term. This conceptual reconfiguration also gives rise to the much-discussed 'substitutability problem', which I explained in Section 2.2 and return to in Chapter 4.

As Salim (2006) carefully teases out, there are subtle differences, however, between Plato's best-known treatment of eros in the *Symposium* and his account in the *Phaedrus*, where he backtracks on the high-minded *Symposium* view. The *Symposium* forces us to decide between the flickering and unstable attraction of a particular erotically desired person, versus the pure light of an eternal form where all our desires for eros and *philia* can be met in an impersonal embrace of ultimate satisfaction. In contrast, in the *Phaedrus*, the erotic love of an individual person is not seen as an option excluding more high-minded love but, rather, as a necessary stepping stone towards that latter kind of love, as we gradually and developmentally climb the *scala amoris*. It is even suggested there that love of an individual person will persist after the heights of true eros have been reached, but only provided the friends have learned to bond through philosophical rather than erotic attraction to one another and refrain, for example, from sexual intercourse (Salim, 2006, p. 46).

So while Plato acknowledges in the *Phaedrus* that *philia* without personally directed eros remains weak and not fully virtuous, and vice versa—nominally supporting Assumption (2)—he does so by starving eros of its everyday connotations (in ancient as well as modern times), evidently reducing either (depending on the textual interpretation) it to a particularly impassioned and enchanted form of *philia* or a stepping stone towards *philia*. Hence, modern readers cannot expect to seek support for Assumption (2), about the ideal concordance of eros and *philia* on standard everyday understandings, in Plato, and he remains completely silent on Assumption (3), that eros can in fact threaten *philia*.

Given Aristotle's penchant for bringing Plato down to earth, to the level of everyday conceptions of 'the many', and to 'naturalise' his most elevated raptures, we could have expected Aristotle to say something practical and constructive about eros and *philia* relations and conflicts. That fact that he hardly does so—and that what he does say about eros in particular seems inconsistent and confused— is, in the words of Nussbaum (1986, p. 371), 'extremely odd'. Some writers have suggested anecdotal or *ad hominem* reasons behind the philosophical taciturnity, such as Aristotle's sexism towards women and, by extension, towards erotic love; his own calm temper and mundanely agreeable, if unpassionate, relationship with his own wife. However, Aristotle was not prone to letting his own personal experiences get in the way of the empirical evidence he garnered from his scientific endeavours and his close study of ordinary human beings. In any case, a study of Aristotle on eros becomes to a large extent a study of where an eminent philosopher goes wrong and what can be learned from his mistakes.

The most puzzling thing Aristotle says about eros is that it is 'an excess of friendship', presumably meaning 'character friendship' (1985, p. 262 [1171a10–13]). Now, although in most cases Aristotle designates an excess of a virtue as a vice (diametrically opposed to the other vice, in the same domain, of deficiency), there are certain places in his texts where 'excess' refers to a bad trait which is nevertheless not a full-blown vice. That said, it goes against the whole grain of Aristotle's discussion of eros and *philia*, and of the different types of *philia*, to consider eros an excess of *philia*. Just as Aristotle connects utility friendships, in terms of prevalence, to old and sour people, he connects eros to pleasure friendships to which, in turn, young and passionate people, guided by their feelings, are most prone (1985, p. 212 [1156a31–1156b6]). That is all fine and well. However, if the view is that erotic love is a sub-species of friendship for pleasure, then it becomes even more bizarre to characterise it as an 'excess' of character friendship, because Aristotle did not consider pleasure friendship as a vice and not even as a bad thing at all. While not as deep and developed, as stable and enduring, as character friendships, pleasure friendships are in general commendable and in no way a deformity, or an excess, of the former, any more than amateur football constitutes the deformity of professional football, although not as advanced. Indeed, character friends continue to have friends for pleasure, just as professional footballers play football with their kids in their gardens also. So in what sense is eros then an excess or a bad thing?

The key probably lies not in the connection to friendship-pleasures but to eros being guided by mere feelings rather than reason. Now, it is not as if Aristotle denigrates feelings morally in a Socratic, let alone a Kantian, way. In contrast, Aristotle is the first philosopher who gave our emotional life pride of place in flourishing and incorporated specific emotions as components in almost all the moral virtues (Kristjánsson, 2018). However, what Aristotle commended were reason- or *phronesis*-guided emotions (namely imbued with, rather than controlled by, reason), not mere intuitive 'thrusts'. So to use a modern distinction between non-cognitive feelings and cognitive (complex, multi-componential) emotions, Aristotle's complaint about eros seems to be that it is based solely on the former but not the latter. Eros, thus, involves defiled or impoverished emotion, rather than defiled or impoverished *philia*, with (sadly) no consideration given to the view that one can love someone erotically in a rational way. That said, this does allow for the possibility that eros can develop into *philia*, for even if the 'beloved's bloom is failing', perhaps one begins to grow fond of her character instead (1985, p. 214 [1157a8–12]). Nevertheless, there is no accommodation in Aristotle, any more than in Plato, of the modern Assumption (2), that the best affection state between partners involves concordance between eros and *philia*.

The non-accommodation of Assumption (2) notwithstanding, Aristotle could have been expected to say something enlightening about Assumption (3), regarding potential eros–*philia* conflicts, particularly because of his sensitivity to the problem of mixing up different types of friendship (recall Section 2.3). The examples he has in mind have to do, for example, with a case where an erotic lover and his beloved, or a teacher and student, begin to clash because while one considers the love or friendship based on pleasure, the other engages in it for utility purposes only (Aristotle, 1935, p. 429 [1243b17–23]). Aristotle seems to miss a trick here, however, by not extending the discussion to a clash between erotic love and character friendship: say, a case where a student seeks the company of a teacher for the sake of establishing an educative character friendship, but the teacher takes this as an erotic advance and proceeds accordingly, potentially with disastrous consequences. The reason for the lost opportunity to explore such 'conflicting loves' (Toner, 2003, p. 259) is, again, Aristotle's idealised view of character friendships and his steadfast belief, which I am challenging in this chapter, that problems that hit at the lower types of friendship leave character friendships untouched.

Because of his deprioritisation of eros, as uninformed by rational emotions, he gives no credence to any variant of modern Assumption (2) about the possibly ideal combination of eros and *philia* in a flourishing life. Moreover, to sum up, because of his idealised view of character friendships, he does not extend his discussion of mixed motivations spurred by eros in incomplete types of friendship to the complete type. Plato does seem to endorse Assumption (2). However, that appearance turns out to be illusory once we realise that the eros he is talking about is not the one of everyday concerns. Furthermore, like Aristotle, he pays no attention to potential conflicts between eros and friendships; hence remaining mute on Assumption (3). All in all, then, despite the invaluable contribution that these two philosophical masters have made to the historical discussion of eros and *philia*, they were not immune to seemingly pedestrian oversights, and in order to evaluate modern assumptions we need to turn to contemporary sources.

For a reason explained earlier, I will mostly confine my attention in the remainder of this section to Assumption (3): the question of conflicts between eros and deep friendships. The obvious case study here is that of cross-sex friendships, where such conflicts are, arguably, most likely to occur. Assumption (3)—which seems to constitute some sort of a received wisdom in modernity—can actually be broken up into two sub-assumptions:

Assumption (3a): Cross-sex friendships are fraught with difficulties and tensions because of the almost inevitable undercurrent of sexual excitement, however faint. Friendship and erotic love thus form an essentially unstable amalgam (see e.g. Vernon, 2010, p. 45).

Assumption (3b): If and when cross-sex friendships mature, they almost inevitably serve as a mere 'tantalising interlude' (Barnard, 2011, p. 199) to the more stabilising relation of erotic love, unless the pair are physically repulsive to each other (see Lewis, 1960, p. 99).

The 'locus classicus' of Assumption (3b), that 'successful' cross-sex friendships are merely incipient erotic relationships, is the film *When Harry Met Sally* (Ephron & Reiner, 1989). While projecting an image that cross-sex friendships are possible, it also depicts them as eventually unsustainable (unless the pair want to end up in the self-flagellating purgatory of the 'friend-zone' which constitutes the worst of all possible worlds). While first enthralled by the lack of sex-fuelled inhibition that a non-erotic friendship between the sexes offers, Harry comes to the conclusion that, eventually, sex gets in the way, and 'no man can be friends with a woman that he finds attractive' (Ephron & Reiner, 00:11:36ff). Inevitably, then, at least in a Hollywood rom-com, Harry and Sally end up in bed.

The *When-Harry-Met-Sally* theme is in no way a specifically modern phenomenon. The historically famous penpalship (*qua* character friendship) between Catherine the Great and Voltaire included a fair amount of sexual intimation (as I tease out in Chapter 7). Even more famously, the close friendship between John Stuart Mill and Harriet Taylor, who eventually became his wife, could only be sustained in their own view because of the mutual lack of sexual attraction. So rather than presenting evidence for the possibility of non-sensuous cross-sex friendships, as Taylor and Mill seem to have wanted it to do, their story is usually invoked as an exception that proves the rule: namely, as a friendship that only worked because both seem to have had unusually low sex drives (cf. Vernon, 2010, pp. 47–8; Schudder & Bishop, 2001, pp. 83–9).

What is the empirical evidence for Assumptions (3a) and (3b), then? The first thing to notice is that, until fairly recently at least, studies of cross-sex friendships were extremely scant or, more precisely, a systematically ignored and anomalous topic in the social-science literature (O'Meara, 1989, pp. 525–7; Reeder, 2000, p. 329). The best sources that I have come across, apart from scattered articles, are two books: one by Schudder and Bishop (2001), an extended dialogical study of their own academic non-erotic close friendship, and an older outlier by Werking (1997), expanding upon the findings of 190 interviews with, and 636 surveys of, self-described cross-sex friends.

After reading through many of the available sources, I would summarise the findings under the following themes:

Frequency. Approximately one-third of friendships in preschool are cross-sex but those have mostly disappeared by the beginning of primary school—only to reappear again in adolescence when the frequency reaches one-third again. 85 per cent of undergraduates have at least one cross-sex friend (O'Meara, 1989; Reeder, 2000; George et al., 2014). While these numbers do not seem to justify the relative academic silence on cross-sex friendship, they may not be as eye-catching as they initially seem because most studies do not differentiate between ordinary friendships and close friendships, let alone Aristotelian character friendships. However, Werking's summary of sources indicate that 40 per cent of men and 30 per cent of women report having *close* friends of the opposite sex (1997, p. 2). That is a significant number. Educational level seems to matter, however, insomuch as cross-sex friendships are to a large degree the privileged province of educated, middle-class people. It has been conjectured that this is because educated people have a greater tolerance of self-complexity and ambiguity (George et al., 2014; Rawlins, 2008, p. 182).

Tensions. It is not a matter for great surprise that a lot of cross-sex friends report tensions about their friendships, although those do not always have to do with sexual 'undercurrents', as suggested by Assumption (3), but rather with a lack of social recognition (see below). Again, not surprisingly, sexual tensions surface more if the friends find each other physically attractive and sexually appealing, although no support has been found for C. S. Lewis's strong suggestion that the pair need to find each other physically repulsive to quench potential lust (George et al., 2014). Indeed, about 40 per cent of women and 20 per cent of men say they intentionally abstain from sexual advances in order to maintain the friendship (Reeder, 2000). Across the board, people experience cross-sex friendship as less stable and less intimate than same-sex friendships—but those findings do not say much because they also include those who have failed to initiate or preserve such friendships (Werking, 1997, p. 24). The fact that almost 40 per cent of cross-sex terminations are characterised by the friendship simply fading away, while less than 25 per cent came to an abrupt end (Werking, 1997, p. 81), indicates that in most cases those friendships do not dissolve because of *When-Harry-Met-Sally*-type crunch moments, but rather for more mundane reasons. Interestingly, self-reported spirituality is associated with significantly lower levels of cross-sex tensions (George et al., 2014). Somewhat paradoxically, male friends seem to experience more sexual tensions than female friends, but at the same time, cross-sex friendships seem to benefit men more (Rawlins, 2008, p. 183; George et al., 2014). Another paradox revolves around marriage and cross-sex friendships, with some studies finding that marriage increases sexual tensions towards the person outside the dyad but others that such tensions are lower if you are currently attached (George et al., 2014; Werking, 1997, p. 3).

Challenges of public approval. The most significant barrier to cross-sex friendships does not seem to be the *When-Harry-Met-Sally* one, encapsulated in Assumption (3b), but rather the 'scriptlessness' of those relationships and a lack of public understanding or approval. The pair typically do not know what the social rules and norms are; and other friends, family and co-workers look askance at these normless encounters. For such friendships to work, then, both parties need to engage in considerable public-perception management (O'Meara, 1989; Werking, 1997, pp. 38, 41, 163). They also need to have considerable tolerance of potential public disapproval.

Characteristics/benefits. Cross-sex friendships tend to differ between the sexes in stereotypical ways. Men do things together, without much emotional attachment, whereas women confide in each other and share emotional resources (O'Meara, 1989). One of the main characteristics (and benefits) of cross-sex relationships seems to be the ability to confound those stereotypes, allowing women to be more masculine, assertive and 'agentic', but men to be more reflective, empathetic and 'communal' (Werking, 1997, pp. 50–3; Rawlins, 2008, p. 111; Schudder & Bishop, 2001; Reeder, 2000). Harry found this characteristic refreshingly 'freeing' (Ephron & Reiner, 1989, 00:42:09ff) before succumbing to the sexual impulse.

To sum up, then, the empirical evidence only partially confirms Assumption (3a). There is nothing inherently unstable about cross-sex friendships. Those are more vulnerable than same-sex ones but more so for external reasons (lack of social recognition) than internal ones (inevitable sexual tensions). Such tensions do exist, however, and need to be taken seriously both academically—when trying to understand the value of, and barriers to, cross-sex friendships—and practically, when trying to initiate or sustain such friendships oneself. Much the same applies to Assumption (3b). There is nothing about cross-sex friendships that turns them necessarily into the eventual *When-Harry-Met-Sally* scenario. However, it is healthy to bear this possibility in mind and guard oneself against it. Even Meilaender (1993), who is overall sceptical of our ability to tame the 'wild and unruly deity' of eros, nonetheless considers it worth a try: 'we have every reason to attempt it, despite its inherent difficulties.' Barnard goes further by suggesting that the very tense and ambiguous nature of cross-sex friendships may give them 'an exciting, precarious edge' (2011, p. 200). Cross-sex friendships have unique benefits and depriving oneself of them for reasons of fear may in the end constitute a greater threat to one's overall flourishing than giving them a fair try.

As an afterthought about the empirical literature that I studied it might be added that most of it was strangely ahistorical. To understand better the complex relationship between friendship and romance, we would probably need to delve more deeply into historical sources: for example exploring how certain socio-historical trends in modernity have prioritised romance and sex over 'mere' friendships.

2.5   Concluding Remarks

This chapter has not aimed at offering a purely deflationary account of Aristotelian character friendships. I have no doubt that such friendships satisfy Owen Flanagan's principle of 'minimal psychological realism': they are, *in principle* at least, possible 'for creatures like us' (1991, p. 32), although *in practice* they are beset by many more problems than Aristotle envisaged. Neither has the aim of the chapter been to discourage the formation of character friendships. Worry is, as someone once said, the interest paid on trouble before it falls due; and despite all the problems explored above, the intrinsic value of successful character friendships is so great that entering into those is definitely a risk worth taking.

Aristotle does identify a *quantitative* problem with character friendships: that they can only be had with a very limited number of people. I have added a series of *qualitative* problems potentially affecting equal or unequal friendships, pointing out that Aristotle either does not mention these problems or never puts the relevant worries about them to rest. It is not only that he seems insensitive to the general fact of the wear and tear of time that naturally dissipates many character friendships unless they are regularly revitalised; he is singularly unconcerned about the more specific psycho-moral and psycho-social issues that pose a threat to their assumed essential stability.

In order to expose this weakness, I drew upon a host of potential problems through a taxonomy of 5×2 categories. I realise that this taxonomy may seem slightly contrived. Another option would have been to focus exclusively on the problems that I myself consider most potentially serious—which happen to be those listed as the first ones in Sections 2.2 and 2.3, respectively. However, as this is, as far as I am aware, the first stab at identifying potential threats to the stability thesis in a systematic manner, I have decided to be as inclusive as possible and simply present all the problems that I could think of, without arranging them in any explicit order of priority or seriousness.

In blowing the whistle on some of those issues, I have stuck my head above the philosophical parapet by drawing on personal experiences and a number of social scientific studies, either directly or obliquely. Readers may not share my experiences, and they may want to draw on alternative empirical sources. I have no problems with either option. All I wanted to do in Sections 2.2 and 2.3 was to encourage avid Aristotelians to consider relaxing their insistence that it is somehow either empirically or conceptually true that character friendships are essentially stable.

Given the sensitivity of Aristotle's naturalistic moral theory to empirical evidence, it is in order, before closing the discussion in this chapter, to say something about why close friendships *do in fact* end. Although current psychological research is not confined to character friendships and does not preselect only those friends whom Aristotle would count as budding *phronimoi*, something would be amiss with Aristotle's restrictive thesis about friendship dissolutions if it did not have a solid basis in reality.

In a nutshell, empirical research elicits lots of facts that do not seem to tally with Aristotelian theory. A common cause for the dissolution of close friendships is that friends simply grow apart as their interactions are no longer psychologically or educationally rewarding. Moreover, close friendships do not simply either continue as such or come to an end; they can be 'downgraded', temporarily or permanently, and then upgraded again. Some people seem to prefer settled long-lasting close friendships while others are more comfortable with 'serial friendships' that change as their life changes. Only about 50 per cent of close friendships among adolescents remain stable over one school year. About 84 per cent of teenage girls report at least one complete dissolution or a downgrade of a close friendship. In general, the trajectory of close friendships is much more fluid, more relative to personality styles and psycho-social preferences, and more subject to the wear of time and subtle changes in external circumstances than Aristotle's discussion suggests (cf. e.g. Bowker, 2004; 2011; Healy, 2015; 2017).

Admittedly, some of the empirical findings can be explained away as applying only to a younger and more eclectic group of people than Aristotle had in mind as his presumed readership of budding *phronimoi*. Others can be related to social circumstances of greater geographical mobility in the modern world than in ancient Greece. All that said, one cannot shake the impression that, given Aristotle's own universalism about human nature, many of these empirical findings would have been the same if Aristotle had conducted rigorous social scientific research in ancient Athens. One must conclude, as I already did in Sections 2.1–2.3, that he may perhaps have been blinded by the lights of his fiery mission to promote (character) friendship as a moral virtue of enormous endurance, vitality and strength.

In Section 2.4, I tried to weave together considerations from the classic writers on eros and friendship, Plato and Aristotle, with references to contemporary sources and empirical findings, in order to cast light on three common Assumptions in modernity. I argued that the writings of Plato and Aristotle are mostly irrelevant to Assumption (1), about the importance of erotic love for psycho-physical wellbeing. Both of them reject Assumption (2), that the best partnership/marriage is between a couple who are both character friends and erotic lovers. Because of the strongly normative nature of Assumption (2), it is difficult to elicit empirical evidence to confirm or refute it. All I can say is that none of the empirical sources I have canvassed provides any backbone to a flat-out rejection of Assumption (2).

Assumption (3) is easiest to handle empirically, and turns out, indeed, to be true in that eros often gets in the way of deep cross-sex friendships—although the further suggestion (as represented in *When Harry Met Sally*) that this is inevitable and unavoidable seems to be exaggerated. Nonetheless, it is a serious flaw in Aristotle's otherwise nuanced discussion of the pros and cons of different types of friendship that he does not discuss the possibility of conflicts between erotic love and character friendships. As sensitive as he is to the unique psychological intimacy that is created through such friendships, it is truly odd that he does not envisage the potential clash between that intimacy and its close cousin: physical intimacy.

3

Friendship with a Filter

The Role of *Phronesis*

3.1 Introduction: The Implications of Friendship Not Being a Master Virtue

If Cicero were right about friendship, there would be no need for this chapter. Recall that, according to him, friendship is an overriding value and possessing the capacity to make friends in the proper way is a master virtue: trumping all others. This is not Aristotle's view. It is not mine either. This is why a neo-Aristotelian account of friendship requires a discussion about value conflicts and value adjudications.

When Aristotle maintains that 'no one would choose to live without friends even if he had all the other goods' (1985, p. 207 [1155a5–6]), he could well have said the same about various other goods, such as health. Possessing all other conceivable goods in life is useless if one does not have the health to enjoy them. This does not mean that health is somehow a master value either, any more than friendship is. It all comes down to the correct arbitration between virtues, where those clash, and in some cases between virtues and other values. Some philosophers seem to think, however, that although friendship does not constitute the trump card in such arbitrations, it serves as a benchmark for the evaluation of general moral theories. An adequate moral theory must, for example, on Badhwar's view, be compatible with the attitudes and practical requirements of friendship, correctly conceptualised (1991, p. 485). If that is the case, there is even more urgent need for a chapter like the present one.

Now, Aristotle is second to none among moral theorists in offering us a passkey to solve moral quandaries. He calls it *phronesis*, and I discussed its workings briefly in Section 1.2. However, discussions of the relationship between *phronesis* and friendship are conspicuous by their absence in Aristotelian and neo-Aristotelian scholarship (although touched upon in Salkever, 2008). Perhaps the reason could be that by acknowledging how (value) judgements and decisions regarding friendships need to be filtered through the intellectual virtue of *phronesis*, virtue ethicists stand to lose what is sometimes regarded as the greatest advantage of virtue ethics over other moral theories.

To explain how, let us do a Bernard Williams redux. In a seminal paper by Williams (1981), which blazed a trail for numerous follow-ups in the two decades

Friendship for Virtue. Kristján Kristjánsson, Oxford University Press. © Kristján Kristjánsson 2022.
DOI: 10.1093/oso/9780192864260.003.0003

thereafter, he argued that both the reigning moral theories of the day, utilitarian consequentialism and Kantian deontology, failed an adequacy test for a similar reason: by compelling us to subject our obvious natural choice to prioritise the needs of a close friend (or a loved one) over those of a stranger, in times of moral danger, to a theoretical decision procedure before coming up with the 'right' reaction. Such requirements of reflective calculation rob us, according to Williams, of psycho-moral reasons to live at all by attacking the source of any integrity-grounding prime motivation that makes us tick. The decision procedure required by these two moral theories—be it the categorical imperative or the utility calculus—inserts a filter (which Williams seems to think of as an artificial gadget or fetish) between the natural moral motivation of any normal person and the decision to act on it. But this interjects what Williams famously terms 'one thought too many' into the moral reaction mechanism and fetishises it in the service of a psychologically overbearing theory. The problem thus lies in the fact that both of the competing moral theories of the day propose determinable methods for considering when goods like close friendship ought to be outweighed by more general requirements of duty or the overall good (cf. Woodcock, 2010, p. 14).

This problem identified by Williams has become known as 'the problem of integrity', but as Williams uses 'integrity' in a somewhat idiosyncratic sense with respect to either lay or philosophical uses (Kristjánsson, 2019), I prefer to refer to it as 'the problem of alienation'. Williams basically urges that being held in thrall by the rationalist demands of the categorical imperative or the amoral assumption of the utility calculus (which considers pleasure as the highest good) alienates us from our most significant others and in the end from ourselves. Juxtaposing this argument with Aristotle's one about the predicament of the vicious who, because they are not capable of loving themselves, also become incapable of loving others (1935, p. 405 [1240b15–19]; 1985, pp. 246–7 [1166b1–25]), Williams turns the psychology upside down: because the moral fetishisers are barred from forming integrity-grounding unconditional commitments to their beloved ones (including their closest friends), they also become alienated from their core commitments to themselves as moral agents that give them any reasons for living or acting at all. The 'one-thought-too-many' argument has become something of a mantra, and I revisit it in more detail in Section 3.2, albeit only insofar as it is relevant for the purposes of the present chapter.

So what are the 'present purposes' then? My aim is, briefly put, to explore a specific assumption that has emerged from the above-mentioned literature. While not explicitly elicited by Williams himself, the lesson that most scholars seem to have drawn from the problem of alienation is that virtue ethics is somehow invulnerable to it and hence better equipped to deal with the desirably realistic features of common-sense morality that make us commit to it in the first place. Needless to say, there are various other features that may draw people towards virtue ethics as an alternative to the other two moral theories—one commonly noted being its facility to make sense of the role of emotions in the morally good life (Kristjánsson, 2018). However, it is typically suggested, or even stated without argument, that the fact that only virtue ethics makes do without a filter between close friendship and moral decisions provides a reason to abandon utilitarianism and deontology and adopt virtue ethics as one's moral theory (see e.g. Card, 2004, p. 149; although he refrains from categorising virtue ethics as a 'theory'). My aim is to problematise the assumption about this unique advantage of virtue ethics. There are many things to like about virtue ethics, but this is, I submit, not one of them.

Notice some odd features about this assumption. First, it is not clearly elicited by Williams himself, as already noted. Second, despite the flurry of responses that followed Williams's piece, none developed in detail—to the best of my knowledge—the positive side of the argument. In other words, the claim that virtue ethics has unique resources to counter the one-thought-too-many argument simply continued to be implicitly assumed rather than argued for. Third, the assumption in question would work if Aristotelian virtue ethics were an intuitionist moral theory, with moral judgements being seen as spontaneous and non-deliberative. However, any intuitionist readings of Aristotle tend to be misreadings (see Section 3.3). Alternatively, it would work if friendship were an overriding master virtue in Aristotle's system, as in Cicero's, but Aristotle blows away any such illusions in the *Eudemian Ethics* when he says that those who unreflectively 'give everything' to a friend 'are good-for-nothing people' (1935, p. 433 [1244a17–19]).

There is, however, as I keep harping on, a meta-virtue in Aristotle's virtue ethical system: namely, the intellectual virtue of *phronesis*. In addition to helping individual moral virtues find means to their ends, *phronesis* helps solve apparent virtue conflicts, and it also informs the content of the virtues, as they are understood by the agent, by bringing them into harmony with an intellectually grounded blueprint of the good life—because Aristotle's is not a Humean theory of moral motivation. I say more about this in Section 3.4. Further, I aim to show throughout that the assumption of friendship being somehow an unconditional, unreflective virtue in Aristotelian virtue ethics is seriously misguided. At the present juncture, it suffices to note that *phronesis* seems to provide a reflective filter through which any virtuous considerations needs to pass—including those of friendship—before they can justifiably issue in either reason-imbued emotion (such as compassion towards a friend) or action (such as helping a friend). It is therefore hard to shake the impression that *phronesis* imports an 'extra thought' between the motivational force of virtuous friendship as a disposition and particular (re)actions of friendship. Does such filtering of friendship through *phronesis* fall prey to Williams's one-thought-too-many argument against moral theories and undermine the assumption about the unique advantage of virtue ethics—or do not all extra thoughts count as 'one thought too many'? These questions call for some sustained analysis.

To anticipate, my conclusion will be that it is worthwhile inquiring what sort of an extra thought counts as detrimental to moral theorising and what sort does not. I argue, in Section 3.4, that although *phronesis* elicits an extra thought, it falls into the latter category. However, at the end of this chapter, my argument still needs a bolstering of its main premise, awaiting Chapter 4.

3.2 Williams Redux: Some Reflections on the Problem of Alienation

As most of the responses that fuelled the lengthy debate about Williams's bombshell argument have come from consequentialists, and consequentialism is logically closer to virtue ethics than deontology (in being teleological in form), I will focus on those responses here. The aim is not to rehearse this debate in any detail, but simply to foreground the features that may be relevant for the discussion in the remainder of this chapter.

The first thing to note is that the problem of alienation is logically distinct from the other standard objection lodged against consequentialist theories, especially of the traditional utilitarian kind: the problem of repugnant consequences (aka 'the problem of victimisation'). The alleged repugnant consequences (e.g. in well-rehearsed transplant and trolley cases) point to *moral* errors in consequentialism, and the typical responses (about the need to focus on long-term consequences, including those of precedents set, or on the threat to overall utility incurred by sacrificing people in lower moral risk zones for people in higher zones) seek to show that consequentialism is not prone to those moral errors. In contrast, the problem of alienation is not first and foremost a moral problem. What sort of a problem is it then? Williams's own words often indicate that it is a problem of *rationality*: namely, that it is '*unreasonable* for a man to give up [...] something which is a condition of his having any interest in being around in the world at all' (1981, p. 14, my italics; cf. Bernstein, 2007, pp. 67–8). However, a closer look at Williams's argument reveals an even more menacing and deep-rooted source, for Williams also introduces the idea of a 'categorical desire', the satisfaction or non-satisfaction of which settles the question of whether the agent cares to stay alive or not (1981, p. 11). For all normal people, Williams assumes, the desire to prioritise the needs of close friends constitutes such a categorical desire. Hence, it is *psychologically* impossible at the same time to suppress this desire, in the interest of a moral theory, and to continue to live: at least live a life that has any meaning. To succumb, say, to the utility-maximising demands of consequentialist moral theories is, therefore, not so much immoral and irrational as simply stretching human psychology beyond the breaking point. It is, in Williams's sense, not alienating only *vis-à-vis* the significant other(s), such as close friends, but self-alienating and self-destroying.

The standard interpretation of Williams's argument is, as Wolf (2012, p. 74) correctly points out, that the psychological impossibility kicks in at the moment of the moral decision. So it is the person who thinks *at the time of action* about what would be morally permissible (e.g. in a case involving a choice to save a close friend/spouse versus a stranger) who falls prey to the problem of alienation, not the person who prepares herself, for instance, as a moral learner for facing moral dilemmas later in life by thinking through various possibilities beforehand, in order to strengthen her commitment to her categorical desires, or to figure out what those really are. Incidentally, I agree with Wolf that this interpretation of Williams's argument is not radical enough, but before elaborating on that point, a few reminders are in order about how consequentialists have tried to parry that argument on the standard interpretation.

Responding to Williams has turned into a whole cottage industry. For reasons of space, I leave out of consideration here Kantian responses (although I would particularly recommend Baron, 1995, esp. pp. 134–5), in order to focus on conse-quentialist ones, as consequentialism is arguably closer to Aristotle's moral theory than Kantianism is. Many consequentialist responses take the form of rejecting the claim that thinking through moral possibilities at the time of action, in cases such as the above, is bound to alienate the thinker from others and then herself. The general complaint is that this argument romanticises and de-intellectualises deep friendships overly and overlooks the continually morally reflective and probing nature of at least some such friendships (see e.g. Railton's classic 1984 piece). This general complaint can then be developed along various argumenta-tive avenues, for instance by illustrating how, at least in the case of two devoted consequentialists, the decision to honour the mutual friendship may be seen as even more precious and noble by the friend if it involves, and is reached on the back of, a lengthy reflection on the general happiness of humankind (see e.g. Conee, 2001; Bernstein, 2007). It is even possible to envisage a conscious pact made between two consequentialist friends that they will never favour each other over others except as a result of rigorous deliberation about the total state of the world, and that they admire each other the more they hold to this pact, even when the friend's decision goes against them in the end. The trouble is that while one can imagine certain people deriving fulfilment from such considerations and such a pact (say, someone like Harriet Taylor or John Stuart Mill), this would hardly generalise to the rest of humankind. Indeed, one would be tempted to invoke here as examples people at, or close to, the autistic spectrum (cf. Dineen, 2019). Williams's argument does not require that *all* people have a categorical desire of the sort he describes; it suffices that the majority of normal moral agents do. Otherwise, the demands of consequentialism are prone to fall foul of Flanagan's criterion of 'minimal psychological realism' (1991, p. 32): of not being feasibly attainable for (*most*) beings like us.

A more promising line of response (also in line with Railton, 1984) is to accept Williams's claim that thinking through moral possibilities at the time of action, in cases such as the one about the friend and the stranger, is likely to be self-alienating, and then to make sure somehow that one's preferred version of consequentialism accommodates this fact. One way of doing that is to adopt rule utilitarianism, rather than act utilitarianism, as one's conscious moral theory, and to argue that many privileged duties to friends are justified by their overall conduciveness to the maximisation of the general good, even if they happen to appear to be utility-reducing in a particular case (see e.g. Telfer, 1970–1971, p. 235). However, rule utilitarianism imports problems of its own, both because of its tendency to collapse logically into act utilitarianism (Lyons, 1965) and because adopting it consciously as one's preferred moral theory seems to call for reflection at the time of action, which is exactly what Williams's argument debars us from doing.

More plausibly, the consequentialist could stick to act utilitarianism but augment it with the *psychological* thesis that considering alternative possibilities to prioritising the needs of a close friend at the time of action is psychologically incompatible with a concern for utility, and such considerations should therefore be forestalled. For if it is in fact true that (even considering the possibility of) not prioritising the friend robs the agent psychologically of the will to live, then there are good consequentialist reasons for *habituating* oneself into prioritising the friend *spontaneously* (as distinct from adopting the prioritisation as a rule to follow). The objection that the world would be better still if considerations of overall utility could be engaged in at the time of action will not cut ice with the consequentialist who has taken this psychological thesis on board, because consequentialism is not a theory about other possible worlds, but just this world, and what 'a consequentialist theory tells us we ought to do is always actually possible' (Conee, 2001, pp. 178–9).

At the risk of getting ahead of my argument in Section 3.3, let me remark here that this response to the standard interpretation of Williams's argument may also seem to make Aristotelian *phronesis* immune to it, at least on one reading of *phronesis*. Some scholars emphasise the developmental function of *phronesis* as an intellectual virtue that prepares agents beforehand to take the right decision by 'metabolising the past to simulate possible futures' (Railton, 2016, pp. 45–6). This would then explain the facility of *phronesis* to get things 'intuitively' right at the time of action. It is not because *phronesis* itself serves as a vehicle of intuition, but rather because it has prepared us so well for what could happen that once we enter into an already-reflected-upon situation, all that *phronesis* needs to do is to activate our sensitivity to identifying this as the sort of situation that calls for a certain reaction, without the need for further deliberation at the time of action. On this reading, there does not seem to be any danger of *phronesis* importing 'one thought too many'. However, this reading does not show virtue ethics to be superior to simple act utilitarianism, provided we grant that the psychological thesis suggested in the preceding paragraph may also save act utilitarianism from the problem of alienation.

What seems to be too good to be true is usually too good to be true. The whole problem to which Williams alerted us seems to have disappeared, simply because initial credibility has been granted to the standard interpretation of his argument. Yet on that interpretation, the argument bewilders rather than enthrals, in particular if it is meant to point towards the superiority of virtue ethics as a moral theory. Snatching potential defeat from the jaws of victory, Wolf explains well, in an intriguing paper, the extent to which the standard interpretation defangs Williams's argument. Williams's intention was much more radical than standardly acknowledged: namely, not only to show that reflecting on what to do, *at the moment of action*, in cases involving friend–stranger conflicts, is psychologically impossible in the sense of being self-alienating, but rather that any reflections on the possibility of betraying the friend will be self-alienating, even if engaged in '*off stage*': be it *prospectively*, to prepare oneself for proper decision making at the time of action, or *retrospectively*, to justify to oneself what one has done. Removing the deliberations from the emotionally charged scene of the action does not rescue the extra thought from being one thought too many (Wolf, 2012). For example, it is cold comfort to me to witness that my best friend refuses to betray me under coercion (e.g. when pressed to by a terrorist) if I know that she agonised over this possible choice beforehand and thus failed to exhibit unconditional commitment to me as her best friend.

On this radical interpretation, there is no way in which the strategy invoked above can rescue consequentialism, because it is impossible to ask the consequentialist to hold all considerations regarding the utility of prioritising friends over strangers (or vice versa) in abeyance, not only during but also before and after the relevant event. That simply goes against the grain of the very idea of consequentialist calculations of the overall good. There must be a time in which those can be engaged in, no holds barred. Wolf's radical interpretation also brings home to us, much more so than the standard interpretation, the sense of 'moral schizophrenia' that Stocker (1976) famously wrote about. For if the moral filter is absent (perhaps because one has developed an automatised, consequentialist disposition of the kind Railton favours), then the agent's motives do not reflect the moral reasons that justify the action, resulting in a kind of 'schizophrenia': she is neither motivated by that which she values morally, nor does she morally value that which motivates her. Notably, Wolf's radical interpretation also casts serious doubts on the facility of Aristotelian virtue ethics to escape from the clutches of Williams's argument, for *phronesis* is surely presented by Aristotle as a method of moral deliberation, and a determinable one at that, although admittedly not codifiable in the same sense as the utility calculus or the categorical imperative (see further in Section 3.3).

The radical interpretation of Williams's argument presents us with the following dilemma, given the aim of the present chapter. Either we accept the argument with respect to *phronesis*, but then we implicitly concede that every extra thought of the kind envisaged above will count as one thought too many, and that seems to do away with *phronesis* altogether (unless we understand *phronesis* as some sort of intuitive artistry, outstripping conscious thought, but that is a misguided understanding of *phronesis* as I argue in Section 3.3). Or we reject the argument with respect to *phronesis*, but then we need to show either that *phronesis* does not import an extra thought into the decision-making process (which I think is impossible) or that although *phronesis qua* filter imports an extra thought, it is not one thought too many for some substantive reasons and hence the 'filter' is not 'fetishising' in the same way as, say, the utility calculus.

While I propose to go down the second avenue in Section 3.4, we can safely conclude at this juncture that there are no obvious escape routes in Williams's argument (on the radical interpretation) that would prevent Aristotelian virtue ethics from potentially being sent to the gallows along with the other two dominant moral theories. However, before that sentence is passed, *phronesis* needs a fair and thorough hearing.

3.3 *Phronesis* as an Intellectual Filter

The important role that the intellectual virtue of *phronesis* plays in all Aristotelian or quasi-Aristotelian forms of virtue ethics is well-known, as already anticipated with the model presented in Section 1.2. In order to answer the question of whether *phronesis* imports one thought too many, various considerations need to be addressed, beginning in this section with some additional reflections on what *phronesis* really is. To cut a long story short, the easiest way to show that *phronesis* does not import one thought too many about close friendship with regard to the (a) nature and (b) content of *phronesis,* would be to argue that (a) *phronesis* does not add an extra thought but simply elicits the relevant moral intuition and moreover (b) that this intuition motivates the unconditional prioritisation of close friendship as a moral concern. I have already provided citations from Aristotle in this chapter and Chapter 1 that seem to rule out (b). However, remember that virtue ethics is a naturalistic moral theory, answerable to empirical findings on how people actually flourish or wilt, and it could well be the case that (b) needs to be revised in the light of new empirical evidence to accommodate a primacy-of-friendship intuition. After such revision, *phronesis* could still potentially be considered to retain the spirit, as distinct from the letter, of Aristotelian virtue ethics. Alternatively, there are variants of virtue ethics other than the Aristotelian one, and some of those could accommodate friendship as a master virtue (cf. Cocking & Kennett, 2000).

It is more difficult to revise (a) by eliciting other variants because the guidance that all leading virtue ethicists in the West tend to follow on *phronesis* has been wrenched from Aristotle, and there is, to the best of my knowledge, no completely un-Aristotelian *phronesis* theory out there (although many theorists rely on MacIntyre's rendering which departs from Aristotle's in some respects; see Kristjánsson, 2007, chap. 1). Not all hope is lost, however, of escaping Williams's curse, for there are almost as many variants of 'Aristotelian' *phronesis* as there are Aristotelian exegetes, and some of those understand the workings of *phronesis* first and foremost in terms of intuitive artistry rather than as an extra *thought*, let alone a thought too many. I will consider two of those variants later in this section, but first some brief rehearsals of Aristotle's own account are in order.

Aristotle's *phronesis* is, as already briefly indicated in Section 1.2, an intellectual virtue (virtue of thought) that serves the purpose of living well by monitoring and guiding the moral virtues. Building on emotional dispositions cultivated through early-years habituation, *phronesis* re-evaluates those dispositions critically, allowing them to truly 'share in reason', and provides the agent with proper justifications for them. In addition to latching itself on to every 'natural' moral virtue, and infusing it with systematic reason, the function of *phronesis* is to 'deliberate finely' about the relative weight of competing values, actions and emotions in the context of the question of 'what promotes living well in general'. A person who has acquired *phronesis* has thus, *inter alia*, the wisdom to adjudicate the relative weight of different virtues in apparent conflict situations and to reach a measured verdict about best courses of action (Aristotle, 1985, pp. 153, 154, 159, 164, 171 [1140a26–9, 1140b4–6, 1141b30–1, 1143a8–9, 1144b30–2]). This is, more or less, where the consensus on what *phronesis* really involves ends and the controversial interpretations that haunt the landscape of Aristotelian scholarship begin. While I want to avoid begging controversial questions about what *phronesis* is, simply for the sake of moving on with the discussion of Williams's argument, I do not think that 'anything goes' in Aristotelian exegesis, and I reserve the right below to reject interpretations that are blatantly un-Aristotelian.

Let me highlight here the oddity that although the topic of *phronesis* is undergoing a revival, not only within contemporary virtue ethics but also in social scientific circles and in various areas of applied professional ethics, no psychological instrument currently exists to measure *phronesis* (although the measure designed by Brienza et al., 2018 perhaps comes close to it, along with my Centre's own preliminary inventory: Kristjánsson et al., 2020; Darnell et al., 2023). This is even more remarkable given the current burgeoning of wisdom research in psychology, which is becoming increasingly focused on *practical* wisdom (Grossmann, 2017; Grossmann et al., 2020). Serious efforts are now afoot, however, to remedy this shortcoming by an interdisciplinary team of philosophers and psychologists (Darnell et al., 2019; Kristjánsson et al., 2021). The advantage of instrument design is that relevant conceptual nuances need to be elicited and the components of the construct under examination identified in detail (Darnell et al., 2023). According to the fairly minimalist reading of Aristotelian *phronesis* by Darnell and colleagues (2019; 2023), it serves at least four distinct functions and thus constitutes what psychologists would call a four-component construct. These four components were explained in Section 1.2 and I refer readers back to that overview.

To be sure, this identification of the four core components of Aristotelian *phronesis* does not dissolve all exegetical disputes about the concept. However, it does help fend off seriously aberrant interpretations, including those which consider *phronesis* a mere outlet for automatic, intuitive (non-deliberative) judgements. Indeed, I do believe the idea of 'phronetic intuitionism' (as espoused e.g. by Kaspar, 2015) involves something of an oxymoron. Let me briefly mention two attempts at 'intuition-ising' *phronesis*, one from the current education literature and the other from contemporary moral psychology.

There is a powerful approach in recent educational theory (harking back at least to Dunne, 1993) which offers an (allegedly Aristotelian) anti-realist, non-foundationalist, perspectivist and particularist account of education: most felicitously described as a '*phronesis-praxis* approach'. I have criticised this approach in detail elsewhere (Kristjánsson, 2007, chap. 1) and will not repeat that critique here except insofar as it relates to an intuitionist reading of *phronesis*. According to Dunne, we need to avoid seeing *phronesis* in terms of 'the *application* of theory to particular cases' (1993, p. 157). In *praxis*, as the sphere of *phronesis*, 'practical-moral universals cannot unproblematically cover or include particular cases' precisely because the universals contain 'an element of indeterminateness' *qua* uncodifiability (1993, p. 311). This is, in Dunne's words, so far from being a defect that it is, rather, 'the great merit' of *phronesis* (1993, p. 314): best captured by terms such as 'particularist discernment', 'intuitive artistry', 'perceptual capacity', 'illative sense' or 'situational appreciation'. *Phronesis* is, in other words, the *eye* of moral experience: the discernment of particular situations that enables us 'to see aright' every time, but which remains ultimately experiential rather than universal 'since the universals within its grasp are always modifiable in the light of its continuing exposure to particular cases' (1993, pp. 280, 293, 297, 361). This intuitionist reading of *phronesis* then allows Dunne and his followers to make sweeping generalisations about the essential uncodifiability of Aristotelian *phronesis*-guided ethical and educational decision making.

The snag is that Aristotle's much-cited assertion that *phronesis* is about particulars and therefore needs perception (1985, pp. 160–1 [1142a12–30]) says nothing about the epistemological priority of perception. A simpler interpretation is that Aristotle considered universal moral beliefs that would be fully capable of taking into account every possible situation to be so complicated—although logically possible—that they would in fact be impossible to learn and apply. Think, for instance, of all the comparisons that would need to be made between individuals with simultaneous, yet diverse, interests. Instead of trying to achieve such a superhuman feat, it would be better to acquire a perceptual awareness that guides us to the right answer in the greatest number of factual situations—as we, more realistically, define only 'as far as we can' (1985, p. 243 [1165a35]). *Phronesis*, while not unproblematically codifiable, because of its 'practical' as distinct from 'theoretical' subject matter, is thus not necessarily (but merely contingently) uncodifiable. A perfect moral theory, which resolved once and for all every question of application, would be possible only for a perfect being. Yet what remains is the 'blueprint function' of *phronesis*, which applies a general blueprint of the human *telos* to diverse, complex ethical situations and furnishes the agent with theoretical tools—an intellectual 'filter' if you like—to think through complex practical situations, rather than having to rely simply on hunches.

A less sophisticated attempt to co-opt Aristotle to the intuitionist camp has recently been made by social intuitionists: the proponents of the currently fashionable two-system (dual-process) theories of moral decision making (see e.g. Haidt, 2001). According to social intuitionism, people typically experience a moral intuition about a given state of affairs—an emotion-driven hunch or an implicit sense of what is the appropriate reaction. Such intuitions normally do not require explicit, effortful reasoning; indeed they seem to persist in the face of contrary rational judgement or of the lack of any rationally grounded conviction. They often arise non-voluntarily and are not fully articulable. Most importantly, they motivate spontaneous action, uninformed by conscious deliberation, although people exhibit a tendency—through motivations such as peer pressure and canonical norms of discourse—to justify their actions retrospectively.

Here would be the proposed Aristotelian corollary, then. Human beings typically act upon motivations provided by general traits of character: vicious, virtuous or somewhere in between. We are essentially creatures of habits (*qua* traits). These traits include emotions (*pathe*) which are the most immediate motivators of action. However, we are not really responsible for our episodic emotions, such as our bouts of anger or pangs of jealousy; those happen to us rather than being chosen by us. Hence, Aristotelian *pathe* are quite similar to what the social intuitionists such as Haidt understand moral intuitions to be. Indeed, those theorists love the idea of 'automaticity of virtue' in Aristotle.

The problem with this analogy, however, is that it is over-simplified to the brink of being blatantly wrong. To be sure, Aristotle does not deny that we may be driven by knee-jerk reactions to events: conditional reflexes and non-cognitive feelings. However, those would not be *pathe* on his understanding, and the claim that *pathe* are not within our responsibility elides important complexities. Let it suffice to say that Aristotelian moral intuitions (*qua pathe*) are part of a learning system that is infused with reason—be it good or bad reason. Moral judgement is in essence an exercise of reason. There is no 'brute' moral intuition in Aristotle, and even what he calls 'natural virtue' is not 'natural' as in either 'genetically preprogrammed' or 'conditioned by the norms of one's society'. 'Natural virtue' in

Aristotle is actually a somewhat infelicitous name for a stage of habituated but non-*phronetic* virtue. True, there is both quick and slow moral decision making in Aristotle, but the difference between the two does not correspond to that between the non-rational versus rational or to emotion versus reason. Aristotle was not a two-system dualist, full stop (see further in Kristjánsson, 2022).

Friendship is indeed a good example here. Early-years habituation, ideally followed by years of autonomous, critical honing of one's dispositions through the exercise of *phronesis*, enables us to react quickly in uncomplicated situations where a close friend needs help. *Phronesis* guides us towards the helping behaviour, almost automatically. However, as soon as the situation becomes more complicated, the decision process slows down, as *phronesis* needs time to kick in and evaluate the situation. Do the needs of the friend conflict with those of another friend, or perhaps a large group of strangers? Has the friend's character changed so dramatically for better or for worse (although Aristotle himself only considered the latter) that the virtue of friendship does not apply anymore? Furthermore, once we are acting through the mediation of *phronetic* rather than just natural virtue, the filter becomes much more demanding, as it requires not only that we comply with the demands of the most immediate virtue relevant to the given situation (in our case, friendship) but that it also takes account of claims proper to other ethical virtues—say, compassion and justice (cf. Müller, 2004).

Friendship as a natural (habituated) virtue may be compatible with your helping the friend for an unjust or foolish cause. However, from the perspective of *phronesis*-guided virtue, the critical dimensions of the virtue of friendship are not determined by the architectonic of that particular virtue only but also by the demands of other virtues. All these different requirements need to be synthesised through *phronesis*, and although that synthesis may appear to proceed fairly quickly and reliably in the case of an experienced moral agent, to get things right the agent still needs to apply the filter of *phronesis* correctly to the concrete situation. There is no room in Aristotelian theory for a *phronetic* decision that is, in principle, unfiltered.

Someone could still argue that because of the essential motivational unity of the *phronetic* agent in Aristotle's virtue ethics, this procedure does not involve the same sort of alienation as in the other moral theories and, hence, some (or perhaps all) of the thrust of Williams's argument can be averted. This consideration is, however, bound to touch even the greatest of Aristotelian aficionados on the raw, for if there is any psychological claim in Aristotle that seems to jar with common intuitions and empirical evidence, it is the one about the motivational unity of the *phronimoi* being such that they never experience regret (1985, p. 246 [1166a27]). Even those contemporary virtue ethicists who go furthest in sticking to the Aristotelian script, such as Hursthouse, admit that there are tragic situations from which even the most virtuous agents cannot escape with their lives unmarred (1999, p. 74; cf. also Carr, 2009). Our ethical outlook as a whole, as well as individual moral virtues such as friendship, need indeed, as Hursthouse points out, to be validated over and over again, 'plank by plank' (1999, p. 165), by appealing to the blueprint of the good life as it comes into confrontation with complex life situations. This is bound to be a painful process, although perhaps not 'pathological' in the strict sense that Stocker's term 'schizophrenia' may indicate (cf. Woodcock, 2010). The pain cannot be averted by avoiding to apply the filter of *phronesis* and simply relying on some raw 'intuitions'. By blocking out the 'extra thought' needed to remain and to continue to develop as a virtuous agent—and a trusted friend—one proceeds to trivialise the message handed down to us by Aristotelian virtue ethics.

3.4 Is the 'Extra Thought' in Virtue Ethics also 'One Thought too Many'?

The preceding section demonstrated the futility of the assumption that, because of the alleged facility of virtue ethics to motivate correct friendship-instantiating moral action directly without the mediation of a theoretical filter, there is something unique about virtue ethics as a moral theory that provides immunity from Williams's one-thought-too-many argument. It turned out that there is no such direct motivation in (Aristotle-inspired) virtue ethics. However, scenting potential defeat at this juncture, it is still possible for the virtue ethicist to argue that although there is an 'extra thought' encapsulated by the *phronesis* filter, as opposed to the deontological or consequentialist filters, it does not involve one thought too many.

What could there be unique about the *phronesis* filter that would leave it untouched by the argument that hits at the other two filters? I explore four possible responses below. The first response builds on the thought that *phronesis* does not offer a filter in the same sense as the utility calculus or the categorical imperative because *phronesis* is just about methods of implementation, not content. The other three responses suggest that although the *phronesis* filter is essentially of the same kind as two competing ones, informing the content of moral decision making (e.g. in the case of friendship, on which Williams fastens), there is something about its content that escapes or at least mitigates the charge of one thought too many.

(1) 'The *phronesis* filter is only about means-end reasoning; it does not impose substantive one-thought-too-many constraints on the moral content of the decision, as do the other two filters; and no moral theory can conceivably work, in any case, without practical advice on how to find the best means to actualising what has been decided. Thus, no one will complain about a close friend taking time to reflect on the best way to help you 'move a body' (Koltonski, 2016). As long as the *phronetic* thought is not about the end (whether to help you), but simply about the best means to achieve this, it will not count as one thought too many.'

This response turns Aristotle-inspired virtue ethicists into pure Humeans about moral motivation. For pure Humeans, reason is irrelevant to the choice of ultimate ends, which is based on non-deliberative desires only. This thesis seems to follow naturally if we take at face value Aristotle's repeated claims about *phronesis* only constituting reasoning about means to ends, not about the ends themselves that seem rather to be formed non-deliberately through the cultivation of (habituated) virtue (1985, pp. 168, 171–2 [1144a6–9, 1145a4–6]). There are other places in Aristotle's texts that do challenge this understanding, however, and there is good reason to take those seriously, because they read as more accurate elaborations, or even corrections, of the general thesis about *phronesis* being concerned with means only. There we are told not only that non-intellectual habituation is insufficient for full virtue but that full virtue requires a decision to choose virtue for itself, and that decision requires *phronesis*. So, although *phronetic* virtue grasps the right ends because the virtuous person has the right desires, those desires require *phronesis* for their creation precisely in order to count as the right desires in the first place (1985, pp. 39–40, 168–9 [1105a28–32, 1144a13–22]). In other words, the transition from habituated to *phronetic* virtue is one of essence: the previously non-intellectually founded desires become deliberative desires, and they are no longer the *same* desires as before, simply dressed up in fancy intellectual clothes, but rather *new* desires, created by *phronesis*. Hence, I agree with Irwin (1975, p. 571) that Aristotle cannot be categorised as a Humean with respect to Hume's thesis that all practical thought depends on non-deliberative desires. Insofar as Response (1) is meant to defend virtue ethics, including the intellectual virtue of *phronesis*, and insofar as *phronesis* is an essentially Aristotelian concept, Response (1) fails to show that *phronesis*, by virtue of its proposed exclusive instrumentality, does not incorporate one thought too many—simply because it is not exclusively instrumental.

(2) 'What makes consequentialists import one thought too many into their thinking about close friendship is their assumption that the only intrinsically valuable good in the world is the maximisation of good outcomes, and that non-intrinsically valuable goods such as friendship need to be measured against it. Similarly, for deontologists, the ultimate moral motivation is derived from respect for the categorical imperative rather than from an intrinsically valuable virtue such as friendship. In contrast, for virtue ethicists, virtues such as friendship are intrinsically valuable.'

In Kantian deontology, the moral motivation to pursue friendship (or any other virtue) does not have its source in the emotional component of the relevant virtue, as in Aristotle-inspired virtue ethics, but in principles of practical reason, encapsulated by the categorical imperative. If the substantive problem identified by Williams's argument is that the crucial moral motivation is derived from the filter rather than the original source of moral concern (here the friendship), then it is indeed true that virtue ethics escapes his charge. However, I do not think the same applies, *mutatis mutandis*, to virtue ethics versus sophisticated forms of consequentialism. Badhwar complains that 'consequentialist teleology defines intrinsic value in morally neutral terms and morality as a means to intrinsic value' (1991, p. 503). While that is, strictly speaking, true, the implications are not as radical as she makes them out to be. For Mill (1998), for example, virtues such as justice (and possibly friendship) constitute essential goods that are parts of the sole source of intrinsic value, happiness as pleasure and the absence of pain, rather than just being instrumentally conducive to it. Those are goods that ought to be valued, whether or not we happen to value them or not, and also goods whose moral value remains intact even in the rare cases when they are out-weighed by other, more salient, essential goods (Kristjánsson, 2006, pp. 146–8). Thus, for the happiness pluralist Mill, the motivation to help a friend would derive from the essential goodness of friendship, rather than from the utility calculus itself. That calculus is only necessary because there are cases where the motiv-ations of different essential goods clash.

There is, in fact, not much to choose between (Millian) consequentialism and virtue ethics here. To love a friend 'as an end', Badhwar says, 'is to place a special value on her—to believe that her value is not outweighed, say, simply by the greater needs of others or the needs of a greater number of others' (1991, p. 484). But this only holds if friendship is the sole intrinsic value in her axiology (see Card, 2004, p. 157) or if she considers friendship as a master virtue, like Cicero. But those are clear departures from Aristotle and from most contemporary forms of virtue ethics, according to which the intrinsic value of friendship can in prin-ciple be overridden by another competing source of intrinsic value (and even Badhwar seems to acknowledge that possibility: 1991, p. 500). *Phronesis* can be defined as excellence in moral deliberation precisely because of its capacity to adjudicate correctly in cases where two such sources seem to clash. In *that particular sense*, it serves the same purpose as the utility calculus. So if there is something about the content of the intellectual filter that separates virtue ethics from consequentialism and protects it against the charge of one thought too many, Response (2) has not identified what that unique content is.

(3) '*Phronesis* allows for preferential treatment but the other filters force us to treat all persons equally. It is the psychologically impossible requirement of non-preferential treatment that makes the other two filters, but not *phronesis*, succumb to the error of one thought too many.'

Is the assumption of impartiality perhaps what makes the filters imposed by consequentialism and deontology import one thought too many, on Williams's understanding (as suggested e.g. by Bernstein, 2007, p. 67)? After all, Aristotle says, in contrast, that it is 'more shocking' to 'rob a companion of money than to rob a fellow-citizen' and to 'fail to help a brother than a stranger' (1985, pp. 224–5 [1160a4–6]; cf. also p. 256 [1169a18–34]).

While it is true that impersonality and impartiality are foreign to the spirit of Aristotelian virtue ethics, agent-relativity is in no way a random, subjective variable in Aristotle. In addition to the somewhat pedantic specific advice that Aristotle gives here (about returning favours to benefactors before favouring a friend and returning debts to creditors before making loans to friends: 1985, p. 241 [1164b25–1165a4]), it is crystal clear that Aristotle's partiality allowances are meant to be calibrated according to demonstrated levels of moral virtue. Firstly, character friends are chosen because of their ethical excellence, and they are to be discarded if they turn bad beyond redemption. Secondly, Aristotle discusses in detail conflicts that arise between the claims that a friend can have on us, versus a virtuous non-friend, and his conclusion is that if the friend is just a utility friend, then her claims on us are strictly limited, whereas the issue becomes more complicated if the clash is between the claims of a character friend and another 'virtuous man', for the former is then also, *ex hypothesi*, virtuous. The overall conclusion seems to be that this has to be assessed on a case-by-case basis but, in any case, simply ditching agent-neutrality and giving everything spontaneously to the friend is what only 'good-for-nothing people' do (1935, pp. 431–3 [1244a1–19]).

These Aristotelian considerations are far removed from the romanticised view of friendship as based on spontaneous preferential treatment that Bernstein (2007), for one, attributes to Williams. Sherman goes as far as to say: 'To the extent that the *phronimos* represents a point of view of experience and reflective judgment removed from irrelevant biases [...] we might say there is something like an appeal to an impartial point of view in the assessment of action', although the point of view is not purely rational in the Kantian sense, devoid of emotional considerations (1987, p. 592). While I consider Sherman's claim slightly over the top—in the sense that the individualisation of virtue, to which Aristotle ascribes (see the fourth response below and further in Chapter 4), builds a certain partial point of view into the assessment process—the idea that the *non-reflective* partiality of friendship holds the key to how Aristotelian *phronesis* escapes the thrust of Williams's argument seems to be a non-starter. To Williams's credit, that idea is not his in the first place, for he explicitly admits that the notion of an attachment to a particular person as a psychological integrity-grounding project, in his sense, protected by a categorical desire, would have appeared 'mysterious or even sinister' to Aristotle (1981, pp. 15–16).

(4) 'The uniqueness of *phronesis* as a filter *vis-à-vis* the utility calculus is that it does not require the maximisation of value. That requirement is the main reason why consequentialism imports one thought too many. Hence, this criticism does not hit at *phronesis*-guided reflections on what friendship requires in particular cases.'

To be sure, although Aristotle places fairly strict moral constraints on the scope of agent-relativity that virtue ethics affords us, there is no hint of the idea of maximisation in his ethics. That is not to say that moral value comes without any quantification, for generally speaking, 'the greatest virtues are necessarily those most useful to others', such as justice and courage (2007, p. 76 [1366b3–6]). Yet virtue comes to us individuality-adjusted according to Aristotle. Some of the well-known things that Aristotle says about the golden mean of action and emotion may seem to indicate that there is an ideal imitable agent whose virtue consists in hitting this mean accurately on each occasion. However, on closer inspection, there is no *unique* blueprint of the perfectly virtuous person to aim for. I will argue in more detail for this claim in Chapter 4, and will need to ask readers to take it on trust for the time being. What I simply want to say at this juncture is that *if* there is no maximisation requirement in Aristotle (because there is no common currency to maximise), this gives us considerable leverage in making wise *phronetic* choices regarding conflicting claims by different friends, or friends and (virtuous) non-friends, and some may even legitimately come down to mere tastes when there is no calculable difference in demonstrated levels of moral worth.

While this response is put hypothetically here, because I still have to argue for its main premise in Chapter 4, I hope readers will agree with me that out of all the responses canvassed so far, this one comes closest (potentially) to explaining the advantage of Aristotle-inspired virtue ethics, in general, and its *phronesis* filter, in particular, in escaping the thrust of Williams's one-thought-too-many argument. That said, I am not convinced that even this response would have satisfied Williams himself, given the radical interpretation of his argument explained in Section 3.2.

3.5 Concluding Remarks

This chapter has explored the common assumption that there is something about Aristotle-inspired virtue ethics that makes it immune to Williams's (in)famous one-thought-too-many argument. I have shown that the idea that virtue ethics has no filter, and hence imparts no extra thought into the moral decision process, is untenable. The reason is the simple one that Mill pointed out to us a long time ago: 'There exists no moral system under which there do not arise unequivocal cases of conflicting obligations' (1998, p. 71). So far is it from being true that Aristotle suggests an exception to this rule that he explicitly provides us with a filter, called *phronesis*, to sort out how to strike a morally justifiable balance between competing sources of intrinsic value, including friendship. To argue that this filter does not import an extra thought, it would have to be shown that *phronesis* is a vehicle for non-deliberative intuitions, rather than an intellectual virtue of adjudication and, furthermore, that the intuition to favour friends trumps all other considerations. However, neither happens to fit Aristotle's system.

At all events, it is difficult to imagine Williams asking for blind attachment to friendship, to which *any* extra thought would be inimical.

The only remaining way to escape Williams's curse is to argue that the extra thought required by virtue ethics is not 'one thought too many'. The presumed advantage of virtue ethics must, in other words, lie in the content of its filter rather than the filter's non-existence (which is in essence a strategy similar to the one Railton, 1984, used in his ingenious defence of consequentialism). The chapter closed with an attempt to show that, contra deontology, the friendship motivation in virtue ethics is derived from the moral virtue, not the intellectual filter, and, contra consequentialism, *phronesis* does not require the maximisation of value (although the latter claim still needs further argument). If it can be made to work, this argument goes some distance in shielding *phronesis* from Williams's complaint. However, I am only half way through making it work so far. The remaining work requires a sequel: Chapter 4.

I frankly admit, even if my eventual argument holds water, the job that still remains for *phronesis* to do, and the way it is meant to do it, would probably still count as a fetish on Williams's understanding, as well as falling under Stocker's sarcastic description of decision filters as 'mental alarm clocks' (1976, p. 458). So there may be no way to avoid a substantive disagreement between a neo-Aristotelian, such as myself, and Williams on what exactly counts as one thought too many. I happen to agree with Woodcock (2010) that balancing our broad ethical obligations with authentic personal motives is bound to remain a non-trivial psychological challenge for any moderately demanding moral theory. I salute Aristotle for having tried to offer us an extra thought to guide our reflections on this challenge, and I maintain that the *phronesis* filter does not deserve the sardonic designation of 'one thought too many'. Filtering friendship through it is a morally justifiable, and indeed necessary, enterprise. It is a tough job, but someone (the moral agent) and something (the intellectual virtue in question) still need to do it.

4

Grounding Friendships

Reconciling the Moralised and Aestheticised Views

4.1 Introduction: Two Views of Grounding

The uniqueness of Aristotle's specification of the only 'complete' form of friendship lies most prominently in grounding it in characterological features: the friend's character as her set of virtues. The virtues referred to there will be mostly the moral virtues—with the inevitable addition, though, of the intellectual virtue of *phronesis* insofar as it synthesises and integrates the moral ones. By 'grounding friendship' I do not simply mean 'explaining its genesis', but rather 'justifying it', 'providing the reason why it is a worthwhile enterprise'. In that sense, Aristotle's approach cannot be seen to be competing with the psychological approaches canvassed in Section 1.5 because, while the latter approaches to what psychologists call 'close' or 'best' friendship seem to pick out a relationship that is extensionally similar to Aristotle's 'character friendship' in terms of interpersonal dynamics, psychologists are loathe to enter into what they would consider a non-scientific discourse on normative grounding. In contrast to this psychological reticence, the standard philosophical assumption, which sets it apart from psychology and motivates this chapter, is that, no matter how hard it may be not to be drawn spontaneously to certain people as friends, 'we do have the capacity to reflect upon just what it is that attracts us to them, and *whether or not it ought to*' (Isserow, 2018, p. 3111; my italics). So, like the last chapter, the present one will be exclusively philosophical rather than social scientific; for it so happens that within philosophy, what I call Aristotle's 'moralised view' has got a formidable competitor that I call the 'aestheticised view'.

The aim of this chapter is specifically to offer an account of the grounding of close friendships within the context of virtue ethics that, while drawing on Aristotle's justification of character friendships, goes some distance in reconciling Aristotle's moralised view with the above-mentioned counterview, according to which we are aptly drawn towards close friends for reasons that are essentially aesthetic, amoral and arational. I argue that there are resources within Aristotelian virtue ethics (although not exploited by Aristotle himself in the context of his discussion of friendship) that enable us to overcome some of the difficulties of his moralised view and bring it into better harmony with common-sense

Friendship for Virtue. Kristján Kristjánsson, Oxford University Press. © Kristján Kristjánsson 2022.
DOI: 10.1093/oso/9780192864260.003.0004

conceptions; yet preserving fundamental aspects of Aristotle's view, such as that vicious people cannot form truly deep and close friendships.

To anticipate, what I will be aiming for could be called an 'individuality-adjusted moralised view' of the grounding of deep friendships: a conciliatory view that still remains closer to an amendment of the moralised view than to a middle-ground synthesis. This conciliatory view also provides the missing link needed to make the argument at the close of the preceding chapter (on why the *phronesis* filter does not require maximisation of value in a consequentialist sense) work, as a response to Bernard Williams's challenge. One more reason for focusing here on the moralised–aestheticised dichotomy is that both views are grounded in strong philosophical traditions with interesting lineages and ramifications that make for compelling comparisons and contrasts.

Although it is a sure sign of the enduring appeal of Aristotle's moralised definition of the most supreme form of friendship that—with deferential stopovers in progenies such as Cicero—the historical debate has to a large extent been couched in Aristotle's terms, it has since the early days of modernity been challenged by the counterview to which I keep referring, of which Montaigne (2015, originally 1580) is perhaps the most well-known historic representative but which has recently been revived with considerable gusto and force in Alexander Nehamas's (2016) book (cf. Telfer, 1970–1971, and Cocking & Kennett, 2000, for slightly more modest versions). His book contains a powerful antidote to common Aristotelian assumptions about friendship: an antidote that could also be potentially lethal to the aspirations of the present work to propose a theoretically touched-up and empirically updated neo-Aristotelian view of friendship.

Interestingly, the Montaigne–Nehamas view of close friendships contains significant parallels with Aristotle's, so much so that the whole debate that unfolds in the following sections is focused primarily on the criterion of how loving close friends 'for their own sake' should be grounded. That criterion is, as already noted, what sets Aristotle's highest form of friendship most apart from the lower forms and gives it the commonly used designation of 'character friendship'. I have called it a 'moralised view' because it considers close friendship to be grounded in the appreciation of certain moral qualities. On the Montaigne–Nehamas view, however, loving a friend for her own sake is not grounded in the friend's moral but rather subjectively experienced, aesthetically appealing qualities. It is worth noting here that there are many possible variants of an aestheticised view of friendship groundings. Some of those variants would not consider the grounding reasons 'arational', although they are aesthetic rather than moral, and they would not characterise the appealing qualities merely 'subjectively experienced'. I am here referring to various objectivist accounts of aesthetic value. In this chapter, however, I focus exclusively on the variant presented by what I call the Montaigne–Nehamas aestheticised view. It might be complained that I am making the job easier by contrasting the Aristotelian moralised view with the option that is most diametrically opposed to it and most radical. My reason is that I have always found objectivist accounts of aesthetic value difficult to fathom, if not simply incoherent. I take myself in this chapter, therefore, to be arguing against the most coherent and plausible alternative to Aristotle's view, rather than a 'soft target'.

Notice the commonalities that both the moralised and aestheticised views share in assuming that the friendship they champion is intrinsically valuable, as distinct from just being extrinsically useful; and on both views, befriending persons contains the normative dimension of evaluating them favourably (cf. Isserow, 2018, p. 3111). The disagreement, however, concerns what precisely it is about them that is being evaluated favourably. While there is something intuitively appealing about close friendships being grounded in moral (or, more specifically, virtue-relevant) properties, there is also something attractive about the view that one is aptly drawn towards friends because of certain personality factors that defy moral analysis and even any rational explanation.

I say 'aptly' here, although neither Montaigne nor Nehamas use that word. Nevertheless, they are clearly doing more than just explaining psychologically what draws us to a friend; they are claiming (implicitly at least) that certain features that *do* so, in fact, *ought* also to do so for anyone who wants to live well. It would be rich, coming from a neo-Aristotelian, to complain about the intermittent collapse of the distinction between the descriptive and the evaluative here. After all, not only does Aristotle fail to bow to the prohibition on value judgements imposed by many current social scientists, the Humean bifurcation of facts and values is entirely foreign to him, as I explained in Section 1.3. This explains why he chooses to take the verdicts of the many and the wise as starting points about what we would call 'value judgements', in just the same way as he does in the case of *other* 'factual judgements'. Those initial verdicts may well need to be rejected if good reasons appear to support their non-validity. However, prevailing views can never be fully consigned into inconsequence. We must engage with them, and the onus is on us to show that they are wrong. So to establish, for example, as Aristotle wants to do, the educational nature of character friendship (see Chapter 5), what is needed is not to elicit a logical connection between the concepts in question or even an empirical one, based on large samples; it suffices to enlist the views of the many and the wise and then fail to come up with plausible evidence to disconfirm them. Analogously, the question of when friendships *are* terminated (by wise people) and when they *should be* terminated is basically the same question for Aristotle.

The preceding paragraph was basically a long-winded way of saying that, in a similar vein to proponents of the aestheticised view, Aristotle takes it for granted that a feature of human psychology which happens to be considered flourishing-enhancing by the many and the wise is thereby worthy of pursuit; the favourable evaluative description of this process already 'grounds it' in a justificatory sense.

The plan for the remainder of the chapter thus involves eliciting the contours, pros and cons of two contrasting views of what precisely grounds friendship according to the best judgements available (rather than eliciting contrasting view on the epistemology of 'grounding') in Sections 4.2 and 4.3, respectively. I offer the conciliatory proposal of an individuality-adjusted moralised view in Section 4.4 and close off, as usual, with some concluding remarks in Section 4.5.

Before delving into the relevant debate below, it is worth pausing to consider a possible objection to how this whole chapter is set up as being anachronistic. First, it is well known that Aristotle did not possess any concept aligning with our modern concept of 'the moral'; hence the term 'moralised' about his grounding of (complete) friendship may seem anachronistic. Anscombe famously remarked (1958, p. 2): 'If someone professes to be expounding Aristotle and talks in a modern fashion about "moral" such-and-such, he must be very imperceptive if he does not constantly feel like someone whose jaws have somehow got out of alignment: the teeth don't come together in a proper bite.' My excuse here is that I am simply making use of a common contemporary philosophical label, for the sake of convenience, but I do specify it below in an Aristotelian way as a view grounding friendship exclusively in the virtuous features of a friend's character. So when I speak of 'moralised' in this chapter, I specifically mean 'characterologically grounded', not anything else that a modern variant of a 'moralised view' might include or entail.

However, this barely touches the core of the anachronism objection. The most serious part of it has to do with the very dichotomy of moralised versus aestheticised, which appears alien from an Aristotelian perspective. It is a platitude that Aristotle considered virtuous actions to be chosen for the sake of the *kalon*: widely translated as 'the beautiful' although 'fine' and 'noble' are also used sometimes (Paris, 2019). Whatever the merits of felicitous English translations in particular places may be, the point of the objection would be that Aristotle already assumes an aestheticised view of virtue: complete friendships are pursued and character education engaged in for the sake of inward beauty: the beauty of one's own and others' character. Hence, the very distinction invoked in this chapter is misleading.

This objection opens up a true Pandora's Box of Aristotelian exegesis, which I will address here as briefly as possible. It is true that there are various interpretations of the true nature of the *kalon* in Aristotle. Irwin (2010) identifies three, one of which states that the *kalon* concept only has one referent, the beautiful, and that virtuous actions are *kalon* precisely when they satisfy the criteria of that referent, just as the beauty of a parrot's feathers are truly *kalon* when they satisfy the concept's same criteria. However, Irwin's own interpretation, which I find persuasive, is different. He considers *kalon* a homonymous word in Aristotle's corpus. It picks out qualities that are beautiful in *either* what we moderns would call an aestheticised sense (such as the parrot's feathers) *or* a moral sense (here having exclusively to do with the fineness of virtue), *or* sometimes both. Simply making use of the same word does not mean that Aristotle did not make a clear distinction between the virtuously excellent picked out as *kalon* and the aesthetically excellent picked out as *kalon*. Hence, Irwin defends his own translation of *kalon* as 'fine' when it refers to virtue and 'beautiful' when it refers to aesthetic qualities only:

> Some things are *kalon* insofar as they are beautiful, others insofar as they are well ordered, and others insofar as they are praiseworthy attempts to promote a common good [...] More specifically, we have [...] no good reason to claim that all *kalon* things are *kalon* insofar as they are beautiful. Aesthetic attractiveness belongs only to a proper subset of *kalon* things. Hence we should not use 'beautiful' to translate *kalon* everywhere.   (Irwin, 2010, p. 395)

While I agree with Irwin's interpretation, I have a Plan B for those who do not, and I will not presuppose either plan in what follows. Even if we insist on *kalon* having had a single referent for Aristotle, the beautiful, and that what I call his 'moralised view' of complete friendship is really an aestheticised view in disguise, it is aestheticised in a very different way from the modern aestheticised view that I identify below and contrast with Aristotle's. The modern view incorporates modernist features of anti-realism about value and about selfhood (as I explain later in this chapter), as well as moral particularism, that are completely foreign to Aristotle. So if readers prefer to couch the distinction invoked in this chapter as one between two different aestheticised views about friendship, I have no trouble with that, as long as we acknowledge that those views are radically different in terms of grounding.

4.2 The Moralised View

Historically there have been many versions of a moralised view of (close) friendships (see e.g. Cicero, 2018, for the most radical version). However, as most of those draw upon or seek inspiration in Aristotle's view of character friendships, which in turn serves as the lynchpin of the present book, attention will here be fastened upon that view in particular, as one that is paradigmatically 'highly moralised' (Cocking & Kennett, 2000, p. 281).

I understand the claim that Aristotle offers a 'highly moralised' view of character friendships to mean specifically that it is considered a *necessary condition* of such friendships that the friends love each other because of the other's *virtuous* state of character (although they may love her for other reasons also), among either fully fledged or budding *phronimoi*. This separates the moralised view essentially from the aestheticised view to be canvassed in Section 4.3, for even if the latter view may allow that—fortuitously—a person is drawn to a close friend because of an appreciation of the friend's moral beauty (say, the coherent elegance of her virtuous make-up), the attraction will be directed towards the qualities in question *qua* beautiful (in a modernist sense) rather than *qua* virtuous.

In addition to Aristotle's remarks, rehearsed in Chapter 2, about how reluctant one should be to terminate a friendship with erring character friends unless they become 'incurably bad' (1985, p. 244 [1165b15–35]), the earlier-canvassed scaling down of the ideal that all character friendships be 'perfect' helps fend off an initial objection to a moralised view of friendship. This is the objection that the moral-ised view distorts the meaning of close friendship by imposing the condition that the good of friendship be extended only to persons who are *morally deserving*. As Isserow (2018, p. 3103) correctly points out, there is something 'inherently dis-comforting' in the thought that friendship is meted out through a moral balan-cing act of that kind. However, Aristotle's moralised view of character friendships clearly allows for cases of friendships between people of under-developed virtue, unequal virtue and virtue gone (non-incurably) bad, in which the friend does not 'deserve' the goods of friendship in the strict sense of rewards due in acknow-ledgement of already attained achievements. A related—but much more serious—problem of essential substitutability, however, remains, to which I will be devoting the remainder of the present section.

Aristotle's own view is clearly that character friends, few and exclusive as they naturally will be, are essentially non-substitutable in the demanding sense of being irreplaceable without significant loss to selfhood, because 'the friend is another himself' (1985, p. 246 [1166a30–33]; cf. Millgram, 1987). This clearly stated view notwithstanding, a common complaint—which I already fleshed out in Section 2.2—is that Aristotle overlooks an obvious implication of his own def-inition of character friendships which makes it in the end look too Platonic. The problem of *essential substitutability* is typically considered to hamper the account of 'Platonic love', even to constitute its 'cardinal flaw' (Vlastos, 1981). In Platonic love—so the standard objection goes—one loves a person to the extent that she instantiates certain admirable universal qualities of goodness, truth and beauty. However, this seems to imply that if another person appeared on one's radar who did an even better job of manifesting those qualities, one's love *would* (and *should* morally) transfer to that new person. There is a rich literature on substitutability, fittingness and romantic love that I cannot do justice to here (see e.g. Howard, 2019), as I need to move the lens from love towards friendship. That said, I acknowledge that there is a lot of overlap and similarity between substitutability problems as they feature in work on friendship and work on romantic love—a topic for another day.

Now, as explained in Section 2.2, Aristotelian friendship is meant to represent fondness of another person *qua* unique person, and thus not fall prey to the sub-stitutability objection. Aristotle's anti-Platonic musings in the *Politics* about how certain personal attachments thrive on their exclusiveness, otherwise becoming too 'watery', are a case in point (as elaborated upon by Sherman, 1987, pp. 603–4). But the question remains of why that should be the case for character friendships, given the contours of Aristotle's own view. Since close friendships can only be forged with few people—hence the need for meticulous selectivity—and the essential grounding of such friendships lies in the appreciation of virtuous qualities, why should a current friendship not rationally be given up, and then 'upgraded' to a new one, if one comes across persons with a more impressive set of virtues? Elder (2013, pp. 83–4) considers the possibility that the same virtuous property gets valued differently when possessed by a friend rather than a stranger, but she concludes correctly that this leaves it mysterious why we become friends with some people but not others.

Whiting (1991) construes this problem, along Platonic lines, as one of the metaphysical loss of a sense of subjectivity, echoing Badhwar: 'That which is *essential* in an individual is universal: that which is *unique* and *personal* in him, is accidental' (Badhwar, 1987, p. 21). There are therefore, in Plato, no individual essences, no truly personal natures, no true subjectivity. Whiting correctly points out that because Aristotle takes the virtuous person's attitudes towards herself as a paradigm for her attitudes towards friends, and given the fact that a person can regard *herself* as a subject, she ought to be able to regard her friends as such (1991, p. 14). However, Whiting misconstrues a moral problem as a metaphysical one. The issue is not that Aristotle—like Plato—conflates abstract qualities with subjectivities, or replaces the latter with the former, but rather that he presents us with a stark choice in only being able to form friendships with a limited number of subjects, and the advice apparently coming from his moralised view is that one should opt for the subjects with the most extensive and impressive virtue-repertoire, from an objective moral standpoint. Yet that advice seems to go against the grain of how real friendships are formed and sustained in the real world.

To call Aristotle's moralised view too Platonic may seem to do injustice to Aristotle's academic patricide committed on his old master. To put the problem of essential substitutability into sharper relief, let me therefore give the example of a contemporary philosopher who is pointing his finger at fundamentally the same fault, but without invoking Plato. Glen Pettigrove (2013) takes to task what he calls a 'proportionality principle' of value, according to which 'our actions and attitudes ought to be proportioned to the degree of value present in the object, action, or event to which they are a response'. I take it that 'being proportioned to' refers to a number of different psycho-moral processes that should ideally be in place: namely, one's acknowledgement of value, one's attachment to it and motivation to seek it, one's willingness to enhance it overall and even to maximise it through education and socio-political engineering. At worst, the agent who fails to adhere to the proportionality principle can be accused of a lack of practical rationality rather than just a lack of moral maturity.

As is most authors' wont, Pettigrove exaggerates somewhat the novelty factor of his discussion—as highlighting 'an important lacuna' in much of the work currently done on value and moral psychology—in order to provide a focus for his own thesis. I would hesitate to go as far as Pinsent, in his commentary (2023), by suggesting that Pettigrove is 'flogging a very dead horse'. He may be flogging an old horse, but scarcely a 'very dead' one. Yet I cannot help observing that much of the historical critique of Plato's theory of love in the *Symposium*, alluded to above, has made similar use of the argumentative weaponry that Pettigrove brands here, and it is not such a long time since Bernard Williams's 'one-thought-too-many' argument (1981), scrutinised in Chapter 3, was high on philosophical agendas, warning against the perils of more or less the same sort of considerations at which Pettigrove directs his animadversions.

Pettigrove's entry-point complaint is that the proportionality principle is 'out of step with common sense': jarring with our moral sensibilities. He subsequently provides a number of examples from different areas of human endeavour to prime our intuitions, for instance, that of parental love, concluding provocatively (citing Marilynne Robinson) that in such love 'the worthiness of its object is never really what matters'. No loving mother would think or say, for instance, to her daughter when seeing her off to school: 'Do your best today, darling, because if you don't, Mummy will be obliged to love you less'.

Intuitions tend to be bit of a double-edged sword, however, as they often need to be pulled a little only, with a slightly different example, to elicit a different set of sensitivities. If the stories that Thomas Markle tells the tabloids about how his duchess daughter Meghan abandoned him without any good reason are true (and that is a big if!), then many decent parents would empathise with Thomas's state of mind in loving his daughter less due to not being the person he knew before; indeed it might be considered a psycho-moral failure on his part (ranging somewhere from co-dependency to the Stockholm syndrome, with a stop-over in Aristotle's vice of excessive compassion) if he did not. Let us not forget that the Parable of the Prodigal Son has probably turned as many people off Christianity as it has attracted followers to it. Pettigrove's 'Mummy example' is simply too trivial to cut any ice as a potential *reductio* of the proportionality principle. No one except some utility calculator on steroids would dream of loving her daughter less just because she did badly one day at school. If Pettigrove wants to provide serious backbone to his sweeping observation that, in the context of love, the proportionality principle is 'at best preposterous and at worst pernicious', he needs a more powerful argumentative arsenal than simple intuitions of this kind. Indeed, Pettigrove ends up acknowledging himself that there is 'something attractive about the idea of proportionality that explains why people have been drawn to it in the first place'.

Pettigrove is not the only one juggling apparently contradictory intuitions about special obligations to friends and loved ones in the context of a potential overarching value system that seems to demand both proportionality and impartiality. To be sure, Aristotle does not subscribe to the proportionality principle in his virtue ethics. However, one needs to engage in some serious Aristotelian justificatory acrobatics (see Section 4.4) to explain why that is the case. The default position for a virtue theory seems to be to remain consequentialist and adhere to the principle in question. I call it the 'default position' because it has conceptual parsimony, simplicity and theoretical elegance in its favour. Take Mill's clever defence of justice as a virtue in his *Utilitarianism*. Nothing in what he says contradicts the very simple principle of utility maximisation along proportionality-principle lines (i.e., the value of the virtue piggybacks on the goodness of utility); yet Mill is able to persuade most readers that they will never in fact be required to abandon justice in any ordinary-life situations in favour of the higher value of overall happiness, because justice is such an important part of happiness that it will take some very far-fetched science-fiction scenarios to put allegiance to justice to the test.

Moreover, if all that is needed to make the proportionality principle more palatable is what Pettigrove calls 'breathing room', then sophisticated Millian utilitarians can provide an abundance of that (as I explained in Chapter 3). They can simply augment utilitarianism with the psychological thesis that considering alternative possibilities to prioritising the needs of a loved one at the time of action is psychologically incompatible with a concern for utility, and such considerations should therefore never be entertained. However, the requirement that one's preferred moral theory be 'self-effacing' in this way is one that troubles Pettigrove and me in equal measure (if perhaps for different reasons), and therefore I agree with Pettigrove that coherent adherence to a virtue theory requires abandoning the proportionality principle in its utilitarian incarnation. But that has to do with more fundamental issues about the individualisation of virtue (as explained later) than just securing 'breathing room' from an overbearing value calculus.

While Aristotle, like Pettigrove, abandons the proportionality principle, he only abandons it within certain parameters and for reasons that are, ultimately, not exactly the same as Pettigrove's, although the initial resemblance is striking. I return briefly to Pettigrove's discussion in Section 4.5. I have simply presented his argument here to show how relevant and topical the discussion of loving values 'proportionally', and seeing them as essentially substitutable, really is, not only within but also outside of the discursive field of Aristotelian character friendships.

If there ever was a case of great minds thinking alike, it comes to the fore in the standard solution to this problem of essential substitutability. Most of the solutions take the form of a *unique-history argument*. To rescue Aristotle, for instance, Brewer (2005), who complains about Aristotle's taciturnity on this issue, offers the consideration that the irreplaceability of our friends 'owes in large part to the history we share with them—a history we could not possibly discover ourselves to share with some stranger'. Friendship is about shared sensibilities, and such sensibilities cannot be brought to fruition except 'through a long series of previous interactions' (2005, pp. 243–5). Brewer's argument offers good reasons for sticking to old friends and not discarding them for new ones. It is not only that such a choice would fail to be cost-effective; it is simply not possible, for deep psychological and historical reasons, to create, *ex nihilo*, a friendship trajectory with a new friend that matches that of one's relationship with an old one. Whiting (1991, p. 22)—who is more tolerant of 'impersonally' grounded friendships than Brewer—nevertheless points out that virtues are always 'the historical accomplishments of that particular person' and 'cannot exist except in embodied historical subjects'. Stern-Gillet observes that each character friendship is 'made unique by the past that it carries with it' and 'the common past that sustains it' (1995, pp. 75, 177). Elder argues that the weight of a shared history can 'exert a pull on friends' and that the value of friendships with unique individuals 'includes both historical and relational properties' (2013, pp. 72, 92, 98).

As far as I can see, however, complementing Aristotle's moralised view of the justificatory grounding of character friendships with the unique-history argument, in order to explain personalised exclusivity, is a strategy that risks diluting or undermining core elements of the moralised view. Notice first that the tricky choice is not between a friend with whom one has a *long* history and another potential, more virtuous, friend with whom one has *no* history. Admittedly, many character friendships do not have long, unrepeatable histories undergirding them; typical university students will form a number of such friendships in their first year of study. That said, it is a *conceptual*, rather than just an *empirical*, condition of all close friendships that they have *some* mutual history behind them. Having a shared history is simply part and parcel of what it *means* to have such a friend.

Suppose I suddenly came across a person more compassionate and generous than anyone I had known before and I set out to befriend that person because of those very qualities. Let us even assume that this person took well to my initial advances. It would still be inappropriate to refer to this person as a 'friend', let alone a 'character friend', until a substantial amount of shared activities and experiences had taken place. Prior to that, the person would resemble more a role model than a friend. So, in that sense, it is a truism that character friendships rely upon a past history. The choice is not between one that does and one that does not, but rather between various potential friendships with past histories where only a few can be pursued deeply and whole-heartedly because of the limitations of time and mental resources available.

The next question to ask, then, is whether something in the past history with the friend (whom one contemplates befriending more closely at the expense of another—or unfriending to stick to the manageable pool of character friends) is relevant to an assessment of the evaluation of that person as a virtuous individual.

If the answer is *yes*, then the unique-history argument does not seem to add anything new to the features that the essential substitutability objection identifies as problematic. The person in question possesses certain virtues, and some of those virtues have been expressed uniquely, well or less well, in historical interactions with me; they then simply go into the general calculation of whether this person is virtuous enough to be worth retaining as a friend or replaced by somebody else who could have an even more admirable history of virtuous interactions with me. However, this was the very crux of the problem that the unique-history argument was meant to overcome. Notice that this is not to underplay the role that a unique history with a friend can play in creating bonds of deep affection and commitment. What I am simply pointing out here is that if we accept the assumption of the substitutability problem that complete friendship should be judged solely on the merit of maximising access to a friend *qua* virtuous individual, then these affective and commitment-forming characteristics of the friendship matter only to the extent to which they can be conceptualised as manifestations of virtue in the other person. One cannot double-count the characteristics in question first as virtue manifestations and then as unique historically conditioned friendship bonds. Incidentally, in Section 4.4 I go on to reject the maximisation assumption, but that deconstructs the substitutability problem rather than salvaging the unique-history argument.

To turn to the other horn of the dilemma, if the unique history, which is meant to justify the continuation or formation of the friendship, *is not* morally relevant, in the sense of mattering for the evaluation of the virtuous make-up of the friend, a further question beckons: are these unique historical-cum-relational features meant to trump the virtue-relevant features or not? If they *are*, then the moralised view has simply collapsed into its anti-thesis, the aestheticised view, or some other competing variant. From an Aristotelian standpoint, those non-virtue relevant properties would simply be idiosyncratic and subjective properties which could not justify the friendship, as only virtue can. If they *are not* meant to trump virtue, on the other hand, virtue is still the differential variable which grounds friendship and the substitutability problem remains.

So the unique-history argument seems to leave us with a couple of intractable dilemmas and, indeed, turn out to be something of a red herring. It is not enough to show that unique historical properties, derived from interactions with a particular person, cannot be transferred to someone else or repeated; what needs to be demonstrated is how these properties can ground particular character friendships in ways that do not undermine, or add alien elements to, the moralised view. Proponents of the aestheticised view that I canvass next will argue that the inability to solve the substitutability problem adds weight to their case. The problem lies—they would say—in the core assumptions of the moralised view itself, which runs the risk of over-rationalising and depersonalising the nature of close friendships. For defenders of the moralised view the task remains of explaining how one can fail to be attracted to form close friendships with paragons of moral virtue, when those are available as potential friends, and how one might want justifiably to stick to less perfect examples of virtue in other current or potential friends, warts and all.

4.3 The Aestheticised View

I focused in the preceding section on the substitutability problem, as a fairly robust objection that could potentially issue in a *reductio* of the moralised view. However, there are other, more general, concerns that may lead to a sense of unease about the moralised view and motivate the endorsement of the kind of aestheticised view that I outline in the present section.

First, a complaint could be made about the moralised view assuming an excessively rationalist and calculated stance on the grounding of friendships: as a relation that can be assessed objectively as appropriate or inappropriate by the respective friends and even second-guessed by an external observer when the friends themselves get it wrong. The complaint could be either that this ignores the arational elements in *all* friendships, or that it fails to account for specifically *modern* understandings of non-rationally grounded friendship as qualitatively different from ancient understandings (Stern-Gillet, 1995, p. 8).

Second, even for those sympathetic to some sort of a moralised view of close friendships, doubts may linger about whether Aristotle got it right. Notoriously, Aristotle seems to have been destitute of any sense of the ineffable and enchanted. There is, for instance, no moral virtue of awe in Aristotle and even his intellectual virtue of wonder is seriously disenchanted (Kristjánsson, 2020, chap. 5). So the more high-spirited moral qualities that some people would see as opening up avenues to close friendships (e.g. moral elevation towards a spiritual guru) may appear to be missing from Aristotle, leaving his version of the moralised view flat and deflated.

Third, there are those who will claim that the moralised view gets its psychology all wrong, as it goes against the grain of everything we can learn about the formation and sustaining of close friendships from everyday life and world literature. Contrary to the moralised view, it is simply a raw psychological fact that we are drawn towards some people for non-rational reasons, much in the same way as we are drawn towards works of art through their subjectively experienced aesthetic qualities. This third 'unease' about the moralised view (as positing rational reasons for friendship) grounds the aestheticised view of close friendship that I flesh out and critique in the present section. It could also be called a 'romantic' view because it understands the attraction to a close friend in much the same way as attraction to a romantic partner is understood in Romanticism: as driven by mysterious psychological forces that are mostly beyond conscious control and defy any rational analysis. It is still worth probing what 'grounds' close friendships through an explanation of individual human psychology, but if 'grounding' is meant to denote what justifies them with reference to the enhancement of moral virtue, then that quest can be given up with impunity, according to the aestheticised view.

The most historically famous and compelling account of the aestheticised view is found in Montaigne's heart-wrenching description of his love for his prematurely deceased friend Étienne de la Boétie. Readers will be struck by how little Montaigne offers in terms of explanation of what made this friend so appealing to him, but perhaps that is the very point of the radically particularist 'justification' (if that is the right word) he offers. Montaigne claims not to know 'what inexplicable and fated power' drew him to the unique mixture of 'manners, parts and inclinations' that set La Boétie apart as a person, except to say: '*because it was he, because it was I*' (my italics). It was, in other words, something undefinable that turned the two into 'one soul in two bodies' (Montaigne, 2015). Elizabeth Telfer, a modern proponent of the aestheticised view, observes that even when we can give some reasons—relating to our tastes and preferences, much as we often can in terms of art—for liking a person and feeling a unique bond with her, 'we cannot further justify those reasons or always explain why they operate in one case and not in another apparently similar'. What is at stake here, is 'a quasi-aesthetic attitude, roughly specifiable as "finding a person to one's taste"' (1970–1971, p. 226). One does not truly *make* friends, on this view, by attuning with them gradually on the moral or characterological plane; rather one *recognises* potential friends and then it is more or less a matter of *serendipity* (namely if the attraction is mutual and the circumstances favourable) whether the initial recognition develops into a full-blown close friendship.

Alexander Nehamas (2016) has done the aestheticised view great service by writing a book-length defence of it in a way that is easily accessible for non-philosophical readers. Through a close and eloquently written study, not only of academic sources but also works of art (most notably the film *Thelma and Louise*), Nehamas provides the aestheticised view with previously unseen detail and backbone. He argues that, try as we might, our best efforts to explain why we are attached to a close friend 'are invariably vague, imprecise, and finally unsatisfactory—banal and incomplete, always leaving out what we strongly suspect are the most essential reasons for our feelings' (2016, p. 109). Nehamas's strongest contribution to the literature is his linking up of aesthetics and friendships as 'mechanisms of individuality' (2016, p. 185). Just as one cannot define art or friendship any better than—to cite A. E. Housman's well-known quip—'a terrier can define a rat' (Burnett, 2007, p. 68), we recognise both unmistakably by the symptoms they provoke in us. Nehamas's book also brought home to me, in a way that I had not realised before, how the increased attraction of the aestheticised view in recent times is tied up with certain conditions of postmodernity, especially the so-called aesthetic turn, through which aestheticisation began to triumph over ethics as a focus of social and intellectual concerns (Harvey, 1991, p. 328). However, in sharp distinction to the lucidity of Nehamas's book, the 'classic' reading on friendship within postmodernism, Derrida's *Politics of Friendship* (1997), is mostly incomprehensible drivel (e.g. about the 'production of ideal objects as the production of omnitemporality, of intemporality *qua* omnitemporality', p. 17), even failing to demonstrate Derrida's ordinary knack for making banality sound profound.

If the objection is raised at this point that the aestheticised view is, *mutatis mutandis*, vulnerable to the same sort of substitutability problem as the moralised view—since one might be tempted to trade one friend for another if the latter presented an overall superior repertoire of aesthetically pleasing qualities—two responses are available. One would be to grant this point but refuse, in a bullet-biting sort of way, to see it as a problem, because friendships are, and should be, fluid and easily exchangeable. However, this is not the tack taken by either Telfer or Nehamas. Aware of the fact that such a radical substitutability thesis would undermine common, deeply held intuitions about close friendships, their strategy is rather to deny the very idea of a calculable 'superior repertoire' of qualities. Thus, as Telfer puts it, 'if I like James because he is witty, gentle, and good at making things, I like him, not as one example of a witty, gentle and craftsmanlike person, for whom another person could be substituted, but as an individual whose uniqueness defies complete classification' (1970–1971, p. 228). Nehamas puts the same idea in terms of the irreducible individuality of the friend: a feature that cannot be accounted for by any list of qualities, however complex, nor aggregated to compare one friend to another as a potential replacement (2016, esp. pp. 121, 125, 180).

One fact which emerges more clearly from Nehamas's treatment of friendship than from previous sources is how the moralised and aestheticised views presuppose competing ontological commitments to the status of human selfhood. Whereas the moralised view assumes a *realist* theory of selfhood, according to which self and self-concept are two different things and we have a stable and underlying objective self which self-concept can capture well (*qua* self-knowledge) or badly (*qua* self-deception), the aestheticised view assumes an *anti-realist* theory, harking back to authors as distinct as Hume and Nietzsche (cf. Kristjánsson, 2010, chap. 2), but best known nowadays within social psychology. While this is not a necessary feature of an aestheticised view (see e.g. Cocking & Kennett, 2000, who do not assume such a theory), it figures prominently in Nehamas's work. On this anti-realist theory, which in Nehamas's case is more Nietzschean (with respect to Nietzsche's musings about self-making and giving style to one's self) and postmodern than Humean, there is no underlying objective self to be discovered or brought into attunement with the self of another person. Rather, selfhood is just a collection of the beliefs we have about who we are: essentially the upshot of existential decisions we make about what sort of 'style' (2016, p. 222) we wish to adopt as our self-image. The self is 'elusive because it is always unfinished business' (2016, p. 134): that is, always in the process of being invented, reinvented and co-created with other persons towards whom, at any given juncture in our lives, we feel aesthetically drawn. Friendship is, in other words, a vehicle of self-fashioning and a mechanism of individuality: of deciding who we are.

In addition to this ontological difference, or perhaps rather as an implication of it, the moralised and aestheticised views presuppose different conceptions of who a person really is deep down and what sets her apart from others. On Aristotle's moralised view, when a character friend loves the other's (moral) character, she loves the friend for who she really is at her core (Aristotle, 1985, p. 211 [1156a16–18]). The aestheticised view seems to have a more capacious view of who one really is and does not assume that what is loved in close friendship is necessarily the core of a person's selfhood (indeed, it does not acknowledge any such 'core'). What typically, or even essentially, characterises us as individuals ('selves') is superficial style rather than deep-rooted moral character (2016, p. 151). One way to put this difference is to say that the two views assume different theories regarding not only the ontological *scope* but also the *content* of selfhood.

As already noted, there is nothing in the aestheticised view that rules out the possibility that one of the things we are drawn towards in a friend are her moral qualities. For example, Montaigne mentions La Boétie's virtues as one of the things he happened to like about him. However, the virtues do not occupy any privileged status on this view *qua* virtues, and it may well be that what appeals to me in a friend are precisely her set of vices (cf. Cocking & Kennett, 2000, p. 286). As a result, treating one's friend properly as a responsible agent—given common-sense views about what friendship entails in terms of actions—can require that one assist her in committing what may in fact be serious moral wrongs, for example helping her 'move a body', as the saying goes (Koltonski, 2016; cf. Cocking & Kennett, 2000: an implication that would have absolutely shocked Aristotle, by the way). Nehamas makes the point repeatedly that (close) friendship is not the prerogative of virtuous people. Just as we may love our friends in spite of their vices, sometimes we may love them precisely because of those vices: 'even the vicious have friends' (2016, pp. 27 and 29). In such cases, friendship serves educationally as a 'school of vice', rather than a school of virtue, as in Aristotle's idealised view of character friendships (2016, p. 60, citing C. S. Lewis). Nehamas then illustrates this with the example of Thelma and Louise whose friendship not only incites them to vices and misdemeanours such as violence, theft, murder and lawlessness but is actually sustained and enhanced *qua* friendship through revelling collaboratively in evil activities, culminating in suicide.

Now recall that the aim of this chapter is to explore the grounding of close friendships from within the context of (Aristotle-inspired) virtue ethics. Section 4.2 identified an unsolved problem at the heart of Aristotle's own virtue-based view of close friendships: the substitutability problem, leading to a potential depersonalisation of friendships. From a virtue ethical perspective, the aestheti-cised view goes much too far in the other direction, however. The problem that virtue ethicists will fasten on here is not only a moral one. To be sure, Jessica Isserow has argued convincingly that a good person *should not* form a friendship with a vicious person because forming such a relationship would indicate 'an objectionable sort of moral complacency, discounting important moral values that ought to occupy a suitable role in her moral priorities' (2018, p. 3101). However, Isserow does not explore the questions of whether a vicious person has good reasons to try to cultivate a friendship with a virtuous person or whether two vicious persons (like Thelma and Louise) can have such reasons for forming friendships with one another. Moreover, her argument will not cut ice with those who are not already committed to being good persons (e.g. on a virtue ethical understanding). What I would want to add to the *moral* argument here is the claim that a vicious person *cannot* form close friendships with anyone for reasons having to do with the *psychology* of vice: reasons that were already elicited by Aristotle.

Recall that the modern proponents of the aestheticised view, such as Telfer and Nehamas, are giving an account of deep or close friendships: a conceptualisation that bears striking resemblance to Aristotle's account of 'character friendships', except for the 'good-character bit' which they reject. So they are not talking about instrumental friendships for mere utility or pleasure—which Aristotle had already acknowledged that the vicious could develop among themselves (see e.g. 1935, p. 389 [1238b8–14]). Rather, the topic under discussion is true soulmate-ship between persons who share common values, engage in shared activities and share joys and sorrows in the most intimate of ways. The question, then, is whether such soulmateship is possible between 'close friends in vice'.

Bear in mind, however, before proceeding further, that because of the anti-realist assumption in the aestheticised view (about selfhood as fluid and transi-tory), a vital distinction that is implicit in the moralised view between essentially *central* and essentially *peripheral* self-traits may be missing in the aestheticised view. So I may, after all, have been too quick to assume thus far that what is at stake between the two views is solely disagreement about what I called, in Section 4.1, the criterion of close friendships that has to do with the *grounding* of the intrinsic love of the friend. They may, in fact, not agree on the *scope* of the 'com-mon values' and 'shared activities' either. The moralised view assumes that those refer to *significant* values and *meaningful* activities, in the sense of being central to 'who we are deep down'. Since someone like Nehamas rejects the self-realist assumption about us being anything deep down that cannot simply be 'fashioned' one way or another, he also seems to allow that the values and activities binding close friends together can be ones that self-realists would see as peripheral rather than self-defining: say the casual enjoyment of sharing a bottle of wine over a nice meal. If that is the case, proponents of the moralised view may well accuse their opponents of not really having a view of close friendship as true 'soulmateship': a concept that, arguably, only has full meaning within a self-realist framework.

The intricacies of the philosophical disagreements between self-realists and anti-self-realists aside, I would argue that it is a conceptual condition—rather than just an empirical one—that close friends exhibit certain moral virtues in dealings with one another, most notably trust, honesty and compassion (cf. Blum, 1980; one could even add generosity, fairness and loyalty to the mix). It would be outlandish of me to claim that I had a close best friend who did not display those virtues towards me; it would indicate my misconception of the very notion of 'close friendship'. If we imagine a Nehamian friend who does not possess those virtues, we would recognise a deeply flawed relationship with dramatic limitations. Nehamas's aestheticised view seems to imply that such severely flawed relationships could pass muster as close friendships, but I do not see why anyone should accept that. If one were to devote significant time and love to someone who consistently lied, showed little or no compassion and was demonstrably untrustworthy, it seems obvious that this would dramatically impair the quality of that person's life as well as detract from the possibilities for having higher quality relationships with people who have the desired traits. This means that even the aestheticised view requires *some* moral virtues to be attached to friendships.

If we grant that it is unacceptable to hold that a putative friend would not be consistently honest, compassionate and trustworthy, it may seem that a compelling counter-argument has already been mounted against the aestheticised view, and that we can simply stop this section here. However, it might be argued in response that the friend who displayed those virtues towards *me* could still be an overall vicious person by not extending them to *others*. In that case, the aestheticised view offers an account of agents as radically and consistently compartmentalised morally, such as being stably and reliably honest towards close friends but dishonest towards others. This response requires me to delve into some Aristotelian observations about the psychology of the vicious. Those are much more complex and controversial than the simple counter-argument offered above to the aestheticised view. I do not ask readers to accept all the details of this Aristotelian psychology. However, when combined with some insights from contemporary situationist and evolutionary psychology, they do add further ammunition to the claim that the vicious may be incapable of close friendships.

Aristotle does not mince his words about the baneful predicament of the vicious. They 'shun themselves' because they cannot stand their own company, and deep down they are 'full of regret'. As their 'soul is in conflict', between appetite for the bad and wish for the good, 'each part pulls in a different direction', gradually tearing them apart (Aristotle, 1985, p. 247 [1166b11–26]). Admittedly, there are many different claims coalescing in Aristotle's description of the psychology of the vicious and it would take another long chapter to tease them apart.

To complicate matters, a group of exegetes claim that Aristotle can be read as consistently (or at least dominantly) arguing *for* the possibility of integrated vice, and that the 1166b text above actually applies to the incontinent rather than the vicious, although this is inadequately spelled out in the relevant context. Suffice it to say here that I have argued elsewhere for the non-possibility-of-integrated-vice interpretation and will refrain from repeating that argument here in any detail (Kristjánsson, 2019).

In short, the key lies, I suggest, in Aristotle's claim that 'vice perverts us and produces false views about the origins of actions' (1985, p. 169 [1144a34]). The vicious thus lack true self-knowledge, including knowledge about what they really want. Furthermore: (a) Because the vicious lack true self-knowledge, they are ultimately 'at odds with themselves' and may even 'destroy themselves' (1985, p. 247 [1166b7–13]). (b) Because of their self-ignorance-evoked disunity, they do not possess any stable traits of action or reaction. As 'the good is simple but the bad is multiform', the vicious 'are quite different in the evening from what they were in the morning' (1935, p. 397 [1239b12–15]). (c) Because of (a) and (b), the vicious are incapable of self-love, love of themselves as bearer of certain stable love-worthy qualities—becoming rather their own enemies (1935, p. 405 [1240b15–19]; 1985, pp. 246–7 [1166b1–25]). (d) Because of (c), they are also incapable of loving others as close friends. Being 'full of caprice' (1935, p. 405 [1240b15–20]) towards potential friends as towards others, it lies in the very nature of their psychology that 'a bad man will injure a bad man, and those who suffer injury from one another do not feel affection for one another'; hence cannot be friends (1935, p. 373 [1236b10–15]). One could grumble that Aristotle is here bundling together under the same umbrella of 'wickedness' various categories of people with flawed characters, ranging from the morally indifferent and inconsistent to the truly sadistic and malicious. While that is true, Nehamas does not place any limits on the category of the wicked who are nevertheless able to have close friends, so any points granted with respect to Aristotle's account of the wicked in general will count as points against Nehamas's view. That said, Aristotle's own view would become more plausible if we could follow Annas (2011, chap. 7) in characterising vice as deep alienation from virtue, rather than simply the absence of virtue.

Schoeman talks about 'a kind of trust that can arise between flawed souls that cannot arise between paragons of virtue' (1985, p. 277). While intuitively appealing perhaps, I cannot see any possible Aristotelian rationale for this view. The same applies to Nehamas's observation (2016, p. 27) that sometimes we love our friends precisely because of their shortcomings (that everyone else may find irritating). That is a distinctively un-Aristotelian view unless the shortcomings in question are just morally irrelevant foibles. I think Arendt basically hit the nail on the head with her famous comments about the superficiality and banality of evil:

It is indeed my opinion now that evil is never 'radical', that it is only extreme, and that it possesses neither depth nor any demonic dimension. It can over-grow and lay waste the whole world precisely because it spreads like a fungus on the surface. It is 'thought-defying', because thought tries to reach some depth, to go to the roots, and the moment it concerns itself with evil, it is frus-trated because there is nothing. That is its 'banality'. Only the good has depth that can be radical.   (1978, p. 251)

While these observations may seem to go beyond any position that could even remotely be described as 'Aristotelian', they do chime in nicely with Aristotle's remarks about the psychological frustrations of the vicious and their inability to form any deep human relationships. Interestingly also, the view of the Enlightenment thinker Voltaire is here closer to Aristotle's than to that of the humanist Montaigne. The 'wicked have only accomplices', he says, 'voluptuaries have companions in debauch', but 'virtuous men alone have friends' (cited in Grayling, 2013, p. 102, from Voltaire's *Philosophical Dictionary*).

I shall not enter the thorny territory here of whether the continent are psychologically capable of close friendships. *Ex hypothesi*, they are not capable of complete character friendships in Aristotle's system, but given what Aristotle says about lower ('mercenary') versus higher (more character-like) forms of utility friendships (1985, pp. 233–4 [1162b23–27]; I say more about them in Chapter 6), one could surmise that some of the advanced utility friendships of the continent would count as 'close' on modern understandings. For present purposes, it suffices, however, to make the point that the vicious are not capable of close friendships rather than insisting on the stronger claim that one needs to be virtuous (in a perfect or developmental sense) in order to engage in such friendships.

One does not need to be a virtue ethicist or take Aristotle's psychology on board wholesale to find the psychological claims about the vicious plausible. The strongest potential Nehamian response would be the one suggested earlier, namely about the possibility of compartmentalised character where an overall vicious persons reserves virtue for close friends and family only, and does so in a consistent and robust manner. World literature seems, for instance, to be replete with such occurrences. What we know from the much-discussed situationist experiments in social psychology is that when people are thrust passively into extraordinary situations involving strong situational norms, they are likely to act 'out of character' (Kristjánsson, 2013, chap. 6). As far as I know, however, none of those experiments have identified situation-specificity of behaviour in the form of consistently exhibiting character trait C towards one person but not-C towards others. The so-called 'local' traits that some situationists acknowledge are local with respect to (a) uniform kinds of situations rather than (b) uniform dealings with particular individuals. Consider the teacher who is honest in the classroom but dishonest when filing tax returns. Indeed, I would find the (b)-sort of consistent situation-specificity of reactions fairly implausible psychologically.

From the perspective of evolutionary psychology, it is not far-fetched to hypothesise that, in order to succeed, vicious traits have developed such as to confound other people. Criminals with consistent action tendencies are likely to be predictable wrongdoers and hence more likely to be apprehended than the ones who avail themselves of motives and means so diffuse that not even they would be able to foresee them. It is thus, so to speak, a 'performance asset' of vice to be disunified. However, such disunification easily, and perhaps unavoidably, spins out of control and overtakes the whole selfhood of the vicious person. They lose track of who they really are deep down; hence their lack of self-knowledge. This is why it seems so implausible to imagine a vicious person who is consistently trustworthy and honest in dealings with one group of people (namely, close friends) but dishonest and untrustworthy towards others. Even world literature offers no consensus here; for every fictional mafia boss who is loyal to friends and family, there is another one who is willing to sacrifice absolutely everything and anyone to further his own ambitions.

It might be urged that, while what has been said above confirms that it is pragmatically risky to try to enter into a friendship with a wicked person, Aristotle did not produce the killer argument needed to establish that such a friendship is impossible. Aristotle would probably have been wise to defer there, as he often does, to the 'natural scientists'. Nevertheless, I find Aristotle's description of the psychology of the vicious plausible. They form utility-based *alliances* and have *accomplices* (partners in crime), but they do not have the psychological wherewithal to develop *close friendships* with others. If that is the case, however, the complete demoralisation (or, if you like, the hyper-personalised romanticisation) that is inherent in the aestheticised view will prove to be its undoing.

4.4 Towards an Individuality-Adjusted Moralised View of Close Friendships

Our scorecard now looks roughly like this. Aristotle's *moralised view* of close (character) friendship, on which virtue ethicists tend to rely, risks producing a disenchanted, depersonalised view of such friendship that does not locate its cause in unique characteristics of friends that make them more intrinsically attractive than other potentially more virtuous people. This evokes the so-called substitutability problem. The main historic competitor, namely the aestheticised view, offers a mystified, demoralised alternative that allows friendships to be forged on the grounds of accidental, even trivial, personal features, opening up the possibility of close and stable friendships between vicious people, while at the same time assuming a controversial anti-realist conception of selfhood as protean and fragmented. From a virtue ethical perspective, in particular, this seems to be a deeply alienating view.

All that said, both views have significant intuitive appeal. The moralised view explains how moral virtues such as mutual honesty and trust sustain close friendships, while writing off the vicious as potentially incapable of such friendships because of their lack of any unifying firmness; 'for the base and evil-natured man is distrustful towards everybody' (Aristotle, 1935, p. 383 [1237b28–33]). The aestheticised view, on the other hand, pays homage to the common intuition that 'friendship obtains only between individuals in all their particularity' (Nehamas, 2016, p. 46) and that friendship produces supra-moral value that cannot be abstracted from its style of expression in an individual's life, for example the person's zany sense of humour.

When two philosophical views clash but both seem to resonate, in part at least, with common intuitions, the natural inclination is to look for some sort of a reconciliation or synthesis. In this case the initial conciliatory idea could be that although moral virtue *constrains* the grounding of close friendship, it *underdetermines* the choice of friends, and that what we need is a combination of virtue in the friend and some attractive non-moral value. What could that value be? From the perspective of contemporary psychology the obvious candidate is amoral *personality* (e.g. as instantiated in a person's Big-Five profile). So what we love in a friend would then be the specific combination of virtue attached to her individual personality profile—or, conversely, we would fail to love a potential friend because, all her virtues notwithstanding, she is for instance just too dreadfully dull. Paula Reiner (1991) has explored this possibility in detail in the context of Aristotelian theory and comes to the unequivocal conclusion that this manoeuver is not available within Aristotelian virtue ethics.

Reiner points out that there is no word in ancient Greek capturing the modern notion of personality as 'character devaluated' (Allport, 1937). More than that, this terminological distinction is just not available, in any shape or form, on the Aristotelian picture of human psychology. In the *Nicomachean Ethics*, for example, Aristotle treats wit as simply one more character virtue with its excess and deficiency forms. Reiner—following the tradition of reconstructive virtue ethics in which Aristotle is 'updated' as needed to bring him into conformity with contemporary social scientific findings—considers the possibility that Aristotle be simply corrected here and amoral personality (largely genetically predetermined) added to his system (cf. also McAleer, 2015). However, Reiner correctly observes that this would be cold comfort, because Aristotle would have to say, in line with his moralised view, that personality would then just represent one of those accidental, non-character-based traits that he himself has excluded from grounding close friendships, such as wealth or good looks. Another way to put this objection is to frame it in the same way as my objection to the unique-history argument in Section 4.2. Adding personality to the grounding criteria elicits the same double dilemma as the unique-history addition did: it either undermines the moralised view or is redundant with respect to it.

I now propose an alternative conciliatory route which—while not satisfying full-blown particularist romantics about friendship—does at least accommodate some of their critical insights into a more 'humanist' virtue ethical view of friendship. The insight I wish to critique here is the way the substitutability problem is normally couched is in terms of a maximisation assumption about virtue. In our lives, according to this assumption, we should try to maximise virtue in the world, and this includes maximising our exposure to virtue as instantiated in potential friends. However, on a closer look, this whole idea of maximisation is totally alien to Aristotelian virtue ethics, which assumes neither the possibility of maximising virtue within or across individuals.

An often underexplored aspect of Aristotelian theory is the radical view of the *individualisation* of virtue. Aristotle is adamant about the relativity of the intermediate state of virtue to *developmental level*, *social position* and *individual constitution*. For example, emulousness is a virtuous emotion for young people whereas adults do not need to emulate role models. Magnificence and magnanimity (*megalopsychia*) are virtues for people blessed with unusually abundant material resources but not for ordinary folks. Temperance in eating is not the same for Milo the athlete as for the novice athlete, because what is intermediate in virtue is relative to the individual, 'not in the object' (1985, p. 43 [1106b1–7]). And, from an educational perspective, a boxing instructor will not 'impose the same way of fighting on everyone' (1985, p. 295 [1180b9–11]).

There is thus no *one* best way across individuals to be, say, virtuously generous as opposed to be being stingy or wasteful. It all depends on your individual circumstance (e.g. being poor or wealthy) and your own inclination towards either extreme, away from which you should try to drag yourself as when one 'straightens bent wood'—with the help of friends. If you realise that your friend is stronger on virtue V than you, and a situation calls for V, then the virtuous thing to do may be to 'sacrifice' the action to your friend rather than trying to exercise your own inferior V (1985, p. 256 [1069a32–4]). Hence, 'it is clear that the good cannot be some common [nature of good things] that is universal and single' (1985, p. 9 [1096a25–9]), and 'each state [of character] has its own special [view of] what is fine and pleasant' (1985, p. 65 [1113b31–3]). This does not apply only to representations of individual virtues. How different virtues cluster and gain greater expression and dominance in each individual's life—yet being constrained by the overarching arbitration of *phronesis*—also depends on the individuality of the virtuous person (cf. Sherman, 1987, p. 609). There is no general master moral virtue in Aristotle's theory, as I have repeatedly stressed.

It is important to distinguish this individuality-adjustment thesis from the idea that we saddle a non-moral feature, such as a unique shared history or a personality profile, onto a fixed virtue profile and then evaluate this 'combo' in terms of whether it appeals to us or not in a potential friend. The individuality thesis proposed here is more radical than this. It claims that there is no description of an individual's virtue repertoire available to us that abstracts from its instantiation in that person in all her psycho-social uniqueness. There is no unique blueprint of the perfectly virtuous person *per se* to aim for. When I love the generosity of my friend, I do not love it as matching well or less well the repeatable generosity of the perfectly generous person, for there is no such generosity *simpliciter*. There is an endless plurality of traits that all make the grade as virtuous generosity, as instantiated in different persons, and there is no way to choose between them in ways that satisfy some ideal condition of virtue-exposure maximisation. Bob is generous in his unique way and Jane in hers. Hence, there is no ideal substitutability available to us. In the end, what I love is the friend as the bearer of a unique virtue make-up that resonates with me. It may well be true, as Stern-Gillet observes, that Aristotle seems to push this uniqueness 'off the centre' in his analysis of character friendships. But it is not, as she hypothesises, because of the 'equation between selfhood, reason and goodness' (1995, p. 73). A realist moralised self-theory is fully compatible with an individualisation-of-virtue thesis. My guess is rather that Aristotle considered himself to have given a plausible enough account of that thesis in earlier parts of the *Nicomachean Ethics* and saw no reason to repeat it in the specific sections about friendship.

In addition to serving as a solution to the problem of essential substitutability, these considerations about virtue individualisation also show why my rejoinder to Bernard Williams on behalf of Aristotle's *phronesis* filter, at the close of Chapter 3, can be made to work. *Phronesis* does not require virtue (exposure) maximisation in the area of choosing character friends precisely because there is no discrete, repeatable set of virtues that can be maximised. *Phronesis* does not import an impartial rationality principle either (except perhaps in the case of rulers of state who need constantly to be mindful of the common good). Moral deliberation under the aegis of *phronesis* is therefore not 'one thought too many'. More generally, the point of view of the *phronimos* is not the legislative one of a view from *nowhere*, or of just *anyone* who might face the given options (cf. Sherman, 1987, p. 592); it is the point of view of a particular virtuous agent with particular virtue needs and resonances. More mundanely, this also shows why we may not be able to befriend someone even though she is a paragon of moral virtue if the emotional spark and the resonance with our own character make-up is not there.

Aristotle himself considers the 'puzzle' of the congeniality in tempers among friends, in terms of whether we are more drawn towards friends who are similar to us or different, but without reaching a conclusion (1985, pp. 208–9 [1155a33–1155b10]). Evidence from contemporary psychology seems to suggest we are typically drawn towards people as close friends who are not too different from us, in terms of objective variables (recall Section 1.5), but rather friends who share certain characteristics with us that still serve to complement our own strengths and mitigate our weaknesses (Yaugn & Norwicki, 1999). However that may pan out in individual cases, the truth does not seem to be the one that Nehamas foregrounds that in our choice of friends, aesthetic values compete with moral ones and often take precedence (2016, p. 216). Choosing friends to complement our strengths is also a moral decision in the sense of one that is conducive to, and even constitutive of, our flourishing as moral beings. It is not a random aesthetic choice. Stern-Gillet is quite right here in that Aristotle pays little attention to the genesis of friendships in spontaneous, non-rational inclination (1995, p. 71). He was not a value subjectivist about friendship. Nonetheless, in the sense explained above, he was a virtue pluralist.

A possible objector could point out that Williams's 'one-thought-too-many' problem (both the initial and the more radical version) were framed in Chapter 3 in terms of deliberation—i.e. choosing what to do in a situation that involves a friend. But the above individualisation solution has been framed in terms of choosing friends. Now, while covering the latter is important for the purposes of explaining how the individuality solution helps to build a response to the substitutability objection—and it was developed explicitly as a response to that specific objection—it may not shed light on how this solution helps to build a response to Williams's problem. Yet I believe it does. I argued in Chapter 3 that *phronesis* constitutes, just like the categorical imperative or the utility calculus, a filter between moral motivations and moral decision making. I also argued that *phronesis* is not essentially uncodifiable as a filter. However, I suggested that it is, nevertheless, contingently uncodifiable and offered a much modified particularist interpretation of it. The individualisation solution has aimed to spell out the nature of the individualisation of virtue which explains this modified particularism. Contrary to the utility calculus, for example, there is no way to deliberate beforehand about how to maximise value in terms of helping a friend or not, or of helping one friend at the expense of another. The virtuous agent will have various thoughts relating to her friendships—before, during and after difficult decision making—but they do not codify the decision making or seek to apply a maximisation calculus to it. Hence they do not fall prey to Williams's objection—for not just any thought is a thought too many.

4.5 Concluding Remarks

The 'reconciliation' that I have been offering here may seem to be moralised all the way down and offer little in terms of making allowances for insights from the aestheticised view. However, that impression is illusory. Although psychological hypotheses about how we generally choose between instantiations of individuality-adjusted virtues in potential friends can be advanced and tested, there will be cases where there is nothing to choose between these different bundles, morally or pragmatically, and the choice may, as Whiting notes, come down to 'mere tastes' (1991, p. 23) that happen to render some of those bundles more appealing to us than others; witness the earlier example of the virtuous but dull person. This does not make the choice 'random', because it is still constrained by virtue (and recall that even wit was a moral virtue for Aristotle), but the constraints provide parameters only within which one must choose, not a decision procedure for choosing. There is nothing un-virtue-ethical about such an 'aesthetic turn', especially insofar as it helps to accommodate common intuitions about a non-rational element behind (some) close friendships. After all, virtue ethics is a naturalist moral theory, as I keep repeating, meant to be sensitive to empirical evidence about what people really feel and think.

Before closing, let me turn briefly to Pettigrove again and explain his own (2023) virtue ethical corrective of a '*modus operandi* account of virtue'. The goods of virtue are, in this account, to be explained not by goods external to virtue but by 'qualities of the agent': her 'characteristic way of being'. Her 'way' all comes down to a certain temperament/style combination. So the unique love of a parent is to be explained by who the parent is and what she is like, not by the child and her qualities or how the parent can attend to and enhance some overall value in loving the child. In sum, 'virtuousness is its own kind of goodness and its goodness is fundamental'. In this account, the goodness of actions and attitudes inherent in virtue is to be accounted for 'simply by reference to a good way of being they instantiate'.

The obvious Aristotelian response to this is to point out that the virtuous person instantiates a certain way of being because it is good in an objective fundamental sense—although the best way to identify virtue is typically to look at how the *phronimos* exhibits it (which is a point about moral learning rather than moral epistemology). After all, virtue is a trait that is at once conducive to and constitutive of human flourishing, and its value piggybacks on that ungrounded grounder. In the Aristotelian system, only the goodness of flourishing is 'fundamental'. His is thus what Pettigrove calls dismissively a 'recursive model' of valuing virtue.

I am not presenting this Aristotelian rejoinder as an *argumentum ad verecundiam*. The point is simply that so much of what Pettigrove says has a strong Aristotelian flavour and it is therefore instructive to explore where exactly he departs from Aristotle. What Pettigrove says bears a resemblance to how Aristotle describes mere 'natural' (read: 'habituated' not 'inborn') virtues whose goodness is, more or less, locked up in silos, without being attentive to the need for *phronetic* integration to take account of overall flourishing. However, once we begin, later in our developmental trajectory (if all goes well!), to act through the mediation of *phronetic* rather than just natural virtue, the intellectual *phronesis* 'filter' of proper decision making requires not only that we comply with the demands of the most immediate virtue relevant to the given situation (say, friendship or love) but that it also takes account of claims proper to other virtues (cf. Müller 2004; recall Chapter 3). Now, exactly how *phronesis* operates may seem a bit of a mystery (as much of it comes down to codification-resistant experience and insight), and it is clearly no mere utility calculus. However, what is clear is that *phronesis* does not only attach itself to individual virtues in individual agents because, as Stangl (2023) puts it, 'love and forgiveness are not self-contained realities'; it acts as a conductor of the whole virtue orchestra (cf. Darnell et al. 2019).

The point of this recourse to Aristotelian virtue theory is to demonstrate how the recursive picture of virtue that Pettigrove rejects is compatible with a rejection of the proportionality principle—a rejection Pettigrove shares with Aristotle—but without giving way to moral anti-realism or radical particularism as part of the bargain. An adherence to the proportionality principle is neither necessary nor sufficient for an appreciation of the excellence inherent in virtue. It is possible to uphold, *in principle*, what Pinsent (2023) calls a 'univocal account' of value—for example one that posits human flourishing as the final end of human life—while fully accepting that, *in practice*, comparisons between values inherent in, say, individuals' virtues are often impossible on a single scale, and that the plurality of possible individuality-adjusted virtue instantiations is large enough to allow for most (if perhaps not all) of the partiality that Pettigrove wants us to be able to accept through his examples of love.

I do admit that parental love presents a trickier case than that of close friends, on which I have fastened above, because we do not choose our children in the same way as we choose our friends. Perhaps there would something noble about Thomas Markle loving Meghan as much as before despite her misdemeanours. Yet the thought of a mother loving her Nazi sadist officer son equally much after finding out about his heinous crimes abhors rather than attracts.

The individuality-adjusted moralised view of the grounding of deep friendships proposed in this chapter does tell us *what* we should love in a close friend but not precisely *whom* we should love. It thus gives us considerable license to choose from a pool of potentially eligible close friends, but without succumbing to the excesses of arationalism and romanticism and the excess of not accepting any lower or upper limit constraining the choice. In this case, villains and gods are excluded. Nonetheless, the moralised view leaves us with considerable space for choice and authentic self-fashioning, although it is not the sort of self-fashioning that Nietzschean or postmodern sympathisers would celebrate.

To sum up, putting gods and villains aside, the virtuous Aristotelian agent can travel 'each and every highway', making other virtuous friends along the way, mostly unfettered by any proportionality principle, and at the end of the day announce proudly and virtuously: 'I did it my way'.

5

How Friendship Cultivates Virtue

Retrieving Friendship as a Moral Educational Concept

5.1 Introduction: Resurrecting Aristotelian Friendship for Moral Education

The ancient Greeks considered philosophy to begin with wonder. Wonder is one of the motivations behind the present chapter, but the other is frustration with the current academic literatures on friendship—even within Aristotelian and neo-Aristotelian scholarship—because of how those tend to relate in unsatisfactory ways (or, in most cases, fail to relate at all) to education in general and moral education in particular.

It is almost a platitude that educational institutions provide the context within which some of the most enduring friendships are initiated and forged, often for a lifetime: among students or between students and teachers. Those contexts and the friendships they engender form a recurring theme in world literature, both 'serious' (such as *Brideshead Revisited*) and 'light' (such as the *Harry Potter* series). A veritable mountain of academic literature exists on the correlations—as causal links are more difficult to establish—between school- or university-formed friendships and various positive psychological variables, most specifically between friendship and (student) wellbeing: typically understood subjectively as happiness but in some cases objectively as flourishing. Moreover, in some studies, friendship is evaluated in light of its effect on educational outcomes, for example grade attainment (see Rawlins, 2008, for a helpful overview). However, only in rare cases is friendship explored in light of its intrinsic educational value, be it intellectual (say, the role friendship plays in one's self-constitution as a reflective being) or moral (say, how friendship may be seen as constitutive of moral growth). While exceptions do exist (see in particular some recent penetrating studies by Healy, e.g. 2015; 2017ab; cf. Ahedo, 2016, and some older ones, such as White, 1990; Friedman, 1993, chap. 7; Bukowski & Sippola, 1996), those are few are far between.

The only serious exception to this rule was provided by the adult-education movement with its heyday in the 19th and early 20th centuries. Forming societies that were meant to educate (aka 'self-improve') working adults through engaged interactions in friendship-grounded activities, the movement was so successful that by 1880, 75–80 per cent of British working-class men belonged to such societies

Friendship for Virtue. Kristján Kristjánsson, Oxford University Press. © Kristján Kristjánsson 2022.
DOI: 10.1093/oso/9780192864260.003.0005

(Smith & Smith, 2002). While undoubtedly, for many, providing a cheap excuse for a jolly with mates in the working men's club down the road, the leaders of the movement had a clear conception of the edifying role of friendship and its transformative potential as an apprenticeship in intellectual, civic and moral virtue.

The few contemporary sources that relate friendship to what could be called 'moral development' or 'moral education', broadly conceived (such as the Healy papers mentioned above), are usually written from perspectives that stand apart from the major paradigms in moral psychology or education, such as Kohlbergianism, neo-Kohlbergianism, socio- emotional learning or positive psychology/education—even character education (despite its Aristotelian provenance). Contrast these modern traditions with the classical Greek conception of friendship as 'a categorical repository for the hope of a mutually *edifying moral* covenant voluntarily negotiated between people' (Rawlins, 2008, p. 13, my italics)—and the difference could hardly be starker. The Greeks in general, and Aristotle in particular, were well-nigh obsessed with the moral educational value of friendship. I use the term 'moral education' here, for reasons explained in Chapter 1, although the Greeks did not have a distinct term for the 'moral'—and 'education for character' would be a more felicitous expression. Friendship, in its ideal instantiation, is seen by Aristotle, along with the other virtues, as enshrining nothing less than the developmental ideal of the 'perfection of man's potential as a rational being' (Pangle, 2003, p. 196). However, for some reason, this educational thread of friendship has become frayed in modernity.

To cut a long story short, the aim of this chapter is to retrieve friendship as a moral educational concept: to explain how moral educational goals ground and sustain close friendships, and how the thorny issue of when friendships should be terminated is best understood in terms of considerations as to whether the friendships have exhausted their educational potential. By arguing that education is the *raison d'être* of close friendships, I want to show how friendship is developmentally constituted and, in its most complete form at least, educationally oriented. There is no such thing as friendship *per se*, but rather friendship at a certain developmental niveau, with its specific developmental assets and liabilities: qualitatively differentiated according to its educational affordances *qua* resources or barriers.

I allow myself to be somewhat upbeat in Sections 5.2–5.3. Their aim is to impart a new edge and added force to the idea that a certain Aristotle-defined type of close friendships (namely, character friendship) may have a unique role to play in facilitating moral growth, above and beyond, for instance, methods of moral-exemplar emulation. That this type of friendship also has its shadow sides is a topic no less worthy of examination and caution, and such an examination awaits in Section 5.4. Aristotle's exploration bespeaks sensitivity to liabilities and barriers in the case of the lower types of friendships, but he brushes most of those aside in the case of character friendships, as I have repeatedly stressed. Yet, greater sensitivity to what may imperil them will add ammunition to the thesis about their essential educational nature: namely, if it can be shown that what typically thwarts them is, precisely, the exhaustion of their educational potential.

Readers should be forewarned that this chapter is more exploratory than the preceding ones, because the topic has been less explored previously. As a means of rehabilitating friendship *qua* moral educational concept, the best way to proceed is to conduct an exercise in talking about friendship in educational terms and see where that leads us. This chapter serves the purpose of such an initial exercise.

Before proceeding further, notice that the list of the defining features of Aristotelian character friendships from Section 1.1 notwithstanding, and especially the unique Aristotelian one of loving the friend's character, I have not really established yet what character friendships are essentially *for* in the same sense as was done in noting the *raison d'être* of pleasure and utility friendships. The standard answer in current psychological theories of close friendships is to fasten on the psychological intimacy involved and postulate that the aim of friendship is to utilise this intimacy in the service of psychological wellbeing (typically defined subjectively and non-morally) and psychological health, as we saw in Section 1.5. The Aristotelian answer, in contrast, draws on the 'loving-her-character' clause.

The Aristotelian *raison d'être* of character friendships is, arguably, both moral and educational. The aim of such friendships is not only the love of character *per se*, but loving it in the service of mutual character development. Character friends become 'better from their activities and their mutual correction' as 'each moulds the other', and through this mutual moulding they become 'more capable of understanding and acting' (Aristotle, 1985, pp. 266 and 208 [1172a11–14 and 1155a15–16]). Friendship of this kind educates by being, in various ways, knowledge-enhancing, virtue-enhancing and life-enhancing, through friends acting as each other's procreators on the trajectory towards full *phronesis* (Telfer, 1970–1971, pp. 239–40; cf. Jacquette, 2001, on friendship's moral motivational force). The dynamics of exactly how this happens, and how it can be made to happen more effectively through educational interventions, is a topic for Section 5.3 and later for Section 8.3 also. For the time being, we can make do with Brewer's crisp illumination of this *raison d'être* as having to do with how 'friends draw each other out and participate in the fine-toothed articulation of each other's character' (2005, p. 726).

Three caveats are in order at this juncture. The first is that this account of the *raison d'être* of Aristotelian character friendships is not indisputable because Aristotle never says explicitly that the fundamental aim of such friendships is developmental-cum-educational. However, bear in mind that the *Nicomachean Ethics* is a manual on making wise choices and living well, and there is a strong educational thread running through it, from beginning to end. Apart from that general point, Aristotle says quite a lot about how friendship in fact educates, and for a dyed-in-the-wool naturalist like himself, there is a short step from 'is' to 'ought'.

Second, although I fasten on character friendship is this chapter, there would be a case for arguing that the lower types of friendships, especially friendship for utility, can have moral educational value also. For example, a utility friend may help me stay self-controlled when facing tribulations rather than lapsing into despondency or vice (say, by deciding to end my life). I say more about this in Chapter 6.

Third, non-character based accounts of close friendships are also capable of postulating educational aims. For example, the aestheticised view, canvassed in Chapter 4, with historic representations in authors as distinct as Montaigne and Nietzsche, could—in principle—assume that such friendships help develop our aesthetic sensibilities and sensitivities in a way that is educationally salient, albeit amoral. Nevertheless—in practice—proponents of the aestheticised view tend to downplay friendship's educational role. For example, Nehamas (2016, p. 199) says that even close friendships 'are often less edifying than the rhetoric that surrounds the institution would have them be' and that 'the bulk of our interactions with friends are, at least at first sight, trivial and inconsequential'. The worry seems to be here that if one acknowledges education as the *raison d'être* of close friendship, one risks letting a moralised (Aristotelian or quasi-Aristotelian) view slip in through the back door.

This worry also motivates Cocking and Kennett's radical rejection of the educational thesis, where they claim that the drawing together that takes place in friendship 'need have nothing to do with character improvement': a concern 'altogether irrelevant to the nature that the interest that friends have in another and in their shared activities' (1998, p. 514). On a sympathetic reading, one could point out that they may not be talking about 'close' friendships here only (although the discussion occurs in a section on Aristotle's 'self-as-mirror' thesis). Moreover, they could be seen to be making the point, with which Aristotle would agree, that close friendships must not be motivated originally by the goal of self-improvement, in order not to instrumentalise the relationship. However, even on those sympathetic readings, there is no denying the fact that Cocking and Kennett are flatly rejecting a moralised view of friendship in general and the view of (moral) education as the *raison d'être* of close friendships in particular. I obviously disagree theoretically—mainly for the reasons listed in Chapter 4—but also personally. For what it is worth, I simply cannot identify with the view that close friendships (may) have nothing to do with self-improvement, or at least self-change through which friendship may, for example, inspire me to drop certain long-term projects or hobbies in favour of other ones, where these may seem on a par objectively speaking but I am still making an *educated* choice. What are 'complete' friendships then for, that distinguishes them from fleeting and shallow friendships for pleasure or utility?

In any case, it is worth reiterating that in order to honour the intrinsic value of (character) friendship and of loving the friend for her own sake, the friendship relation must not be entered into instrumentally, with the explicit aim of incrementally enhancing one's character through interacting with, and thereby learning from, the friend. However, again, this poses no serious threat to the thesis of moral education as the *raison d'être* of character friendship. Consider, as an analogue, Millian utilitarianism, according to which happiness is the sole intrinsic value. This does not mean that one's life is best led in direct pursuit of happiness where one asks oneself at every turn what will be most pleasing here and now. What Millians tend to recommend, rather, is engaging in worthwhile activities and then enjoying happiness as it supervenes upon those activities. Like the person who does not think about health as the *raison d'être* of swimming each time she goes to the pool (although it is), one ideally chooses friends and enjoys their company without asking oneself what they can contribute to one's character development. Yet the ultimate point of the institution of character friendships is mutual self-cultivation of virtue. This also explains why people will hardly ever offer the educational *raison d'être* as the explicit motivation for initiating or engaging in friendship. Education acts as a 'regulative ideal', an implicit guiding background condition on our motivation to pursue character friendship, rather than as a direct source of motivation, just as in the case of the utilitarian who is best advised to forget the *raison d'être* of his ethical theory (except when engaging in a philosophical debate about it) in order not to instrumentalise it (cf. Railton, 1984).

As only a privileged group of people, 'brought up in good habits' (Aristotle, 1985, p. 6 [1095b4–5]) and already (being) conditioned into virtue from an early age, stand a reasonable chance of developing virtue-based character, Aristotle's references to what we would nowadays categorise as the general moral educational value of character friendship are limited to this narrowly defined group. Moreover, when Aristotle elaborates upon those features as the defining criteria of character friendships, some of his discussion smacks of idealisations—similar to those that mar his account of when character friendships are/should be terminated, as we saw in Chapter 2. Take, for instance, the stringent conditions that Aristotle places upon character friends' willingness to expose themselves (including their foibles and weaknesses) to one another and their ability to do this through accurate self-knowledge; or the romanticised view of the unproblematic concord between friends as having 'one spirit' (Aristotle, 1935, p. 403 [1240b1–5]). One almost pines for an injection of some deflationary Nietzschean antidotes here.

Cooper explains the penchant for idealisation as part of a teleological bias in Aristotle's thinking that induces him to define things with respect to their most fully realised instances (1977, p. 629). So despite his thinly veiled digs at the cardboard idealist Plato and the latter's vantage point of secure distance from real life,

Aristotle cannot always avoid falling into the same trap. Pangle (2003, p. 131), on the other hand, sees Aristotle's idealisations as a pedagogical ploy that aims to avoid breeding any whiff of cynicism among his readers as young budding *phronimoi*. Whatever the reason, Aristotle ends up underplaying the fiery impulsiveness and precarious happenstance that characterise all friendships, even of the most complete and educationally rewarding type. Incidentally, many popular (e.g. literary) accounts of what people nowadays would simply refer to as 'close' or 'best' friendship share this aura of romantic invincibility, so for those readers without a full command of the Aristotelian concept of 'character friendship', it will suffice in what follows—as previously in this book—to think of the contemporary concepts of 'close friendship' or 'soulmateship' instead.

To end this introduction, here is a possible slight modification of the thesis that educational value of friendship is reserved for people brought up in good habits. It is not unreasonable to suppose that Aristotle had the potential educative influence of character friends in mind when he made his uncharacteristically positive remark about how even 'the bad man, if he is being brought into a better way of life' is able to 'make some advance' so that he might eventually 'change completely' (1941, p. 32 [13a22–31]). This remark has been seen to contradict Aristotle's alleged early-years determinism about the supposed effects of bad or good upbringing that can never be wiped off (see Kristjánsson, 2015, chap. 5). At all events, what Aristotle says about the role of the character friend as a source of moral learning is likely to be accepted or rejected in the measure in which readers accept or reject his more general virtue ethical assumptions about what constitutes character development and its facilitating conditions.

5.2 Learning from Character Friends (Soulmates and Mentors) versus Learning from Role Models

Let me say something about what we could call, to paraphrase Vygotsky, the zone of proximal development of character friendships: the zone in which moral (character) education can take place through scaffolding by my friend—in between the two zones where I can, and cannot, cultivate my character on my own. Simply put, the zone in question comprises people brought up in good habits who are neither too good nor too bad. A human does not befriend a god, although the god could figure as a role model, and similarly, two *phronimoi* (perfectly virtuous people) do not engage in what we would normally consider to be *moral* education, although it could be considered 'education' of a kind. At this extreme top end of the zone in question, then, the friendship relation involves an evolving bond within which the friends simply affirm each other's evaluative outlooks and engage in a 'running appreciation' of their 'jointly produced sensibilities' (Brewer, 2005, pp. 726, 730, 758).

The idea here is that just as the *phronimoi* no longer need emulousness as a virtuous emotion (because they have nothing left to learn from role models), they no longer need to learn from each other either, but can simply relish each other's virtuousness and affirm it. One could argue that Aristotle is here once again trading in undue idealisations, and that he should have been more mindful of his own examples of how even the highly virtuous can go wrong (Curzer, 2005). So, on a plausible Aristotelian account (although not Aristotle's own), the *phronimoi* would still need lifelong moral education in the ordinary sense (see e.g. Brewer, 2005, p. 726, who talks about Aristotelian character friendships as 'lifelong sources of [...] ethical education'; cf. Vakirtzis, 2014, on the continued need for 'interpretative *mimesis*' *vis-à-vis* character friends among the fully virtuous). It is nonetheless worth bearing in mind that the threat of the redundancy of friendships among the fully virtuous does hover over moral-growth theories of friendship, as forcefully brought home by the early feminist writer Mary Astell (1666–1731), although she probably never read Aristotle (see Broad, 2009).

However, even if we take Aristotle's own description of friendship between fully fledged *phronimoi* at face value, it does not subvert the thesis that moral education is the *raison d'être* of character friendship, for the *phronimoi* would not have got to where they are without having traversed the relevant moral developmental trajectory with the help of character friends. At the present time, they are simply exercising their virtues in the company of friends, making sure they do not lie fallow, in much the same way that some people might go to the gym with mates to stay at their ideal fitness level, without the motivation or need to improve. Moreover, the fully developed *phronimoi* are, through their character friendships, engaging in flourishing-enhancing activities by enjoying the specific kinds of pleasures that attach themselves, subsequently, to successful characterological achievements. They are, so to speak, savouring the icing on the educational cake, which may also count as an educational activity of a sort: namely, its culmination. To be sure, this is a slightly unusual understanding of 'education', but it is not a true counter-example to the main thesis of this chapter.

More relevant for present purposes are, however, three cohorts of people—all budding rather than fully developed *phronimoi*—who engage in character friendships that are essentially moral educational in nature according to the prevailing current understanding of the term. Those are people of (a) equal social status who are either (a1) equal in virtue or (a2) unequal in virtue, and (b) people of unequal social status who are unequal in virtue. Consider, for (a), two undergraduates who become friends in the first year at university and help each other grow in virtue, either because, (a1) being equal in virtue at the outset, they share experiences on parallel tracks, or because (a2) the one who is more virtuous at the beginning helps the other catch up while also developing herself. For (b), consider a professor and a student who both grow morally from their mutual interactions but where the more virtuous professor has more to give in terms of moral knowledge, yet more to take back in terms of gratitude and admiration.

Empirically minded educators will obviously want to know what age ranges we are talking about here. It would be untenable, according to Aristotle, to claim that very young children are capable of character friendship (although Aristotle is usually not precise in giving age limits for developmental transitions). Such friendship presupposes some minimal 'comprehension or [at least] perception' of the moral character of the other to be cherished and admired (1985, p. 230 [1161b26–7]). Other than that, Aristotle is at his most elusive here. He does say that, while the old and 'sour' are prone to mere utility friendships in order to make sure they are cared for, the cause of friendship between young people 'seems to be pleasure' (1985, p. 212 [1156a31–3], and 216 [1157b14–15]; cf. 1935, p. 371 [1236a35–7]). On the other hand, he also states that 'the young need [friendship] to keep them from error' (1985, p. 208 [1155a10–13]), and he is clearly not talking about friendship for pleasure there. Despite this textual evidence, the standard view is that Aristotle did not consider children capable of character friendships (see e.g. Jacquette, 2001) because they do not yet really possess virtues as relatively stable (but amenable to further development) traits of character.

I cannot resist the temptation to remark that the standard exegetical view seems fairly weak. In the *Rhetoric*, Aristotle unambiguously refers to some 'virtues' that virtuous adults should ideally possess but do come more easily to young people for reasons of developmental psychology. The young are thus typically *open-minded* and *optimistic*, tending to look at the good side rather than the bad side of things, as they have not yet 'seen much wickedness'. They *trust* others readily 'because of not yet having been much deceived'. They are also more *courageous* and *guileless* than the old are, and have more exalted notions, not having yet been 'worn down by life'. Moreover, they are *fonder of their friends* than older people are and have not come to value them for their usefulness (2007, pp. 149–50 [1389a16–b3]). The virtues referred to here are obviously not *phronesis*-infused virtues, but rather what Aristotle would designate as 'merely habituated' ones, but they are virtues nevertheless, making up character (cf. Kristjánsson, 2007, chap. 8).

In any case, whatever Aristotle's view may have been, current empirical evidence seems to indicate that, at least in late childhood, children may be capable of mutually edifying character friendships (cf. Healy, 2011, for an even-handed discussion of the literature, pro and con). For example, an empirical study of 9–10-year-old children in the UK (Walker, Curren & Jones, 2016) revealed that those children often claimed to identify and choose friends on the grounds of their moral qualities; more specifically, virtues such as honesty, generosity, helpfulness and kindness. Indeed, 'the language of virtue seemed to come naturally to many of the children' (2016, p. 296; cf. Wagner, 2019, for similar findings about early adolescents, and a more surprising study which finds some understandings of moral aims linked to friendship among pre-schoolers: Afshordi & Liberman, 2021). Notably, Walker and colleagues refer to the sort of friendship described by many of their respondents as 'eudaimonic friendship', perhaps to avoid the strictness of the criteria associated with Aristotelian 'character friendship' and avoid becoming embroiled in exegetical debates. Nevertheless, I consider their evidence to add backbone to the view that the educative value of character friendship can emerge prior to adolescence—a view which also suggests a more optimistic view of the usefulness of reflective moral education among quite young people than that often ascribed to Aristotle (e.g. by Burnyeat, 1980).

Now, while reams have been written about Aristotle's theory of friendship, and there is a current bandwagon of interest in Aristotelian or Aristotle-inspired methods of character education, few attempts have been made to bring the two literatures together (as correctly pointed out by Hoyos-Valdés, 2018), at least for practical educational purposes as distinct from moral theoretical ones. At the same time, another related Aristotelian method, about which Aristotle actually says much less, namely the emulation of moral exemplars (aka moral role modelling), has become the hottest ticket in town, with major recent contributions from within moral philosophy (Zagzebski, 2017), moral psychology (Damon & Colby, 2015), moral education (Campodonico, Croce & Vaccarezza, 2019) and even popular trade books (Brooks, 2015). I am only able to offer educated guesses about the reasons why. Perhaps modern amoral (e.g. aestheticised) views of friendship have blinded us to its moral value; perhaps role-model methods are easier to administer in formal educational contexts as 'interventions' than the cultivation of (the right kind of) friendship; perhaps friendship as an educational strategy cannot be fully understood or operationalised without simultaneously making sense of advanced *phronesis* development, which has baffled many moral educators because of its sheer complexity (Darnell et al., 2019).

In any case, Hoyos-Valdés (2018, p. 66) argues in her challenging paper that the 'overemphasis on role models is misguided and misleading, and a good antidote draws on the Aristotelian concept of character friendship'. As noted just now, this discourse is—in direct contrast to Aristotle's own emphasis—almost exclusively about role-model education as distinct from learning from character friends. While there is no reason to take Aristotle as gospel on any of those issues, his conceptualisations are well suited, as ever, to serve as starting points of the discussion. The current discourse on role-model education, insofar as it is conducted within a character-education tradition, typically draws on Aristotle's well-defined emotion of emulation (*zelos*), or emulousness as a trait. Emulation, says Aristotle, is

a kind of distress at the apparent presence among others like him by nature, of things honoured and possible for a person to acquire, [with the distress arising] not from the fact that another has them but that the emulator does not (thus emulation is a good thing and characteristic of good people, while envy is bad and characteristic of the bad; for the former [person], through emulation, is making an effort to attain good things for himself, while the latter, through envy, tries to prevent his neighbour from having them).   (2007, p. 146 [1388a29–38])

Emulation, as we gradually learn from Aristotle (cf. Kristjánsson, 2007, chap. 7), is an unusual emotion in that, although its *valence is overall negative*, that is, distressful, with the pain being caused by the emulator's perceived inferiority *vis-à-vis* the emulated person (i.e. the role model, in today's language), it is *overall positively evaluating* in that the emulator prefers the option of the role model retaining her superiority over the option of surpassing her by making her inferior. What the emulator wants is just to *equal* the role model, not to *supersede* her or take anything away from her; this is why emulation must be strictly distinguished from the overall negatively evaluating emotions of envy and begrudging spite. Aristotle does not consider the possibility, however, of an emulator who aspired to be 'at least as good' (rather than 'just equally as good') as the role model.

Aristotle is not terribly enlightening in explaining the psychological processes leading from emulation to the internalisation of the emulated characteristics of the role model. However, by tidying up his account and adding bits and pieces to it where necessary, it is possible to make sense of those mechanisms, at least in rough outline (see Zagzebski, 2017; Kristjánsson, 2020, chap. 7). One can thus hypothesise that the process of role modelling starts with the overall positively valenced *admiration* of an exemplar, which leads to a conception of oneself as lacking the admired qualities but desiring to possess them, which in turn evokes *emulation*—that is, as long as the admiration is strong enough to elicit *inspiration* rather than just inert admiration from a distance of some glorious hero, deemed far beyond reach. Notably, admiration and inspiration do not feature in the simple story that Aristotle tells about the emulation of moral exemplars; those emotions will need to be added to make the story more psychologically nuanced and plausible. I have elsewhere complained about the lack of attention in Aristotle (and, for that matter, in the revisionary account by Zagzebski, 2017, also) of *another route* to moral learning: elevation *vis-à-vis* abstract moral ideals where one is inspired, so to speak, by exemplarity itself rather than an exemplar (Kristjánsson, 2020, chap. 7). However, I have another complaint to make here, drawing on Hoyos-Valdés general misgiving (2018, p. 67) about reducing all moral learning from inspiring others (including character friends) to Aristotle's emulation-model or Zagzebski's admiration-emulation one.

Sherman (1987, p. 610) explicitly states that character friends 'are eminently suited as models for emulation'. Although this claim follows her rehearsal of Aristotle's *zelos*, it is not entirely clear whether Sherman is using 'emulation' in Aristotle's technical sense or a broader colloquial sense in which it simply indicates that character friends are ideal models for moral learning. While the latter is somewhat platitudinous if one endorses Aristotle's view of what character friends are about, the former claim is problematic because it falls afoul of the following intuition that I hope readers share with me.

It strains credulity towards the breaking point to think of the way our character develops through interactions with friends simply in terms of positively valenced admiration and negatively valenced emulation. I may be inspired to internalise the virtue of forgiveness to an enhanced extent by admiring Nelson Mandela's display of it, and then feeling inadequate in not matching him in this respect. However, given the psychological intimacy with a character friend and the idea of her as 'another self', it seems simplistic, at best, perverse, at worst, to consider my gradual internalisation of a stronger trait of forgiveness through my interactions with her in terms of simply, on the one hand, admiring her from the outside, as it were, and then, on the other, feeling bad that I am not as developed as her *qua* forgiver. This model may work perfectly for what are normally called 'role models' (of the Nelson Mandela or Mother Teresa kind) in the character-education litera-ture, but surely the psychological processes of learning from a character friend are much more complex, having to do with the affection shared between the two par-ties, to the extent that my relationship with her is qualitatively more advanced than the one I have with the standard role model.

I will try to entangle some of the possible processes involved in learning from a character friend in the following section. However, to make initial sense of the conceptual and empirical distinctions that I want to draw, I am persuaded to offer here a model of persons as sources of character development (seen from the per-spective of the beneficiary, see Table 5.1) that involves considerable tightening of ordinary language, in the service of clarification and precision, especially with regard to the concepts of a *role model* and a *moral exemplar* (as a 'good' role model). Notably, I am no great fan of radical departures from the common usage of terms, however unsystematic that usage may be, because such departures can easily trap theorists inside ivory towers and hinder practical applications. However, I ask readers to bear with me, for the purposes of the present discus-sion, and give the following conceptual distinctions a fair hearing, even though they may not like the particular terms I use to convey them.

Table 5.1 Persons as sources of character development

	Morally equal character friend	Morally unequal (superior) character friend	Morally superior non-character friend
Role model	∅	∅	Moral exemplar, e.g. Nelson Mandela
Non-role model	Soulmate	Mentor, e.g. parent, teacher, professor, more virtuous peer	(Lots of people who might, but do not, influence me)

Recall that, for Aristotle, a relationship with a friend must be entered into non-instrumentally: for example, not with the primary intention of securing incremental character gain rubbing off from the friend. Moreover, the goodwill must be reciprocated: the friend must value/love me in the same non-instrumental way as I value/love her. In unequal friendships Aristotle adds the condition that the stronger party be 'loved more than he loves, for when the loving reflects the comparative worth of friends, equality is achieved in a way' (1985, p. 221 [1158b26–9]), but this does not subvert the point that the stronger party also loves the weaker one non-instrumentally.

In contrast, then, let me stipulate that a relationship with a role model is (a) instrumental in nature: initiated for the sake of character development and (b) asymmetric (or unilateral) in the sense that the (perceived) benefactor is not also at the same time a beneficiary of the (perceived) relationship, nor reciprocates the beneficiary's feelings. This obviously rules out the possibility that a role model can also be a character friend, which narrows down the ordinary-language meaning of 'role model'—although it still allows for the possibility that a role model can be a friend for utility and/or pleasure. Unequal character friends may seem to present an intermediate case, in terms of psychological proximity versus distance, but they still count as 'friends' rather than 'role models' in the above model because they fail to satisfy conditions (a) and (b) for role models. I think the term 'mentor' is most felicitously reserved for those friends. In fact, mentoring was first described in the *Iliad*; the English word is derived from the Greek name of the man who guided Odysseus's son. Not all mentors are friends but all unequal character friends *qua* benefactors are mentors (cf. Lunsford, 2017). The friendship between Immanuel Kant and his tutee Marcus Herz provides a gloriously intoxicating example of mentorship where the mentee felt indebted to the mentor (Kant) for his 'entire self'. Without him, Herz says he would have been 'nothing' (cited in Barnard, 2011, pp. 109–10).

In the suggested model, a role model is a non-character friend, and insofar as she is morally superior to the beneficiary, she counts as a 'moral exemplar'. Parents, teachers and professors can fall into this category but, *ex hypothesi* in the present model, only in those cases where they are not character friends of the beneficiaries. This model may seem to have the counter-intuitive implication that common claims about a parent being at the same time 'my best friend and my greatest role model' do not make sense anymore. However, the reason we find this implication counter-intuitive is, I submit, because of our impoverished language in describing the processes of learning to develop one's character through interactions with friends *qua* mentors rather than role models, and because of how bloated the term 'role model' has become in everyday discourse. The aim of this classificatory model is not so much to close down linguistic avenues as to open up new ones, which will be explored in the following section.

It is well known from the role-model literature that role modelling is a rickety ladder to climb because of the inter-related threats of uncritical hero-worship, moral over-stretching and moral inertia (Vos, 2018; Kristjánsson, 2020, chap. 7). There is good reason to conjecture that those threats will be mitigated when the benefactors are morally superior character friends (mentors) rather than just role models, precisely because of the greater psychological intimacy and mutual self-knowledge among character friends, where *co-ordination* with the friend replaces *conformation* to a role model (cf. Hoyos-Valdés, 2018, p. 77).

Finally, in this model, I reserve the term 'soulmate' for a morally equal character friend from whom one learns to self-improve. There is nothing wrong as such with a broader understanding of 'soulmate' as covering all character friends *qua* kindred spirits (as I have used the term earlier in this book); my intention is not to disrespect ordinary language by recoiling from it and suggesting that it must be replaced, across the board, with a new technical vocabulary. We simply need a handy term to operationalise the notion of a morally equal character friend as a character developmental benefactor, and 'soulmate' fits that purpose well in this model.

5.3   The Mechanisms of Learning from Character Friends

No one has, to the best of my knowledge, written in any detail about how one develops one's character through interactions with close friends, let alone 'character friends' in the specific Aristotelian sense (barring some general suggestions in Telfer, 1970–1971, and Hoyos-Valdés, 2018). Despite its underlying educational focus, what Aristotle says about this himself is very meagre. In the absence of either a clear theory or specific empirical evidence, this section, on the putative mechanisms or processes of learning from character friends, must therefore be seen as exploratory and tentative. I have in mind for now mainly examples of equal character friendships *qua* soulmateships. Most of what I say could plausibly apply to unequal character friendships as mentorships also, but further caveats and conditions would then have to be added for which there is no space here. Drawing broadly on the spirit rather than the letter of Aristotle's account, I propose to separate the mechanisms in question into three categories: *emotional*, *cognitive-linguistic* and *epistemological*.

Character friendships arguably involve an *emotional connection* that is uniquely conducive to moral learning in terms of character improvement. The pride of place that Aristotle gives to emotions as part of the good life is well known (Kristjánsson, 2018). While he does not single out emotions that are specific to character friendships, some candidates suggest themselves easily (cf. Martínez-Priego & Romero-Iribas, 2021, on a whole potential hierarchy of emotions linked to character education). One is trust and, most notably here, *mutual trust*, understood as equal self-disclosure and confidently confiding in one another (Thomas, 1987). A moral learner can also place trust in an elevated role model, but in most cases such trust will not be mutual; the standard role model may not even be personally acquainted with the learner. Trust is also an essential emotion in some non-friendship-based social relationships, such as between a doctor and a patient, but there it is grounded in quite different motivational and dispositional structures to friendship and manifests itself differently (cf. Cocking & Oakley, 1995, pp. 93–4). The unique feature of mutual trust, which is grounded in psychological intimacy and soulmateship, is that it steadies the mind, by providing what could be called existential security, and lowers psychological barriers of self-disclosure and self-receptivity, some of which are inimical to moral learning. For example, to meet someone who unhesitatingly bears moral witness to her faults and the temptations that she is facing can be an eye-opening experience for someone fighting the same demons. It will all be part of a mutual learning journey.

The second mechanism of learning that I propose to highlight here is *linguistic and/or cognitive* and has to do with the mutual corrections that take place between friends as they discuss or debate their understandings of virtue terms (facilitating 'virtue literacy') and how the virtues are best applied in daily life. Mary Healy puts this in terms of young friends learning to practise their non-egoistic 'moral reasoning' with one another (2011, p. 449). There is an old saw that dialogue is only a Socratic, not an Aristotelian, method of moral education, but that seems ludicrous when we think of early-years Aristotelian habituation with a moral tutor (who will surely explain her moral exhortations rather than just rely on the carrot and the stick), and even more so when we think of the advanced cultivation of *phronesis*-guided virtue that is ideally instantiated among character friends as soulmates (Kristjánsson, 2015, chap. 6).

Paramount here is the notion of a 'critical friend'—with the friend being not only a supporter but also a challenger (Gibbs & Angelides, 2008). While that ideal may seem more at home in unequal character friendships, where the mentor gently 'corrects' the mentee (cf. Andrew, Richards & Fletcher, 2020), any constructive dialogue between equal character friends about how to deal with life's exigencies will involve critical engagement with the friend's point of view. Otherwise the friendship degenerates into what Brewer calls a 'static and complacent mutual admiration society' (2005, p. 726) and its very *raison d'être* is lost. As Cicero put it, to 'graciously give and receive criticism is the mark of true friendship' (2018, p. 155). Accepting criticism may even become a catalyst for profound epiphanic self-transformation (although Aristotle himself was sceptical of radical self-change in adulthood, see Kristjánsson, 2020, chap. 6). To accept, unquestioningly, the friend's character flaws, without trying to correct them, is not a sign of true character friendship but rather its opposite: an attitude that in today's academic parlance would probably best be referred to as unhealthy 'co-dependency'. This does not exclude the possibility of some epistemic impartiality in friendships

(Stroud, 2006), but such cases would have to be limited to situations in which the impartiality does not stand in the way of the friend's moral progress.

The critical engagement required by true friendship would, by Aristotle's lights, be guided by a mutual recognition of objective normativity inherent in the natural world in which we live. While understanding a soulmate involves understanding that person's unique self-narrative (Hoyos-Valdés, 2018, p. 71), it thus also involves understanding that narrative against the background of shared character-relevant values. Nehamas's point (2016, p. 76, drawing on C. S. Lewis, 1960), on how, in painting, friends tend both to look ahead, whereas lovers stare into each other's eyes, may be seen to represent this commitment to a common moral vision which not only is subjective, and not even relational in a dyadic sense, but lies beyond personal selfhood.

Speaking of 'selfhood' brings us neatly towards the third learning mechanism that I wish to foreground here, which I call the *epistemological* one, by drawing on Aristotle's much-cited locution of the friend as 'another self'. Debates have raged about what exactly Aristotle meant by this metaphor. Just as in Section 1.1, I want to avoid getting embroiled in those exegetical debates here and just focus on two of the educational implications that Aristotle's locution is evidently meant to alert us to. To start, here is the most relevant 'Aristotelian' quotation (I take it that the *Magna Moralia* was written by Aristotle or at least a faithful follower):

> Now we are not able to see what we are from ourselves […]; as when we wish to see our own face, we do so by looking into the mirror, in the same way when we wish to know ourselves we can obtain that knowledge by looking at our friend.
>
> (1915, 1213a15–22)

The first thing to note here is that although Aristotle was a self-realist, believing that selfhood is objectively identifiable and not reducible to mere self-concept, he also subscribed to the 'soft realist' credo that self-concept forms part of actual underlying selfhood, in the same way that the mirror which mirrors the furniture in a room is also part of that furniture (Kristjánsson, 2010, chap. 2). Aristotle thus considered it of paramount interest (e.g. in terms of our potential character growth) that our views about who we are correspond to who we really are 'deep down'. What Aristotle is referring to here is accurate self-knowledge, not in the somewhat esoteric modern philosophical sense of having knowledge of one's mental states but in the more ordinary sense of having knowledge of one's abilities and character traits (Gottlieb, 2020). He realised that we are often lacking in self-transparency in this ordinary sense and need someone who knows us well to correct our self-conceptions. This is why contemporary neo-Aristotelians are sceptical of self-report instruments to 'measure' character and recommend peer-reports and other more objective performance measures for triangulation (Kristjánsson, 2015, chap. 3; cf. Wright, Warren & Snow, 2021).

So the first educational implication to be drawn from Aristotle's self-theory is that character friends are invaluable for self-knowledge in the sense that they (often) know us better than we do ourselves. For example, a soulmate is likely to notice much earlier than I do that I have lost my zest for life and am sinking into depression. In general, 'we are able to observe our neighbours more than ourselves, and to observe their actions more than our own' (Aristotle, 1985, p. 258 [1169b33–5]). Because of the mutual trust involved, I reveal aspects of myself to the friend that I am not even fully aware of myself and she then reflects those back on me as needed. The reciprocity of self-disclosures need not be about the same sorts of things (Thomas, 1987, p. 226). One friend might be worried about her sex life, another about her career; the magic of close friendship is that you become interested in, and gain insights into, the other's self-relevant concerns although they may not happen to be your own.

There is a second and perhaps more controversial implication lurking inside the above *Magna Moralia* citation, about which Andrea Veltman (2004), for one, has written a penetrating paper. Because of the co-ordination and resonance of souls, involved in true soulmateship, Aristotle clearly thinks that I can learn facts about myself—including my current state of character and its potential for growth—by looking at how my character friends react and act, as their reactions are likely to mirror mine (although the latter will be opaque to my own introspection). So there are actually two reasons for why 'the self-sufficing man will require friendship in order to know himself' (1935, 1213a23–6).

I said that the second reason may be more controversial because it seems to assume that (a) we have privileged access to an understanding of other people's character traits—when we see those being exercised in action—that is somehow, in principle, unavailable in the case of our own traits, and (b) we can identify those viewed traits as being the same as our own, although lack of direct self-knowledge prevents us from having immediate access to the self-traits with which we are meant to juxtapose the friend's traits. Aristotle seems to forget here his own insistence on how good character is individually adjusted to persons' different temperaments and social situations so that people who would count as overall equal in virtue and able to form character friendships as soulmateships could, in fact, be very different in terms of detailed character profiles, rather than just being character-look-alikes. One of them, could, for example, be strong already in compassion but weak in honesty but the other strong in honesty while weak in compassion.

My qualms over the second of those implications notwithstanding, Aristotle does make a strong case for self-examination being dependent upon other-examination, and self-knowledge upon other-knowledge: in particular the intimate knowledge that the character friend has of who I am. We are beings prone to self-deceptions and positive illusions about ourselves. Friends can correct those, to a certain extent at least, either by direct criticism, as noted in the second mechanism of moral learning above, or simply by being there for us as a 'mirror' to look into. There are even hints in Aristotle of the thesis that one is epistemologically barred from exercising certain virtues if one is not able to share them with others as friends in an educational sense (cf. Kreft, 2019, p. 198), which lends further backbone to the close association between friendship and moral education. We must, however, avoid over-intellectualising the process of gaining knowledge about ourselves through the friend as 'another self'. Contra Houston (2020), who understand this mechanism in terms of a (uniquely human) contemplative second-order awareness of oneself in another, I understand it not so much in terms of a metacognitive intellectual skill but rather in terms of experiential doing things together with the friends through shared activities.

In any case, this many-folded epistemological mechanism holds the key to understanding the highly contested claim about character friendship that it cannot be forged with vicious people: a claim that turns some theorists off Aristotle's moralised account of close friendship and towards an aestheticised one, as we witnessed in Chapter 4. One can understand this claim fairly superficially as a counter-example to the proverb that the sun never becomes worse for shining on the dunghill. It may attest to character flaws in oneself to want to mingle with the vicious and doing so can, then, exacerbate those flaws. Such interactions would represent 'an objectionable sort of moral complacency' (Isserow, 2018, p. 3101). However, Aristotle is making a more profound claim here than just warning against the contagious perils of moral pollution. He offers an extended argument, which I summarised in Section 4.3, showing that complete vice precludes self-knowledge, which in turn precludes self-love; and as lack of self-love prevents one from loving others in the *philia* sense (Aristotle, 1985, pp. 246–7 [1166b1–25]), the very foundations of any edifying character friendship have been shattered.

So the educational upshot of Aristotle's the-friend-as-another-self conceptualisation is actually quite radical. It is not only that we need character friends to achieve self-knowledge which, in turn, is necessary to enable us to (continue to) reform our character. Even more importantly, without some measure of (developmentally growing) self-knowledge, we are unable to make true friends in the first place as, bereft of the capacity to love ourselves because we do not know who we are, we are also unable to extend those feelings to others and to identify a rightful place for them in our lives.

5.4 How Socially Equal and Unequal Friendship May Lose Their Educational Value and Become Dissolved

Recall once again Aristotle's claim that a friend's characterological shift into incurable vice warrants the termination of friendship. He never explicitly tells us why. Yet, seen from the perspective of close friendship as an educational concept, two reasons explained at the close of the preceding section suggest themselves again. Despite the implicit acknowledgement of educational ruptures, I cannot endorse McCoy's contention that 'Aristotle exhibits a tremendous sensitivity to human moral weakness in his account of friendship' (2013, p. 146). It is not all bad news, however. Having explored his educational rationale of character friendships above, we can now use Aristotle's defining characteristics to hoist him with his own petard, in terms of the potential causes of character-friendship terminations that he overlooks.

In Chapter 2, I suggested ten different reasons, beyond those identified by Aristotle himself, for the dissolution of character friendships. I called those reasons 'un-Aristotelian' in the sense of not being invoked by Aristotle, although many of them seemed to be potentially compatible with his general theory of friendship. By drawing on the thesis proposed in previous sections of this chapter about education as the *raison d'être* of close (character) friendships, it is now possible to probe some of those reasons in more detail. In the present section, I first explore some educational reasons for the dissolution of socially *equal* character friendships and, subsequently, I scrutinise the demise of some socially *unequal* character friendships.

Aristotle does admit, albeit briefly, that in addition to drastic departures from the path of virtue, circumstances may intervene through which friends become separated—including increased disparities in wealth (1985, p. 221 [1159a33–4]). However, he remains reticent about the specific problems that can beset character friendships between people of an equal social standing that exhibit inequalities in virtue. I will focus here on *divergent developmental paths* amongst people who begin as social and virtue equals but who become increasingly distanced from each other as one of the pair turns in a direction that may ultimately induce the other friend to pull up the friendship drawbridge. From an educational perspective, one could argue, for example, that continuing to pursue soulmateship with a person who is on a slow but steady trajectory towards moral decline may do irreparable damage to my own virtuous make-up. The respect and commitment to the friend notwithstanding, we seem at least entitled to modify Aristotle's thesis to say that one has good reasons for stamping out friendship with a friend who is on such an unstoppable trajectory, even long before the friend has wound up in a state of complete wickedness.

I will not be elaborating upon this sort of example of divergent developmental paths, however, but rather on a different one. Let me invoke as a case study a perspicuous novel by the best-selling author Meg Wolitzer, *The Interestings* (2014). This work has all the ingredients of a blockbuster novel, but it also contains unusually penetrating observations regarding the complexities of relationships between friends, as their fortunes tilt precipitously during the course of their life journeys. Depicting the trials and tribulations of a group of six Americans who become friends during a teenage summer camp in 1974, and most of whom harbour (varyingly realistic) artistic aspirations, the book offers glimpses of lives that—to keep readers absorbed—are more tempestuous than most ordinary lives of ordinary people; yet not far-fetched enough for readers to cease identifying with them.

With various narrative detours and a troupe of protagonists too numerous to explore here, the three most interesting characters, for present purposes, are Ethan and Jules, as well as Jules's best friend, Ash, whom she also met at the summer camp and who ends up marrying Ethan. The dynamics of the Ethan-Ash-Jules triad, where Jules tries to preserve her friendship with Ethan while avoiding making her best friend Ash jealous, is juicy enough to merit a discussion of potential eros–*philia* conflicts. However, the more relevant dimension here of the (ultimately) fraught and tenuous friendship between Jules and Ethan is how Ethan's life takes a developmental turn that strains the friendship with Jules almost beyond the breaking point. To be sure, the friendship does endure—for otherwise the author would have had to bring the narrative to a premature end. However, it is easy to envisage an alternative trajectory where what happens to Ethan would have sufficed to dissolve the friendship completely by exhausting the friendship's educational potential.

Notice first that both Jules and Ethan are kind and caring people, 'brought up in good habits', in Aristotle's sense. While neither are full *phronimoi* (Ethan is for example badly lacking in the virtue of courage), both would fall securely into the category of budding *phronimoi*. The very rationale of their friendship, which nourishes and sustains it, is their unremitting care for each other and eagerness to help, advise and strengthen each other for the other's sake, as well as learning from the one another's experiences. In this sense, they are typical character friends, and there is not a whiff of charlatanism about their soulmateship. However, while Jules has to give up her artistic dreams for a modestly rewarding career as a therapist, Ethan becomes shockingly successful as an artist, 'gilded with specialness and privilege' (2014, p. 347). Because of his strong moral self-identity, Ethan channels his riches into philanthropy and other charitable causes, turning himself into what Aristotle called a '*megalopsychos*': one who because of largesse-enabling external fortunes can afford to be magnificent and grandiose in giving and in assisting others, not simply mundanely generous.

Although being a *megalopsychos* is, by Aristotle's lights, a mixed blessing (because of the strain that being a busy public benefactor places on one's intellectual resources; see Kristjánsson, 2020, chap. 4), the moral developmental path of the *megalopsychos* is ethically more advanced than that of a (budding) *phronimos* and involves the possibility of blessedness in life, rather than simple flourishing. However, here is the moral of the story: Jules becomes increasingly disengaged from Ethan because she can no longer identify with him and learn from him— nor give him advice relevant to his new life circumstances. The issue is not so much Ethan's raised status in life or his wealth *per se*—which by itself might just have subtly changed the character friendship with Jules into one of social inequality rather than equality while still retaining its characteristic ethical quality. The issue, rather, is that Ethan gradually grows into a 'thicker, finalized adult self' (2014, p. 4) that does not allow for mutual correction and reinvention with Jules's self because their capacity for moral action has taken such different turns that the educational basis of their friendships has become eroded. Whenever Ash and Ethan 'cooked a chicken, it would feed a subcontinent' (2014, p. 50); whereas Jules's attempts at good deeds remain limited to offering her close friends and her own ailing husband (a chronic depressive) some modest comfort. She feels she wants to be 'as good as' Ethan is (2014, p. 122), but she falls desperately short because of a lack of personal and financial resources, and that discrepancy gradually creates a wall between the two of them.

The friendship between Ethan and Jules changes 'into something so different from what it had originally been as to be unrecognizable' (2014, p. 135). The imbalance between them is 'suddenly, jarringly evident' (2014, p. 236). The almost 'telepathic mutuality' (2014, p. 171) between them is lost, not because Ethan becomes irredeemably bad but rather because his goodness achieves heights that Jules cannot share with him as a soulmate. If they met now, 'they would never become friends' (2014, p. 241). The lesson is that lives can divide, and even the best of friendships can become threatened, for a reason that is the diametrical opposite of the one that Aristotle foregrounded. The possibility for mutual education and self-cultivation in character friendships is parasitic on there being a shared area of experiences and activities that can inform the sensibilities of both parties and help them to correct each other. If one person becomes 'too good', it can create a barrier that is just as insurmountable as the one that results from the person becoming 'too bad'—because, in either circumstance, the shared zone of proximal development that serves as the relevant educational crucible disappears. Bear in mind here the Aristotelian assumption, which I happen to share, that material resources can augment moral virtue—make it greater—rather than simply increasing one's capacity for displaying a disposition that is already in place.

Another instructive example has been elicited by Alexander Nehamas from the play *Art* by Yasmina Reza (Nehamas, 2016, pp. 142–85). Understandably, Nehamas uses this example to illustrate his own view about the grounding of close friendships in the aesthetic qualities of the friends, rather than, as in Aristotle's view, in their moral character. However, the example can easily be reinterpreted in the service of a moralised-cum-educational account of close-friendship groundings. Having previously shared their appreciation of art, the three friends Marc, Serge and Yvan fall out when Serge pays a fortune to buy a painting that the other two find aesthetically worthless. Marc accuses Serge of pretentiousness, maintaining that he has just bought the painting simply because it is in vogue; Serge in turn takes Marc to have become a paternalistic *besserwisser*. Nehamas sees this example as indicative of the precariousness of best friendships insofar as they are based on essentially fleeting phenomena, such as one's taste in art. Lack of aesthetic harmony can thus easily undermine friendships, as friendship is more about a common characteristic 'style' than a common moral 'character'.

As an Aristotelian, I read the lesson of the story quite differently. If I were Marc, what would worry me is not the sudden incompatibility between my aesthetic tastes and those of Serge. Rather, I would see Serge's gesture as indicative of a more profound change of character profile: from authenticity to pretentiousness. While such a transformation falls short of a debilitating descent into vice, I still would worry that I had nothing more to learn from Serge and that we would no longer be able to hone each other's moral sensibilities. In other words, the educative rationale of the friendship would be lost—and I do not mean educative as in 'aesthetic education' but rather as in 'moral education'. While I say this as a neo-Aristotelian, I repeat my discontent that Aristotle himself did not consider non-extreme character shifts of this kind as offering valid reasons for the discontinuation of close friendships but fastened instead on more radical and rare examples.

That said, Marc may have been too quick in seeing the change in Serge as a reason for terminating their friendship. When friends change their values, we have the option of also changing our values accordingly rather than just rigidly sticking to our guns (as Rorty, 1993, explores). Still, even in such cases, the decision is educational as much as psychological. We need to ask ourselves about the additional educational resources such a change would create in our trajectory towards self-cultivation, and also weigh the educational barriers that it might potentially erect.

Because dissolutions of friendships on grounds of subtly changing developmental paths are probably much more common than Aristotle envisaged, and such dissolutions are often profoundly painful, one may have some sympathy with the UK head teacher who discouraged pupils from forming 'best friendships' so as to avoid the pain and upset caused by fallings out (as reported in Healy, 2015, p. 196, n. 1; cf. more recent worries in the UK about Prince George attending a school where best friendships are frowned upon, see Vernon, 2017). While, from an Aristotelian perspective, this would count as an over-reaction (throwing the baby out with the bathwater), providing grist for the head teacher's mill are extensive research findings that highlight the long-term negative consequences of (close) friendship-endings for pupils' socio-moral development and school success (Healy, 2015, p. 187).

Isserow is quite right that on any plausible account of the grounding of close friendships, enhancing their credentials 'is not something to be swiftly achieved by cutting ties with those friends who are deemed morally sub-par, and replacing them with the good Samaritans and humanitarians of the world' (2018, p. 3107). In that sense, Aristotle was on target about the unique endurance of character friendships. However, once the friendship has become perverted from its educational purpose, this may legitimately lubricate the slide towards its dissolution (or at least its downgrading to a mere pleasure or utility friendship) long before the friend has turned incurably bad.

The thesis about education as the *raison d'être* of close friendships has, I submit, even more initial plausibility in the case of unequal friendships, such as between a teacher/professor and a student. World literature teems with examples of young learners soaking up wisdom and reflective virtues from mentors while the mentors rejuvenate their own character with inputs from the youthful exuberance and open-mindedness of their mentees. To avoid unnecessary controversy, let me focus in the remainder of this section on unequal friendships of the kind that are most explicitly educational, in order not to beg the questions whether all are. I am thinking here of friendships between teachers/professors *qua* mentors and their mentees. Two penetrating studies provide examples of such pedagogical friendships (cf. also Kakkori & Huttunen, 2007). Amy Shuffelton (2012) recounts the friendship that she, as a teacher, developed with an artistically inclined, nerdy and lonely elementary school pupil in Krakow (a friendship that still persists), with the young man in his late twenties when the article was written. Paul Weithman (2015) elaborates on 'academic friendships' between professors and the undergraduate students in their classes. Weithman refrains from defining those as full-blown character friendships in the Aristotelian sense, as they normally disband at the end of the academic year. Instead, he relies obliquely on references in Aristotle to a higher form of utility friendships that 'would seem to depend on character' more than one sees in ordinary 'mercenary'-type utility friendships (Aristotle, 1985, pp. 233–4 [1162b23–7]). However, Weithman fails to account for cases where the student continues to rely on the mentorship of the professor long after graduation and where their friendship even lasts as long as both live, as is not infrequently the case in my own experience. It would be churlish to deny such associations the status of unequal but complete character friendships in the Aristotelian sense. Another way to put this point is to say that the 'terminating conditions' of friendships between professors and (graduated) students are not as clear-cut as those, say, between a doctor and (cured) patients (cf. Cocking & Oakley, 1995, p. 94).

Shuffelton (2012) spends considerable time discussing the objection that friendships of this kind breach the teacher's duty of impartiality towards all her students. She correctly argues that a teacher can give all her students excellent service while giving some of them (who, for some reason, need personal friendship rather than just instruction) more of it. In some cases of particularly vulnerable students, the truly caring teacher will rush in unhesitatingly where others are unwilling to tread. In Chapter 2, I identified specific barriers that unequal mentor–student friendships may encounter. For one thing, because such friendships tend to be motivated by concerns that involve enjoyment by the mentor in spending time with a young person, as well as considerable academic benefits accruing to the mentee from the association with the more learned person, there is serious danger of the friendship never reaching the higher level of character friendship or, worse still, of degenerating gradually into mere pleasure or utility friendship, even if it does actualise the higher ideal at the outset. For another thing, because of the well-known phenomenon of role inertia, standardly scrutinised in social psychology, it is highly likely that even after the mentee has caught up with the mentor in terms of character development, their association continues to be stuck in the terms in which it was originally forged. In such cases, a potentially equal character friendship becomes misconceived by one or both parties as unequal, thus undercutting its capacity to (continue to be) educationally productive. Furthermore, as noted in Section 2.4, Aristotle is reticent about possible eros–philia conflicts that often lurk around the corner here as in other kinds of character friendships (Shuffelton, 2012, p. 220). While modern scholars have studied this problem in detail (e.g. Werking, 1997; Schudder & Bishop, 2001), none of them has focused specifically on the detrimental effects of eros–philia conflicts on the educational 'regulative ideal' of character friendships. I return briefly to this issue in Section 8.3.

I will end this section with a brief discussion of a problem that is explicitly educational and to which, I submit, unequal character friendships of the kind I have been considering are particularly susceptible. This is the *problem of paternalism*, already introduced in Section 2.3. Since the Enlightenment, the ideal of education as the cultivation of the critically reflective, autonomous individual has permeated almost all respectable educational theories in the Western world, in one guise or another. Any educational interventions smacking of paternalism are anathema to the ideal of autonomy. Obviously, the ideal of autonomy was not familiar to Aristotle in its modern form. However, he famously demanded that virtuous persons not only perform the right actions but also perform them for the right reasons and from the right motives: knowing them, taking intrinsic pleasure in them and deciding on them for themselves (1985, p. 40 [1105a30–4]). The underlying assumption is that ethical acts do not have moral value unless they are guided by the agent's own *phronesis*; and although *phronesis*-guidance cannot be equated with autonomy in the modern sense, it is incompatible with the idea of a moral agent being paternalistically controlled by an external puppet master.

Despite the high-brow ideals to which both Aristotelian educators and—more radically still—their modern counterparts are meant to aspire according to the *phronesis* and autonomy mantras, every seasoned educator knows that no educational activities can get off the ground without some measure of paternalism involved. In a sense, all students beginning the study of a new topic subject themselves to initiation into certain qualities of mind, hitherto unknown to them, by putting themselves under the teacher's authority and guidance. As Weithman (2015) unapologetically puts it, the professor should try to make her partnership with students formative; it is her job to *form* their intellectual tastes. However strongly the ideal of autonomy figures as the eventual goal, and however much the learning process is conceptualised as subjection to normativity itself rather than subjection to the teacher's authority as a guide to that normativity, there is no escaping the fact that the pedagogical relationship involves, by its very nature, elements of paternalism—even if that paternalism is self-chosen and fully complied with by the student. This fact forces upon the teacher, whether she wants it or not, certain motivational and dispositional structures (cf. Cocking & Oakley, 1995, p. 93) that seem to be quite alien to a relationship between character friends, even of the unequal kind. For example, it is incumbent on the teacher to impart certain knowledge, a particular mindset and specific skills, and the measure of whether or not that has been successful or not seems to have very little to do with the mutual collaborative self-cultivation of character that is meant to be the *raison d'être* of Aristotelian character friendships.

What I have been saying here is not that the role of a teacher/professor is essentially incompatible with the role of an unequal character friend in Aristotle's understanding. There are, I believe, countless examples of mentor–mentee friendships where those two roles have been brought into alignment. I am simply calling attention to a warning signal that failed to register on Aristotle's radar. Although character friendships with a socially superior party are often entered into precisely to avoid the paternalism that typically characterises unequal associations, there is great danger that the friendship with a teacher/professor becomes liable to perversion into the very vice that it was created to resist. It is not so much that friendship with a student undermines the teacher's paternalistic authority (Jarvie, 2019), but the other way round: that the teacher's authority can undermine the friendship.

The aim of this chapter has been to retrieve (close) friendship as an educational concept. While the most obvious place to pan for gold is Aristotle's account of character friendships, whose value is essentially moral educational, I have focused in the present section on the negative side of the story: how viewing friendship as an educational concept helps make sense of why many close friendships are so vulnerable to dissipation and rupture. In a nutshell, putting an educational construction on friendship comes with as many liabilities as assets, and those may in some cases not only enfeeble the specific friendship in question but fully cancel its advantage. To be sure, one of the glories of Aristotle's moral and educational theory is its focus on the value of friendship; at the same time, however, one cannot but wish that his assessment of its pros and cons had been more measured and even-handed.

5.5 Concluding Remarks

We become friends by practising friendships, just as we become harpists by playing the harp. The process of learning to become friends is thus essentially an educational process. Those are perhaps little more than truisms. However, I have proposed to make a more radical claim in this chapter: namely, that making close friends for character is not only an educational process but rather that its ultimate *telos* is educational at its very core. Aristotle's obscure references to the character friend as 'another self' are probably not best understood as references to human selves interwoven in some 'woolly pseudo-mystical way' (Hitz, 2011, p. 17), but rather as reminders of the fact that cultivating close friendships is an integrated collaborative activity, involving both an educational process and an educational outcome. As iron sharpens iron, character friends sharpen each other and contribute towards collaborative moral growth, conducive to both individual and communal flourishing. Educators, at all levels of the school and university system, need to take note.

I will end this chapter with two observations. The first is that the somewhat rose-tinted view of character friendships as one-sidedly rewarding 'schools of virtue' that one finds in Aristotle may be but one more instantiation of his general over-estimation of the characterological stability of people brought up in good habits. The idea of the (increasingly) unified moral agent on an (unproblematically) upwardly mobile trajectory towards full *phronesis*, with the help of trusted friends on the same journey, belies the extent to which human life is rarely a quiescent stretch, characterised by psycho-moral integration, but rather is one that bends with the winds of time and fortune—and where dilemmas lurk around every corner: including dilemmas about how to best interact with one's friends. Because we keep changing subtly as persons, as we enter new unforeseen situations, it is no wonder that the educational benefits we derive from associations with different friends fluctuate and may, in some cases, make us drift apart from people who, at previous junctures, were our 'other selves'. The very point of education is to *enact change*, and it would be remarkable if the change that my friend enacts in me, or vice versa, always kept us close together rather than prying us apart. In many cases, drifting from one another will be a slow process, just as the effects of education rarely hit us in an epiphanic instant. In the words of Samuel Johnson (cited in Barnard, 2011, p. 228), the 'most fatal disease of friendship is gradual decay, our dislike hourly increased by causes too slender for complaint, and too numerous for removal'.

The second observation is that education is not, by its nature, an essentially comfortable process. Socrates did not only liken himself to a midwife but also to a gadfly and a torpedo fish. Even when moral educational guidance is provided by a character friend non-paternalistically, it may touch a raw nerve. In the words of novelist Patrick White (cited in Vernon, 2010, p. 74), friendship is 'two knives'. 'They will sharpen each other when rubbed together, but often one of them will slip and slice off a thumb'. There are times when we are simply not ready to have our thumb sliced off and where guidance from our friends is seen—rightly or wrongly—as being surplus to requirements. Friendship for virtue, just as education itself, is rarely straightforward and easy.

6

Friendships for Utility

Their Moral Value and an Online Example

6.1 Introduction: Context and Questionable Assumption

This chapter aims to explore one fairly specific question: can so-called *friendships for utility* have moral value? I take Aristotle's account of utility friendships, as one of his three main friendship types, as my starting point because of its historical importance and logical nuance. In a sense, then, this is just, like Chapter 5, an exercise in Aristotelian retrieval. However, my ultimate answer here goes—much more so than in Chapter 5—beyond anything Aristotle says explicitly, although some of its main ingredients are extracted from his texts. In order to situate my question and elicit its relevance, both for the moral discourses on friendship and on Aristotelian virtue ethics, some context-setting is in order.

There is one area of discourse in which Aristotelian friendships are being excitedly and painstakingly discussed at the moment in ways that are non-exegetical and highly practical: the discourse on the merits and demerits of *online friendships*. While many of the participants in this discourse are in fact academic philosophers, it seems to have largely escaped attention within the comfort zones of mainstream philosophy. Some of the relevant participants have adopted a style of writing that is vexingly dystopian, homiletic and characteristic of moral panic (see e.g. Deresiewicz, 2009). More typically, however, the quality of argumentation in this ongoing debate is measured, well informed (with respect to Aristotelian theory) and rigorous (see e.g. Vallor, 2012, debating Kaliarnta, 2016, on whether online friendship can constitute character friendship). This debate deserves recognition and development within mainstream moral philosophy, and although I will not to pay homage to it in any detail until Chapter 7, I derive my main illustrative example in Section 6.4 from an online context.

It is instructive for present purposes to identify an assumption that tends to be taken for granted in this literature, both by friends and foes of online friendships *qua* character friendships. This assumption states that the lower forms of friendship (compared to character friendship), especially friendship for utility, do not 'merit the label "genuine friendship"' and thus do not 'qualify as morally valuable' (Fröding & Peterson, 2012, p. 201). Rather, friendships for utility are just about taking advantage of one another in amoral or immoral ways (Bülow & Felix, 2016, p. 27).

Friendship for Virtue. Kristján Kristjánsson, Oxford University Press. © Kristján Kristjánsson 2022.
DOI: 10.1093/oso/9780192864260.003.0006

I happen to consider this assumption questionable or even largely misplaced. Yet the standard interpretation, not only in the recent discourse on Aristotelian online friendship but in the general friendship scholarship, is that this assumption is actually Aristotle's own reasoned view. While that interpretation has surface credibility at least, given various unsympathetic and dismissive things that Aristotle says about friendships for utility, I do believe there are potential resources within Aristotelian theory to reconsider and reject this assumption, but that those resources remain hidden (even to Aristotle himself) for various reasons that I explain in the following section.

In all events, my motivation for writing this chapter is substantive rather than exegetical. I propose to offer counterweight to the assumption in question and do so in a way that is at least not fully alien to the spirit—as distinct from the letter—of Aristotle's account. Aristotle aside, I go against the grain of the standard ploy of ruling friendships for utility out of moral court. I have only found one article that proposes to do anything remotely similar to what I aim for. Thus, I agree fully with James Grunebaum's contention that utility-based friendships 'have been unjustly undervalued by philosophers' (2005, p. 203). However, I propose to go beyond Grunebaum's argument in various ways and offer a different take on the value of (Aristotelian) friendships for utility.

Upsetting the applecart is always an exciting prospect for a philosopher. However, my aim is not so much to achieve a conceptual reshuffle of standard friendship classifications as it is to open up new avenues of thought regarding some of Aristotle's less-than-optimal (compared to the ones charted in Chapter 5), but still commendable, paths to ethical development. Prior to the analysis of utility friendships in Section 6.3 and the illustrative examples in Section 6.4, I therefore need to devote the second section to a rehearsal of some Aristotelian developmental themes that bear on the subsequent argument and give it traction.

6.2 Some Aristotelian Concepts and Complexities Regarding Moral Development

The very question about the potential *moral* value of utility friendships may seem like a non-starter from an Aristotelian perspective, as Aristotle famously had no concept of 'the moral' at his disposal (Kraut, 2006). Consider, for example, the insight from current 'moral-domain theory' that the development of children's judgements about morality, issues of social convention and personal matters follow independent courses of maturity rather than being stage-based (Smetana, Jambon & Ball, 2014). The issue here is not so much that Aristotle would have disagreed with this view (or that neo-Aristotelians should), but rather that Aristotelian theory lacks the conceptual repertoire to draw any clear lines between these three domains. Not only is there no distinction in Aristotle's vocabulary between the 'moral' and 'non-moral', there is no distinction to be drawn from his works between (moral) character and (non-moral) personality; ancient Greek simply had no specific word for 'personality', as I pointed out in Chapter 4. Aristotelian developmental theory thus lacks the relevant conceptual resources to engage in some of the elementary debates about issues that divide contemporary moral psychologists (cf. Darnell et al., 2019).

There is, on the other hand, a clear distinction in Aristotle between positive traits that relate to character (*ethikos*) and those that do not. Thus, he often refers to commendable qualities, such as compassion and righteous indignation, as traits that are 'characteristic of good people' (see e.g. 2007, p. 142 [1386b8–12]) rather than as 'virtues of character', and to the inability to experience such qualities as blameworthy deficiencies rather than as 'vices'. However, this distinction is not serviceable for present purposes, as the traits Aristotle has in mind here are mainly emotional ones which fail to pass muster, in his (somewhat flaky) view, because (a) of the way emotions *happen to* us rather than being deliberately *chosen* in a fully responsible way and (b) they may fail to reach completion through *action* as true virtues should.

If this particular distinction were couched (in more modern terms) between (1) moral traits relating to character and (2) moral traits not relating to character, friendship for utility would seemingly fall on the side of (1), because such friendships are clearly chosen by us and result in action, so the key to the distinction between friendship for character and utility would fail to emerge. Some Aristotelian scholars, especially those of a practical bent, seem to use 'moral' for any quality that is conducive to the overall goal of life, namely *eudaimonia*, but that understanding of 'moral' is too broad to be helpful for present purposes, as it would turn various strokes of luck, such as being of good health and being born into a well-off family, into 'moral' qualities or conditions. Moreover, it would make the claim that friendships for utility have moral value trivially true.

In order to make sense of—and be able to argue against—the received wisdom that friendships for utility do *not* have moral value, as a view that is more than just trivially false, I need to stipulate a meaning of 'moral' that accommodates contemporary conceptions but still has some reasonable place within an Aristotelian, or at least a neo-Aristotelian, system. Let us try this: consider a trait or quality 'moral' (in an educational context) if it *at least* aims at mitigating vice or incontinence in people, for their own sake, without *necessarily* making them virtuous. While this a fairly broad definition, which obviously includes a wide range of traits in addition to the standard character virtues, it does not make the claim that friendships for utility have moral value trivially true, because it is still open to sceptics to argue that friendships for utility simply do not have this aim. Indeed, that is what most of them seem to want to argue, given their understanding of the concept of 'friendship for utility' as amoral, typically taken to be derived from Aristotle (see e.g. Fröding & Peterson, 2012). This definition also gives me leverage to argue—as I propose to do—that friendships for utility have moral value insofar as they help turn vice into (at least) incontinence, and incontinence into (at least) continence, although they may not produce virtue. Educationally, they may aid friends in keeping one another on the straight and narrow by helping each other fight contra-ethical inclinations, provided the friends are not already fully fledged *phronimoi* who have no contra-ethical inclinations to resist anymore. As readers will have noticed, I follow Aristotle in speaking of friendship (here for utility) either as a relation between people or a trait of character (here: the capacity to form friendships of a certain sort). While the former understanding is probably more common in ordinary English, it is not outlandish to speak of 'friendship' as a positive characteristic of a person.

In spite of Aristotle's inability to avail himself of the word 'moral', he could have made this point about friendship for utility if he had wanted to by using terms that were available to him, for example by talking about it as a relationship that is, at its best, 'characteristic of people striving towards goodness or flourishing'. The reasons why he chooses not to do so are, I would argue, somewhat complex and have to do both with the intended readership of the *Nicomachean Ethics* and Aristotle's (related) lack of interest in non-virtue-routed developmental paths that lead to less than full *phronesis*. I need to say something about both those reasons before proceeding further.

General readers of the *Nicomachean Ethics*, uncorrupted by too much academic philosophy, may easily get the impression that it was written as a self-help manual for ordinary people who want to learn to flourish—much like, say, Martin Seligman's (2011) contemporary bestseller on flourishing—and that the two extensive chapters on friendship are meant to help people 'like us' make and sustain healthy friendships. This impression is erroneous, however, as I have intimated at earlier junctures. The *Nicomachean Ethics* is specifically written for a discrete and fairly small group of people: aristocratic young men 'brought up in good habits' (Aristotle, 1985, p. 6 [1095b4–5]) and already (being) habituated into virtue. Even more specifically, the message of the book is geared towards readers who are later to become statesmen or entrusted with the moral education of the young. While these points have been made repeatedly by Aristotelian scholars (see e.g. Pangle, 2003, pp. 10–13), they tend to become breezily swept under the carpet when the overall ethical message of Aristotle's work gets distilled and analysed.

The *Nicomachean Ethics* plots a unique developmental path for young men blessed with constitutive 'moral luck'. After the habituation process, which presumably requires considerable systematic guidance by a parent/mentor/educator, a process of *phronesis* development follows, in which the budding virtues mature into fully fledged *phronetic* (*phronesis*-guided or *phronesis*-infused) moral virtues with the help of character friends. We later learn, much to our surprise, in Book 10 that not even this suffices for the fully flourishing life; complete moral virtue complemented by the wherewithal of abundant worldly resources to do good (as in the case of the notoriously blasé but supremely good *megalopsychoi*) leaves people unfulfilled unless they can practise the somewhat esoteric activity of pure contemplation (see Kristjánsson, 2020, chap. 4).

From the point of view of contemporary developmental psychology, even this main path plotted in the *Nicomachean Ethics*, for its prospective elite readers, remains so curiously under-developed that it resembles a dance-of-seven-veils mystery. The standard Burnyeat (1980) interpretation of two distinct developmental phases, habituation *qua* mindless conditioning, followed by critical and reflective *phronesis* development, turns the whole process into the famous 'paradox of moral education' (of learning uncritically and heteronomously to become critical and autonomous, see Kristjánsson, 2007, chap. 3). Even if one opts for Sherman's (1989) more rhapsodic interpretation of the habituation process as being reason-guided and critically stimulated from the word go, there remain urgent questions about *when* (namely at what age) and *how* the external guide becomes overtaken by character friends and what the powerful intellectual virtue of *phronesis* really assumes and incorporates by way of intellectual and moral faculties—leading to a plethora of conflicting contemporary interpretations (Darnell et al., 2019).

Why is Aristotle so reticent and sketchy about this developmental story? For one thing, he simply may not consider it necessary to retell the obvious; after all, this is the way good young men in Athens are being brought up, so you just need to look around yourself for examples. Or he wants to defer to 'the natural scientists' the psychological details of the story (cf. Aristotle, 1985, p. 181 [1147b5–9]): a naturalistic remark that may sound like music to the ears of current empirically minded psychologists but is somewhat ironic, given the fact that Aristotle himself was probably the leading natural scientist of his day. As a third possibility, Aristotle may have fleshed out this developmental story in his book on child-rearing, known to be lost.

I have grappled with many of those puzzles before (Kristjánsson, 2007, chap. 3; 2015, chap. 4) and will not dwell further on them here except to observe that I have concerns about the extent to which current writers on the qualities of friendship types in Aristotle typically remain oblivious to the fact that, in his account of friendship, Aristotle is guided by the lights of his mission to give advice to a privileged group of moral learners and moral educators, and that this account may thus bear the marks of a forced assimilation to a very unique developmental project—a project from which most ordinary people are actually barred.

There are two other developmental paths described in the *Nicomachean Ethics* (I omit here the subhuman and superhuman paths that are just mentioned in passing). One is for those brought up in bad habits and habituated into vice. It must be admitted that Aristotle is not optimistic about the possibility of their moral reform. I bent over backwards in Chapter 5 to seize upon an anomalous paragraph in an obscure textual place that seems to open up the possibility of a bad person having a radical conversion and rising like phoenix from the ashes of vice (Aristotle, 1941, p. 32 [13a22–31]; cf. Kristjánsson, 2015, chap. 5). But that is clutching at a straw. Aristotle's cohort of badly brought up, vicious people are most likely to end up as a basket of deplorables, simply because they will not understand the need for character reform or comprehend the terms in which such a need would be formulated (Aristotle, 1985, p. 292 [1179b11–31]). Their only hope lies in being constrained by law and punishment; they might therefore progress, at least intermittently, up to the superior levels of the incontinent or continent, driven by the intellectual virtue of calculation (*deinotes*). What holds the vicious back is not only their lack of virtue literacy, so to speak, enabling them to grasp what is being said to them, but also the fact that they are unable to form mutual character friendships, according to Aristotle (1985, p. 215 [1157a18–20]), because of their arrested development, and that Aristotle does not allow for the sort of spontaneous transcendent epiphanies—where you grasp moral truths in a flash—that his mentor Plato would have suggested as a propitious way towards moral reform (Kristjánsson, 2020, chap. 6).

If the *Nicomachean Ethics* had been written as a handbook for the general public on living well, Aristotle would have needed to spend more space on the developmental levels of incontinence and continence, as those happen to be the levels most ordinary people are at, in his own estimation (Aristotle, 1985, p. 190 [1150a15]). He would also have had to initiate a discussion of the best kinds of friendships suited to those levels—and their further development. The curious disparity between Aristotle's acknowledgement of the preponderance of incontinence and continence, together with his lack of interest in helping those people become better, can only be explained, as before, by the specific group for whom the *Nicomachean Ethics* was written.

Notice that incontinence and continence are not natural developmental levels between habituated virtue and *phronetic* virtue; Aristotle's is not a Kohlbergian stage theory where all stages need to be traversed in the same order. Incontinence and continence are rather aberrations or second-best tacks for those who for some reason take a wrong turn in the developmental trajectory towards *phronetic* virtue, perhaps because, while enjoying a decent upbringing, they are not exposed to quite good enough moral exemplars or quite systematic enough habituation (or they are born with unusually unruly passions) but still retain a vision of the right moral ends, ingrained in their moral identity. They, then, try to force themselves, unsuccessfully (the incontinent) or successfully (the continent), to comply with the right moral ends. Continence can be a relatively stable state; it is not destined to degenerate into vice, although every lapse may enfeeble the mind (cf. Stern-Gillet, 1995, p. 95); nor is it likely to mature into virtue, although it may do so in some cases. At all events, contra Kant, Aristotle clearly did not think that the best way to become virtuous was to fight temptations.

Retaining continence in the face of temptations, at least with 'limber elegance' rather than 'crude effort' (Steutel, 1999, p. 133), is a tricky ladder to climb, and Aristotle fails to tell us which intellectual virtue the continent draw upon in their delicate balancing acts. It is not *phronesis*, which is reserved for the adjudication of moral virtues, and it is hardly *deinotes* either, as that virtue has to do with means-end reasoning that can be amoral or immoral. The coherently continent need an intellectual virtue reserved for moral acts (but not virtuous because theirs are forced and not embellished by the characteristic pleasures of virtues). I have argued elsewhere that we may need to complement Aristotle's taxonomy of intellectual virtues with a specific virtue fit for that unique purpose, and I have called it 'integrity' (Kristjánsson, 2019). I have also argued that since Aristotle's conception of full virtue is an unhelpful idealisation (cf. Curzer, 2017), we should allow for the possibility that people with a mixture of continent and virtuous traits can enjoy a satisfactorily ('good-enough') flourishing life (Kristjánsson, 2020). In any case, continence seems to be a seriously undervalued trait of character, as long as we study the *Nicomachean Ethics* out of its proposed reading context, and that gives us considerable leverage to complement Aristotle's discussion with insights—especially, in the present context, insights about friendships—that do not breach the general drift of his account—be those insights, as Pangle puts it, that Aristotle saw no reason to 'broadcast to his noble-minded readers' (2003, p. 150).

Before setting out my case for the moral value of Aristotelian utility friendships for the weak-kneed and those fighting temptations, a couple of new but instructive conceptual distinctions are in order. Some Aristotelian goods, such as health and friendship, are at the same time instrumentally and non-instrumentally valuable *vis-à-vis* the good life. Aristotle's focus is, as we see later, on the non-instrumental value of (solely) one type of friendship, namely character friendship, for *eudaimonia*, and this is often couched in terms of the intrinsic value of that kind of friendship versus the mere extrinsic and instrumental value of others. However, I believe there is good reason to distinguish between intrinsic and non-instrumental value and also between extrinsic and instrumental value. An illustrative example can be drawn from an unlikely source, namely Mill's type of utilitarianism, according to which some 'higher' goods (for instance desert and freedom) are non-instrumentally related to the greatest good of happiness. They are contingents *parts of* happiness rather than just *instrumentally conducive to* it. However, since in Mill's simple view happiness is the only intrinsic good, even those non-instrumental parts are extrinsic to it and may, in dire dilemmatic circumstances, have to be sacrificed for the greater good, albeit at considerable pain to the agent. We can call those non-instrumental but extrinsically valuable goods 'painfully expendable', in contrast to mere instrumental 'lower' goods—say bars of chocolate—that are non-painfully expendable when competing with more essential goods. We can further call the latter non-painfully expendable goods 'fungible': we may easily substitute them with something else. So if a good is purely instrumental, it is *ex hypothesi* fungible, but if a good is non-instrumentally related to the intrinsic good, it may be only painfully expendable even when extrinsic to that good.

Aristotle's theory of the nature of *eudaimonia* is obviously much more complex than Mill's account of happiness, but I would argue that some of the same conceptual distinctions would be equally at home there—although those are not made by Aristotle himself. *Eudaimonia* has many intrinsic and non-replaceable goods attached to it: say, love of character friends. It also has many instrumental goods that are conducive to it but which are pretty painlessly replaceable (i.e. fungible); I would, for instance, not mind replacing all the chicken I eat for my nourishment with fish. However, some goods are part of who I am now and would only be painfully replaceable (i.e. not fungible). For example, I can imagine myself giving up my love of Liverpool football club; being a Liverpool fan is not an intrinsic part of who I am, or who I would potentially be as a fully flourishing agent. However, being a Liverpool fan is more than instrumentally related to my current self-identity (*qua* self-concept); it is part of *who I am here and now*, albeit an extrinsic one, and giving up on it, even for some good reason, would not be easy at all.

The fundamental point made here is that it is in the interest of conceptual clarity not to understand 'non-instrumental' as synonymous with 'intrinsic' and 'instrumental' as synonymous with 'extrinsic', and that there is also a helpful distinction to be made between painfully 'expendable/replaceable' goods, on the one hand, and 'fungible' goods on the other.

6.3 Levels of Friendships Beneficial for Flourishing, Including Friendships for Utility

As noted in Section 1.1, there is one more *philia*-type virtue in Aristotle's *Nicomachean Ethics* that lies outside of the tripartite typology elaborated upon in the sections on friendship. This is the social-glue virtue of friendliness in casual social encounters (1985, pp. 107–9 [1126b11–1127a12]; cf. Kristjánsson, 2007, chap. 10). Although this 'virtue' fits the architectonic of an Aristotelian quantitative mean, it is somewhat remarkable that it makes the grade as a virtue, because it fails to satisfy the standard Aristotelian condition of a moral virtue of being underwritten by a discrete emotional component (as a golden mean of feeling). To exercise this 'virtue', say, towards the janitor who opens the doors of the office building every morning, a friendly smile and a nod suffice—without any emotion-imbued 'reciprocated goodwill'; hence it does not qualify as a virtue of friendship. Friendliness thus appears as something of an anomaly in the *Nicomachean Ethics* (whereas one might possibly have expected it to be mentioned as a valuable civic trait of concord, camaraderie or fellowship in the *Politics*). Its anomalous standing notwithstanding, friendliness does serve as a helpful reference point for an attempt to make sense of a more subtle account of levels of *philia*-type virtues than Aristotle accomplished himself, and I therefore include it in my below classification of friendship-or-friendship-related character traits that have benefits for human flourishing (although Aristotle makes no suggestion himself that it is related in any way to utility friendships).

A cursory reading of Aristotle's many but scattered references to utility friendships creates the initial impression of a relationship characterised by 'mean-spiritedness, manipulativeness, and pettifoggery' (Stern-Gillet, 1995, p. 65). However, a more careful reading identifies *potential* layers of complexity in utility friendship and *potential* qualitative differences between them. Thus, Aristotle says that 'one type of friendship of utility would seem to depend on character, and the other on rules', with the latter being confined to 'mercenary'-type associations whereas the former is 'more generous' (1985, pp. 233–4 [1162b23–27]). That former types presumably include the relationships that Aristotle notes often form between 'fellow-voyagers and fellow-soldiers' (1985, p. 224 [1159b27–8]). Konstan interprets this as a clear distinction between 'two sorts of utilitarian *philia*' (1997, p. 78; cf. Yuanguo, 2007, p. 300, on 'legal' versus 'moral' Aristotelian utility friendships). While that is quite a bold exegetical claim, which I would hesitate to endorse, I propose below to *reconstruct* the Aristotelian notion of friendships for utility to tease out the notion of two different utility levels; one instrumental and the other non-instrumental (while both are extrinsically, rather than intrinsically, valuable).

More specifically, what I aim to do below is offer an account of five levels of friendships beneficial for human wellbeing as *eudaimonia*. I use the slightly ambiguous term 'beneficial for' here because I include in this classification, for the sake of comparisons and contrasts, one level beneath utility friendships, as Aristotle defines them, and two levels above them, namely levels of (complete) character friendships, explaining how those are beneficial for wellbeing in ways that go beyond the lower levels. In order not to open up a can of worms, I leave friendships for pleasure out of reckoning here. Those are problematic both because they include the category of erotic friendships, which have a well-known tendency to complicate non-erotic ones in various ways, and because the type of pleasures referred to in 'friendship for pleasure' will have to be distinguished clearly from the characteristic pleasures that supervene upon (all) virtuous activities. In Table 6.1, I summarise the characteristics of the five posited levels. Each of them is also delineated in more detail in the text below.

Notice that 'level' is not meant to denote 'developmental stage' here. Just like continence is not a developmental stage in a trajectory towards virtue, but rather a level that well brought-up people can bypass (see above), so virtuous people do not typically 'move up' from Levels 0–2 to Levels 3 and 4, although they would be

Table 6.1 Levels of Aristotelian friendships, beneficial for human flourishing

	L0: Friendliness	L1: Lower level of utility friendship	L2: Higher level of utility friendship	L3: Imperfect (developing) character friendship	L4: Perfect character friendship
Acquaintance- ship (A) or friendship (F)	A	F	F	F	F
Character friendship (C) or not (N)	N	N	N	C	C
Perfect (P) or non-perfect friendship (N)	N	N	N	N	P
Only instrumentally valuable (I) or not (N)	I	I	N	N	N
Extrinsically (E) or intrinsically valuable (I)	E	E	E	I	I
Fungible (F) or non-fungible (N)	F	F	N	N	N
Morally valuable (M) or not (N)	N	N	M	M	M

expected to move from Level 3 to Level 4 as their *phronesis* progresses. However, the difference from the general developmental story is that whereas the best educated virtuous people will, mostly or fully, eschew the levels of incontinence and continence, Aristotle assumes that even fully fledged *phronomoi* will still have the need for utility friendships with various people although they have got a supply of good character friends to rely on.

Level 0. I prefer to refer to the first level as Level 0 as it involves the potted or at least unusual 'virtue' of friendliness, as previously described, rather than genuine friendship. We could call the relationship involved 'acquaintanceship'. X, who works in a big company, has janitor Y open the door for her every day, which is clearly conducive to X's wellbeing. X exchanges niceties with Y every morning and kind of likes Y, but Y's value to X is purely instrumental and Y, while useful, is fungible. X would simply transfer her friendly manner to the next agreeable janitor who came along. As Telfer notes, 'being friends with' is not the same as 'being a friend of' (1970–1971, p. 223).

Level 1. This is what could be conceptualised as the lower level of friendship for utility. X and Y are colleagues in a company and work on projects together. They have developed reciprocated goodwill towards each other and quite like one another's company. They enjoy a beneficial working relationship, which also includes the occasional social interactions outside of work, for example in the pub. However, with the practical 'cause of their being friends removed', the friendship would be 'dissolved too', on the assumption that the friendship aims merely at a practical end (Aristotle, 1985, pp. 211–12 [1156a19–23]). This friendship, which is simply instrumental and extrinsically valuable, is what Aristotle calls 'mercenary' and what Grunebaum (2005) dubs as 'fair-weather friendship' and Vernon as friendship of 'convenience' (2010, p. 6); I have also heard it being referred to as 'go-to friendship'. What leaps to the fore here is that the reciprocated goodwill, while potentially wide-ranging, does not penetrate deep enough into X's and Y's psyches for it to be deemed morally valuable (in the earlier explained post-Aristotelian sense). It does not steer away from vice or incontinence, although the Level 1 utility friend might give me some virtue-relevant advice, such as not to throw my trash on the ground, in much the same way as a non-friend could. To be sure, X would miss Y if she suddenly changed her job, but without severe pain, and Y would be fairly soon forgotten if an equally competent and agreeable workmate came along; hence (the friendship with) Y must count as fungible.

Level 2. A straight, if by no means an uninterrupted, road leads from the first level of friendship for utility to the presumed second level (cf. Alpern, 1983). While Aristotle is nowhere explicit about this distinction, as I have repeatedly stressed, and some might claim it is out of its exegetical depth, I refer back to the suggestion that a higher level of utility friendships can be carved out of the material yielded to us by Aristotle's text. X and Y are workmates, as before, but in this scenario their friendship has been elevated to the level of sharing of 'distresses and pleasures' (Aristotle, 1985, p. 246 [1166a26–7]). X shares with Y some of the troubles she has with her spouse and relatives and receives helpful advice. Y also persuades X not to cut corners at work, which X is tempted to do. Neither X nor Y have been habituated into virtue and, hence, they cannot count as character friends in the 'complete friendship' sense, let alone as 'perfect' friends of that sort. However, they help each other stay on the straight and narrow. Gradually, they become as close as the best of fellow voyagers, and their friendship is anything but mercenary. Rather, it is a utility friendship that 'depends on character' (1985, p. 233 [1162b24]), as Aristotle puts it, and mutual 'trust' (1985, p. 234 [1162b31]), although (good) 'character' is here *ex hypothesi* used in a broader sense than the standard Aristotelian one of a repertoire of virtuous traits, probably referring more to the fact that an ethically relevant *choice* is being made rather than to a virtue being exhibited or enhanced. It could be objected that I have smuggled into my description above interactions that go beyond the examples that Aristotle himself takes of utility friendships (which tend to be about the exchange of goods and favours), in order to put an ethical spin on them, but the truth is that it is almost impossible to envisage close workplace interactions between utility friends that pertain to non-moral issues only. Close workplace interactions tend to be permeated with moral concerns.

Because only character friends are intrinsically valuable and irreplaceable as parts of one's flourishing, Y's value to X cannot count as intrinsic. However, Y is not only instrumentally valuable to X in an out-of-sight-out-of-mind sort of way; the friendship with Y is constitutive of X's psycho-moral self-identity, as it is here and now, and a loss of that friendship (say, if Y suddenly passed away) would be accompanied by considerable pain and grief, although X might find a suitable replacement for Y in due course. X's friendship with Y is thus both non-instrumental and non-fungible; for, as Konstan (1997, p. 72) puts it, their 'affection is not reducible to the mutual appreciation of one another's serviceability'. 'Eudaimonic friendship', a term invoked by Walker, Curren and Jones (2016, p. 290), might helpfully describe the relationship in question: a term that straddles the distinction between character friendships and Level 2 utility friendships—as would be seconded by those who believe that *eudaimonia* can actually be achieved without perfect virtue (see e.g. Kristjánsson, 2020). Moreover, having Y as a friend is clearly *morally valuable* to X in the sense given to that locution in the present chapter. It helps prevent X lapsing into incontinence or vice, by reminding her of what she stands for and what her principles are. The friendship might even, little by little, shade subtly into one of character friendships (Level 3), at least if we are slightly more optimistic than Aristotle himself was about the possibility of people unhabituated into virtue early on in life seeing the light at a later stage (Kristjánsson, 2015, chap. 5).

Yet I would flatly reject the claim that Level 2 friendships are simply budding Level 3 friendships or Level 3 friendships in disguise. It is much too developmentally 'optimistic' to think that all morally relevant Level 2 interactions between utility friends will, if all goes well, progress towards a mutual interest in developing each other's virtue. Some people are firmly stuck, their whole lives, at the levels of continence or incontinence. Indeed, that is where Aristotle thought most people are at (1985, p. 190 [1150a15]). In some cases, being stuck at those levels is not so much a moral developmental issue as a practical, institutional one. For example, although it is heart-warming to read Karches's (2019) Aristotelian musings about how a physician and patient ought to help one another develop the virtue of temperance, which would for instance motivate the patient to quit smoking, Karches himself acknowledges that such an idealisation is unrealistic in the modern world of health care. I do not necessarily see that as a problem of professional ethics, as long as the interaction can be characterised as a Level-2 one—and this does not mean that the physician and patient cannot learn to practise true virtue, as distinct from mere continence, with close friends in other areas of their lives.

In any case, I hope to have shown that Level 2 utility friendships can meet the desiderata of a relationship that is 'morally valuable' in a sense that was not terminologically available to Aristotle but does matter significantly for any contemporary account of the moral value of friendships. It goes without saying that the overall credibility of the argument proposed in this chapter hinges to a large extent on the plausibility of Level 2 types of utility friendships, as described here, because Level 2 drives an exegetical and substantive wedge between the standardly acknowledged Aristotelian levels. Notice finally, as an aside, that although I used an example of two non-*phronimoi* friends at Level 2, there is nothing standing in the way of two *phronimoi* pursuing Level 2 utility friendships with another—simply because that is all their current interactions require—although they have other *phronimoi* as character friends at higher levels. Hence, the mere presence of *phronetic* virtue in an individual does not in itself suffice to distinguish higher level friendships from Level 2 ones.

Level 3. Here we re-enter more mainstream Aristotelian territory. Level 3 marks the emergence of 'complete' (namely, character) friendships. Those can only develop between people habituated into virtue: who are cultivating or have cultivated a virtuous self-identity. X and Y are workmates and soulmates who are both concerned about growing as persons of good character and who bolster each other's efforts in that area by mutual contributions to the growth of *phronesis* (which turns merely habituated virtue into perfect *phronetic* virtue). While not yet having reached Level 4 of perfect virtue, 'each moulds the other in what they approve of', and this effect 'increases the more often they meet' (Aristotle, 1985, p. 266 [1172a11–14]). Here—to return once again to Aristotle's famous another-self thesis—X has become 'related to his friend as he is to himself, since the friend is another himself' (1985, p. 246 [1166a30–3]). This is why, in character friendships, the friend is not only non-fungible but irreplaceable in the sense that because of Y's unique blend of character and individual traits, no one can replace the part that Y plays in X's character make-up. This then moves the nature of the friendship up from the extrinsic to the intrinsic level. It is precisely at this point that Aristotle's theory becomes more 'complex' than Mill's, as I put it earlier. While Levels 0–1 might seem to correspond to Mill's lower goods and Level 2 to his higher goods, there is no space for other goods at Mill's level of the intrinsically (as distinct from essentially) valuable than happiness itself. For Aristotle, however, character friendship belongs to a category of various intrinsically valuable goods, constitutive of *eudaimonia*.

It is worth mentioning here in passing that not everyone agrees that even true character friends are intrinsically valuable in Aristotle's axiological system. Hitz (2011), who subscribes to a hard intellectualist interpretation of *eudaimonia*, based on a literal reading of Book 10 of the *Nicomachean Ethics* according to which only contemplation has intrinsic value for the good life, argues that character friendships belong to a category of goods that she names 'integrated goods'. Those involve a mixture of intrinsic and extrinsic value, but where the former (here resting on engagement with friends being constitutive of the good person's virtuous practical activities) is still not their key feature and diminishes with greater contemplative excellence. On Hitz's axiological interpretation of Aristotle's friendship theory, it may seem even easier to downplay the difference between Level 2 and Level 3 than I have made it out to be: namely, to see higher-level utility friends as functioning in much the same way as character friends, since both would presumably fit into the same category of 'integrated goods'. However, I do worry that Hitz's interpretation throws the baby out with the bathwater. Inclusivist or intellectualist readings of *eudaimonia* aside, rejecting the pure intrinsic value of character friends and relegating them to the group of 'the replaceable', albeit painfully so, simply goes against the grain of the whole tenor of Aristotle's idealised discussion of character friendships both in the *Nicomachean* and *Eudemian Ethics*. The final thing to note about Level 3 is that this is the level where *phronesis* begins to kick in. Understanding how people progress to Level 3, either directly from 'habituated virtue' or (possibly in some cases) via the developmental level of continence, will thus hold the key to solving the aforementioned 'paradox of moral education'.

Level 4. This is the final level of complete friendship which is also 'perfect' and on which a lot of Aristotle's idealised description of fully internally and externally unified character friendships is focused. X and Y and are soulmates and *phronimoi*. While X needs no encouragement from Y not to go astray (as X has no temptations in that direction) and X's virtuous make-up is already fully mature, what X gains from the relationship is to have her evaluative outlook affirmed 'unreservedly and unconditionally' (Brewer, 2005, p. 730), as explained in Chapter 5. Like Cicero—drawing heavily on Aristotle as always—put it: 'The reward of friendship is friendship itself' (2018, p. 63).

I have now tried to account satisfactorily for all the variances between the levels of friendships, beneficial to wellbeing, in Table 6.1. I consider it a disparagement of both ancient and contemporary accounts of friendship that they do not acknowledge the moral value of what I have dubbed Level 2 utility friendships. I have explained already what the reason for that may be in the case of Aristotle-based accounts. As alluded to in the above comparisons with Mill, Aristotle has a complex and nuanced theory of utility or usefulness. There seems to be a tendency among scholars to read Aristotle as a Kantian, prioritising intrinsic goods over utility (as critiqued in O'Connor, 1990). However, there are many kinds of utility in Aristotle and although they differ in terms of instrumental versus non-instrumental and intrinsic versus extrinsic value, all are beneficial for the agent's own *eudaimonia*. The utility of friendliness and friendship at Levels 0 and 1 may refer solely to the agent's basic necessities and bodily goods. At Level 2, however, utility begins to benefit the goods of the agent's soul: her moral development. That level still remains within the confines of what modern philosophy would define as 'enlightened self-interest'. Things get more complicated at Levels 3 and 4 because of Aristotle's theory of the character friend as 'another self'—an *alter ego*—obliterating any simple distinction between the self and the other. Nevertheless, although we here move into the realm of the intrinsically valuable and of intermingled selves, the concept of usefulness does not become redundant. Character friendship is useful because it is useful for the friends to become better people. Character friendship 'includes' utility (1985, p. 220 [1158b5]). Indeed, a character friend is, other things equal, the most 'useful' friend of all. According to Aristotle, the best form of self-love is the love we have for the best part of ourselves, though not to the detriment of the 'lower' parts of us. So too the useful. The highest form of usefulness serves the 'highest' part of us (our intellectual and moral virtues), but not to the detriment of the lower, necessary, parts. Aristotle's discussion benefits here from being unpolluted by latter-day debates about narrow and exclusively instrumentalist forms of utilitarianism (and also by notions of a sharp line between selfishness and altruism, see Salkever, 2008, p. 66). He is neither shy of the notion of the useful nor sees it as antithetical to intrinsic value.

It is in order to end this section with a comparison to the only article located that has explicitly proposed to defend the moral value of utility friendships. James Grunebaum (2005) very much follows the same strategy as I have, of crowbarring morally valuable utility friendships into Aristotle's system through a more modern understanding of 'moral' (rather than just sweeping the Aristotelian stables), by positing a distinction between two sorts of utility friendships, where the second one passes muster in this respect. However, he does this without invoking the extrinsic–intrinsic or instrumental–non-instrumental distinctions, or the one between friendships that are simply replaceable versus fully fungible. Whilst his article offers suggestive and astute forays into the subject, it fails in my view to make adequate use of available Aristotelian resources and instead invokes an under-motivated distinction.

Grunebaum begins helpfully by distinguishing relationships of mere friendliness from what he calls fair-weather friendships and which I attributed to Level 1. He also points out correctly that Aristotle's own 'unkind descriptions' of all utility friendships seem to be geared towards only the mercenary, exploitative and occasional kind (2005, p. 209). The originality of Grunebaum's manoeuvre lies in distinguishing between utility friendships involving 'restricted and unrestricted goodwill' and in justifying the latter morally (2005, pp. 210ff). What I called Level 2 utility friendships involve, on Grunebaum's characterisation, friends who 'guard and preserve each other's prosperity' in unrestricted ways and operate with a long-term perspective, much like character friends do (although the psycho-moral 'objects' being guarded and preserved are slightly different). He also notes, convincingly, that unrestricted utility friends may conceivably have 'an even higher degree of morality than virtue friends' (2005, p. 211), given a modern conception of morality, because what I called budding Level 3 character friendships, especially among young and merely habituated virtue learners, may actually be less morally demanding than the continence-guarded, and more Kantian-like, moral commitments mutually reinforced at Level 2.

Grunebaum makes an additional observation about the possibility of entertaining mutually beneficial friendship relations with a much greater number of utility friends than character friends. It must be admitted, however, that Aristotle himself is not consistent on this point. On the one hand, he says that utility friendships enable us to 'please many people': on the other hand, he advises us that friends for utility should be limited 'since it is hard to return many people's services' (1985, p. 218, [1158a17–18]; cf. p. 261 [1170b25–7]). All in all, Grunebaum defines unrestricted utility friendships as being motivated by goodwill 'aimed at a friend's complete overall well-being' (just as in character friendships), whereas restricted wellbeing is aimed at only 'a portion of well-being' (2005, p. 208).

Grunebaum is clearly onto something here, but I consider the terms 'restricted' and 'unrestricted' too imprecise and bloated to capture what is at stake in Level 1 versus Level 2 utility friendships. First of all, even Level 1 utility friendships may well be 'unrestricted' in the sense that X harbours *general goodwill* towards all aspects of Y's life. X would feel sad, for example, if Y lost his wife or was undeservedly sacked from her job. The fact that X would recover gradually even if the friendship with Y were lost does not mean that the *goodwill* itself is somehow necessarily restricted while the friendship lasts—although other aspects of the friendship could be said to be restricted (see my earlier characterisation of Level 1).

On the other hand, on another plausible understanding of 'unrestricted', the friendship between X and Y is also restricted at Level 2 in that it does not extend to the mutual appreciation, and polishing, of moral character *qua* virtues (cf. Salkever, 2008, on how all utility friendships are directed at 'partial aspects' of the friend's life, p. 64). Grunebaum goes too far when he contends that 'the unrestricted goodwill of [some] utility friendships enables friends to complete their individual characters by acting *virtuously* to each other' (2005, p. 213; my italics). Of course, a virtuous person will act virtuously towards anyone, friend or non-friend, and in that sense 'complete' her own character. However, since that is trivially true given the definition of a virtuous person, Grunebaum must mean that in some utility friendships friends act virtuously towards one another in order to help the friend cultivate or complete her character. This conflates an important and valid distinction between Level 2 (which still counts as 'incomplete' friendship) and Level 3, not to mention Level 4.

So while Grunebaum is quite right in that 'more value resides in utility friendships than Aristotle concedes' (2005, p. 213), he fails to avail himself of a more nuanced conceptual repertoire than simply a distinction between 'restricted' and 'unrestricted' goodwill. This complaint signifies more than a quibble about terminology. I have argued in this section that making use of distinctions between instrumental versus extrinsic, non-instrumental versus intrinsic, and fungible versus (painfully) replaceable carries more hope for making sense of the distinction between two qualitatively different levels of utility friendships in ways that are relevant to contemporary 'moral' concerns and remain at least minimally faithful to an Aristotelian system of ethical development.

6.4 A Brief Online Example

As noted at the outset, I realised that something was not quite right about the contemporary discourse about Aristotle-inspired views of types of friendships when I delved into the growing literatures on online friendships (or on lack thereof). It is therefore fitting to append to the theoretical discussion an illustrative example, derived from cyberspace, which I believe bolsters my above case about the nature of Level 2 utility friendships and their moral value. I hope I may be forgiven for relying here on a personal example that is close to my heart. There is nothing particularly unique about this example by virtue of it being based on my anecdotal experiences: I simply chose it because of my familiarity with it.

In August 2018, I suddenly developed overnight, and without any prior warning, a condition called sudden sensorineural hearing loss ('sshl'). I recounted some of the details of this gruelling episode in the Preface. As with many sshl sufferers, an aggressive steroid treatment did not bring my hearing back, and I was also left with some disabling side-issues. This is a little-known and badly understood condition, not only among the general public but also in the medical community where it is normally termed 'idiopathic' (i.e. without a known cause), although a virus infection of the inner ear is probably most often the culprit, as was hypothesised to be in my case. To cut a long story short about this disorder, sufferers often feel misunderstood, badly treated by the health system and in general more disenfranchised than many other patient groups.

Early on, I was lucky enough to be able to find and be admitted to two closed Facebook support groups for sshl sufferers. Those groups gave me a lifeline. As the sufferers often know more about the nature and repercussions of this syndrome than health-care professionals, those support groups provided me with invaluable information, not available to me elsewhere, and personal support. I quickly found out that these groups are about much more than just a simple exchange of information and encouragement, and in many cases, members make a serious effort to get insights into each other's lives and circumstances (even moving from Facebook to personal messages) in order to be able to 'put a face to' and 'individualise' the support provided. As I argue below, a lot of this support was of the *moral* kind. Although I have now turned into more of a giver than a receiver in these groups, paying back some of the care and attention that I was given at the outset, I still keep in Facebook contact with some of the people who encouraged me most at the beginning and consider them as my friends. I cannot say that I would have chosen to get to know them if the choice had been mine before the illness, but at the moment they form part of my self-identity as an sshl sufferer, and even if I were miraculously cured overnight, I think I would continue to participate in the support groups, since being disassociated from what I would call the Level 2 utility friends I have met there would cause me considerable pain. Being associated with them is not an intrinsic part of my *eudaimonia*, but it does not only have instrumental value either.

So what sort of friends are they? I would hesitate to call them 'character friends' for at least three reasons. One is that they represent just a random sample of the whole population who happen to be hit by this illness, and as we know from Aristotle, were few people actually reach the level of character friends. The second reason is that virtue considerations are rarely referred to in the advice and support given. Words such as 'compassion', 'gratitude', even 'courage', seldom appear. Even when, in a spontaneous act of what we could call 'generosity', a rich sufferer decided to donate a hearing aid that was insufficient to him to an uninsured US patient, the exchange between them remained at the level of a mutual benefit discourse. I could not spot a sense of virtuous 'flow' in the benefactor, nor did the beneficiary utilise virtue terms in response. The most common terms used in these groups are for amoral performance skills such as persistence, resilience and grit. The most frequent phrase encountered is something like: 'This is tough, but please hang in there and do not give up; things will get better'. Notably this advice is not only meant to avert psychological surrender but a moral one too. Sufferers, especially those left with unbearable tinnitus and vertigo, have been known to commit suicide, and suicide is normally considered an act of moral despondency, not only a psychological one. Thirdly, and perhaps most obviously, the scope of 'shared activities' in these online support groups is much more limited than what one would normally see among character friends, and the relevant 'activities' are typically pursued with the group as a whole rather than with a distinct individual (although in some cases, as I mentioned, participants prefer to exchange private Facebook messages away from the group web).

Notice that some support groups may aim higher than this by explicitly encouraging virtue development in their members and hence pave the way for true character friendships. In traditional non-online contexts there are support groups that are known to do this, most famously Alcoholics Anonymous. However, my point is simply that even in groups that do not have such a high-minded aim, true moral support may be provided—and by 'moral support' here I do not only mean support of the 'morale' of the sufferer but support that strengthens the sufferer morally.

Here is a recent testimonial lifted from one of the support groups to which I belong:

> One year ago today, I woke up violently ill with vertigo and no hearing in my right ear. Since then, the vertigo has mostly subsided, but I still have no hearing in my right ear. This past year was a rollercoaster and probably the hardest year of my life. I sincerely want to thank each one of you for helping me through this crazy ordeal. When things got bad, you all were always there to listen to me vent, answer my questions, let me cry, and even made me laugh. I don't know what I would have done without you! This group is amazing! Thank you all and if there is ever anything I can do to help you through this, please do not hesitate to ask.

In light of this testimonial and others, I find it difficult to identify with Fröding and Peterson's claim that although social network sites 'can sometimes be of mutual advantage to their users', they lead to false expectations about friendships in ways that are morally objectionable and even fail to qualify as examples of Aristotle's 'lesser friendships' (2012, p. 206). Of course, social network sites *may* have this effect, but why *necessarily* so? I am not the first person to notice how online support groups, which tend to lurk at the outskirts of the web and only be accessible through invitation, help people deal with traumatic experiences (see e.g. Vallor, 2010; Vernon, 2010, p. 110). However, I believe mine is the first attempt to illustrate how the friendship enacted in Facebook support groups exemplifies neatly the sort of utility friendship that I have associated with Level 2 above: extrinsically but non-instrumentally valuable from a moral point of view.

6.5 Concluding Remarks

There is no doubt that Aristotle was right that many, perhaps most, utility friendships are of the mercenary kind, going for 'the quick wins and low hanging fruit' (Vernon, 2010, p. 233, citing Emerson). However, in this chapter, I have argued for a higher form of utility friendship that binds up some of the psycho-moral lacerations inflicted upon us by life's exigencies. I have argued how the benefits of those (Level 2) utility friendships can count as *moral*, in that they steer us away from moral despondency, incontinence and even vice. I have given an example from a domain (cyberspace) at which theorists often look askance precisely because of its potentially morally debilitating effects.

I would like to add a brief consideration here as an afterthought, but one that would be worthy of further exploration, even a book-length study of its own. There exists a proverbial debate about the virtue of political or civic friendship that Aristotle claims is based on 'concord' (*homonoia*), keeping city states together (1985, p. 208 [1155a23–8]; pp. 249–50 [1167a22–1167b15]) and urgently needed there in addition to procedural justice. Concord—and by implication the civic friendship that it motivates—is 'concerned with advantage and with what affects life' (1985, p. 250 [1167b2–4]), Aristotle says, which seems to place civic friendship in the category of utility friendships. Even more explicitly, in the *Eudemian Ethics*, Aristotle maintains that civic friendship 'is constituted in the fullest degree on the principle of utility' (1935, p. 415 [1242a5–8]; cf. p. 421 [1242b20–3]), built 'on a footing of equality', and that it is 'more necessary' than character friendship, although the latter is 'nobler' (1935, p. 427 [1243a32–6]). This view of civic friendship as a form of utility friendship grounds, for example, Irrera's (2005) interpretation in her rich and detailed study. Fowers (2019, p. 81) agrees—because civic friendships 'inevitably include people with a wide range of character' and must, therefore, not be conflated with character friendships.

At the same time, the aim of political associations and science is to attend to 'the character of citizens, to make them good people who do fine actions' (Aristotle, 1985, p. 23 [1099b29–32]), which seems to elevate civic friendships to at least Level-3 character friendships. Indeed, those remarks, and various others in Aristotle's *Politics*, which indicate that virtuous people are distressed when their fellow-citizens lack virtue, have swayed Curren towards the strong interpretation that civic friendship 'is based in virtue and not merely utility' (2000, p. 133). Irrera acknowledges these remarks but refuses to let go of her utility-friendship interpretation, although she concedes that it is a 'peculiar' or *sui generis* kind of utility friendship (2005, pp. 567, 572).

There are powerful but competing considerations here dragging Aristotelian scholars in opposite directions. On the one hand, the vast number of potential political friends and the impossibility of spending intimate time together with all of them in mutual activities, or sharing joys and sorrows, points in the direction of civic friendship as standard utility friendship. Moreover, Cicero's scepticism (2018; discussed by Lynch, 2005, chap. 3) about civic friendships, because of politicians' penchant for power games and cronyisms, offers general warning signals about the characterological foundations of political life. On the other hand, the nature of ideal political associations in a well-ordered state requires citizens to be deeply concerned with each other's goodness and its development—a key feature of character friendships. Nehamas's quick rejection of the very idea of civic friendships (2016, pp. 52–6)—in conjunction with his dismissal of Aristotelian character friendships—have made me reconsider Curren's strong interpretation, which I previously dismissed. Since I take Nehamas to be wrong about character friendships, he might be wrong about the civic ones also.

Once again, I do not think there is any unproblematic reinterpretation of Aristotle's texts that makes this difficulty vanish. However, if we reconstruct Aristotle's utility friendship as consisting of two levels, Levels 1 and 2, as I did above, we can accommodate the moral intentions and aspirations inherent in true civic friendships at Level 2, without succumbing to the temptations of extending the scope of character friendship (which after all is a very exclusive category for Aristotle), in order to make sense of fellow citizens caring deeply about, and contributing to, each other's moral goodness (cf. also an interesting distinction between 'instrumental friendships' and 'democratic friendships' in Yeste et al., 2020, and thought-provoking, if essentially un-Aristotelian, suggestions about how the democratic area needs to be depoliticised but friendship-resurrected, in Talisse, 2019). The reconstruction of utility friendships, suggested above, would help accommodate Aristotle's educational remarks about civic friendship— namely, about the promotion of such friendships as a task of political science and political leadership—and, in a way, reinforce the developmental thread running through the whole discussion of friendship by extending it beyond character friendship to the utility kind also.

There are a couple of reasons why I confine the discussion of civic friendships here to a few afterthought paragraphs in a chapter about utility friendships. One is that, as already intimated, the topic is too large to cover in the present work because it would require engagement with Aristotle's extensive writings on political constitutions and associations, as well as with his specification of civic (or 'political') virtue, which is considerably more permissive than his definition of moral (or 'ethical') virtue. The second reason is that this topic would no doubt induce me to go head-to-head with a pervasive conspiracy theory about the recent surge of interest in character and character education as being motivated by a neo-liberal agenda, only concerned with fixing individual character faults while shying away from necessary social change. In a recent book, for example, Jerome and Kisby (2019) build a whole skyscraper of accusations, directed at the neo-Aristotelian character research centre where I work, upon a pinprick of evidence about our implicit neo-liberal agenda.

No doubt they will see the present book as one more indication of the focus on the individual rather than the ethos.

Anyone who is vaguely familiar with Aristotelian moral and political theorising will know, however, that Aristotle was as far from hustling a neo-liberal, individualist agenda as any theorist can be; and his view of flourishing—of which the virtues, including friendship, are meant to be constituents—was socio-political all the way down (Kristjánsson, 2020; Peterson, 2020). In any case, I am afraid that a thorough treatment of civic friendship would necessitate an extensive engagement with these conspiracy theories (as well as the current social-justice discourse in education which is a complete mess, see Arthur, Kristjánsson & Vogler, 2021) but, at the moment, I consider my resources better invested elsewhere.

That said, I do not exclude the possibility of writing about civic friendships in the future because the political dimension of friendships opens up a whole new avenue of issues (cf. Digeser, 2016; Smith, 2019; Ludwig, 2020) that cry out for a neo-Aristotelian overhaul. Take, for example, the question how, and then in what sense, states or other political bodies can be considered as 'friends'—witness the (in)famous 'special relationship' between the UK and the USA. Or take Curren's powerful argument that civic friendship, based merely in utility, could not unify a state in the way that Aristotle himself envisions (2000, p. 133)—meaning that whatever Aristotle explicitly said about civic friendships, they require an element of true character friendships to fulfil the function that Aristotle assigns to them. I would probably want to argue that Level 2 utility friendships suffice, but that requires a more detailed look at the concept of 'concord' within states—including Western multicultural democracies (cf. Cheng, 2019).

To conclude, I have argued in this chapter that utility friendships are (contra Millgram, 1987, p. 374) not just related to character friendships in the same way as toy ducks are related to real ducks. Rather, higher-level utility friendships partially blunt the force of a clear distinction between the benefits of utility and character friendship for ethical formation, although I would not want to go as far as Grunebaum in ascribing virtue cultivation to them. We humans are weak-kneed beings, and good utility friends are the morally unsung heroes of the friendship literature, harking back to Aristotle. Would that Aristotle himself had been more alert to that insight.

7

Online Character Friendships

The Example of Epalships

7.1 Introduction: Character Friendships and the Cyberworld

A lively debate has been playing out over the last decade or two about whether various forms of online friendships pass muster as instantiations of character friendships in the Aristotelian sense. As often in philosophy, there is a formidable anti-camp (see e.g. Cocking & Matthews, 2000; Vallor, 2012; Fröding & Peterson, 2012; McFall, 2012; Sharp 2012) but also a formidable pro-camp (see e.g. Elder, 2014; Kaliarnta, 2016; Bülow & Felix, 2016), with both offering palatable and initially persuasive arguments. It could be argued that this debate has reached something of a saturation point and that expending further intellectual energy on it would be redundant. While my sympathies happen to lie, roughly speaking, with the pro-camp—about which I speak more carefully later—my rehearsal of the general terms of the existing debate will be reduced to a stage-setting critical overview.

Much of the relevant debate used to be driven by examples of friendships forged on social media platforms such as Facebook (see e.g. Deresiewicz, 2009; Elder, 2018; Jeske, 2019). The rapid developments and fiendish intricacies of those platforms, especially in light of their commercial nature and potential abuse, muddy the intellectual waters considerably when delving into a theoretical or conceptual issue, such as the one at stake in the Aristotelian friendship debate. Moreover, the debate has later branched out to include other kinds of platforms such as massively multiplayer online role-playing games (MMORPGs, see e.g. Munn, 2012). My eventual aim is to refocus and extend the discourse even further by looking at sustained and deep email correspondence, or *epalship*, as a potential venue for the creation, development and maintaining of character friendships, and to do so by drawing an analogy with historically famous *penpalships*.

Most well-read people have heard about the unique bonds formed between penpals such as Harriet Taylor and John Stuart Mill, Johannes Brahms and Clara Schumann, and Voltaire and Catherine the Great. While I have yet to come across a paper explicitly arguing for those 'bonds' as ones of complete character friendship in the Aristotelian sense, it is difficult to shake the impression that the correspondence between those somewhat unlikely pairs of people comes as close as

Friendship for Virtue. Kristján Kristjánsson, Oxford University Press. © Kristján Kristjánsson 2022.
DOI: 10.1093/oso/9780192864260.003.0007

anything can get to exemplifying genuine and close friendship of the most mature kind. In Section 7.4, I look closely at the friendship between Voltaire and Catherine the Great and explain the way in which it satisfies some of the salient criteria for Aristotelian character friendships. I then suggest, by analogy, that an epalship (email-penpalship) between these two historic greats—had that been available to them at the time—would have offered at least an equally satisfactory outlet for character friendship.

A sceptic could claim that this argument by analogy constitutes at best a red herring and at worst a *non sequitur*, because it assumes that penpalships suffice as vehicles for character friendships, but that is something which representatives of the anti-camp mentioned above might flatly reject, with arguments similar to those mounted against modern-day online friendships. At the close of Section 7.4, I therefore argue that epalships allow for various technological extensions in the cyberworld of today that were not available to Voltaire and Catherine, for example, and that augmented with those extensions, there is even more reason for seeing epalships as potentially making the grade as true character friendships than traditional penpalships.

Prior to the eventual aim noted above, a preliminary and subsidiary aim of this chapter is to systematise in a clarificatory way, and to offer a critical assessment of, the main arguments for and against online friendships as character friendships (in Section 7.3): an aim preceded (in Section 7.2) by a brisk tour of the relevant conceptual and empirical background, harking—as always—back to Aristotle. I conclude by arguing, in Section 7.5, that despite being potentially categorisable as character friendships, mature epalships are vulnerable to the same problems and pitfalls as other examples of character friendships, and perhaps even more so. Despite that caveat, this chapter is meant to make a positive contribution to the pro-camp regarding the question of the overall nature of online friendships as potential character friendships.

7.2 Some Problematics of Aristotelian Friendships in Online Contexts

Some of the hues and cries about how the cyberworld is destroying friendships, which I briefly referred to in Section 6.1, are directed at any genuine forms of friendship as reciprocated goodwill—the idea being (and typically woven into a more general moral-declivity thesis about the cyberworld) that online friendships are replacing, corrupting or eroding the very constitution of friendships in the real world (Deresiewicz, 2009). The debate relating to this broader question, which would overstretch the limits of the present chapter, is subsequently about whether 'the web is a boon for friendship, or a place where it falls apart' (Vernon, 2010, p. 12). In contrast, the more nuanced writings see online friendships as threats not so much to friendship *per se* as to Aristotelian character friendships in particular, with more and more people now allegedly settling for the inferior forms (McFall, 2012)—meaning that online friendships, however pleasant or useful, may be damaging our 'ability to develop as fully virtuous members of society' (Sharp, 2012, p. 231).

The advice from the robust naturalist Aristotle would definitely be to go out and inspect the empirical evidence for these claims. The problem is, however, that despite the rapidly growing mountain of empirical literature on the cyberworld and virtue (see e.g. overviews in Harrison, 2021; Morgan, Fowers & Kristjánsson, 2017, as well as a broad philosophical discussion in Vallor, 2016), very little of it is geared towards online friendships in general, let alone Aristotelian online character friendships in particular (a concern raised e.g. by Kaliarnta, 2016). The latter lacuna is not unique to online friendships as putative character friendships. As we have seen at previous junctures in this book, there is simply very little empirical evidence available about Aristotle's three famous types of friendship, and how they do or do not play out in the real world (yet see Anderson & Fowers, 2020). We know that the frequency of self-reported friendships is on the rise among adults (Vernon, 2010, p. 118). However, we must take such findings with a pinch of salt, both because the self-reports might be inauthentic as a result of our notorious lack of self-transparency, and because the frequency of friendships does not say anything about their quality and does not add argumentative weight, either way, to the Aristotelian debate about the relevant types of friendship and their respective worth.

Given the current state of friendship research, I am not sure we need to accept Vallor's contention that 'what philosophical and ethical discourse exists trails well behind the available empirical data' (2012, p. 186). Firstly, the empirical data that would be relevant to the question of whether online friendships can constitute character friendships is simply not available. Secondly, even if such data existed or were gathered presently, it would in any case be accepted or rejected by scholars in the measure in which they accept or reject the conceptual taxonomy on which Aristotle's theory of friendship types is based. I would, therefore, argue that the lively debate about Aristotelian online friendships, to which I referred in the opening paragraph, has generally been carried out along sound methodological lines, although these have mostly been theoretical: by identifying features of Aristotle's friendship types and arguing, typically by dint of intuitive or anecdotal evidence, about how they do or do not materialise in online friendships. Conceptual analysis is, after all, what philosophers are best at; and it does help when such analysis is backed up by psychological insights (see e.g. Gulliford & Roberts, 2018), even if they are mostly confined to the 'armchair-psychology' kind.

Despite being in broad agreement with the manner in which the current discourse has been conducted, I have identified four contestable assumptions that tend to be taken for granted by most friends and foes of online friendships *qua* character friendships: (1) (Aristotelian) virtue ethics is far better equipped to account for the moral salience of any close friendships than ethical theories such as utilitarianism and deontology that demand impartiality. This is precisely why it matters so much for the defenders of online friendships to show that those can be brought within the rubric of Aristotle's highest level with respect to virtue (see e.g. Vallor, 2012, and Kaliarnta, 2016, who otherwise disagree on whether this is possible). (2) The lower forms of friendship, especially friendship for utility, do not 'merit the label "genuine friendship"' and thus do not 'qualify as morally valuable' (Fröding & Peterson, 2012, p. 201). (3) Only friendships between equals, and more specifically equals of 'perfect' virtue, count as true character friendships (McFall, 2012, pp. 222–3; Bülow & Felix, 2016, p. 24). (4) If we can demonstrate that (some) online friendships count as character friendships, we have demonstrated their true value as virtuous because such friendships are inherently stable and commendable from the perspective of wellbeing, as *eudaimonia*, and virtuous living (which is simply a reiteration of Aristotle's claim that character friendships are the only 'complete' type).

I consider those assumptions questionable either in themselves or as interpretations of Aristotle. Aristotle himself is the culprit behind the 'inherently-stable' part of Assumption (4) because he was singularly oblivious to the exigencies that can threaten and dissolve even the most mature of character friendships. This has been one of the major themes of my discussion in previous chapters so I do not need to say more about it here, although I return to it briefly in Section 7.5. Aristotle is not guilty for Assumption (3), however, because two of the main threads running through his long discussion of character friendship are about how such friendship is also possible between unequals (given certain conditions), and how it plays a significant role in not-yet-perfectly-virtuous people helping each other make further progress on the road to full virtue. Again, this is a point I have made previously in this book and do not need to argue further for here. Aristotle did not have Mill and Kant to compete with so he remains understandably silent on Assumption (1). However, Chapter 3 provided ammunition against this assumption if understood in the sense that Aristotelians can rely on 'unfiltered' moral decisions about friendship.

Chapter 6 was an attempt to challenge Assumption (2), not only in the context of online friendship (although my main example was derived from there) but more broadly conceived. The upshot was that Aristotelian friendships for utility are typically undervalued (as valueless or even as value parasites) from a moral point of view in the friendship literature, and that if the aim is merely to demonstrate that online friendships can have 'moral value', on a plausible modern terminological reordering of Aristotle's developmental account, then the bar is set too high by focusing solely on character friendships. That said, the present chapter aims higher than simply reiterating or bolstering this point. I thus argue in what follows that some forms of online friendships have the potential to satisfy the stringent demands of character friendships, and I demonstrate this with the example of epalships as augmented penpalships in Section 7.4. Prior to that, however, it is instructive to explore briefly the standard arguments against the overall possibility of Aristotelian online character friendships.

7.3 For and Against Online Aristotelian Character Friendships

Given the quantity and quality of the general discourse on arguments for and against the possibility of online 'character friendships' in the Aristotelian sense, I only offer a brief systematisation and critical classification in the present section, with the odd additional observation, and I limit myself mostly to considerations that I can revisit serviceably in the following section where I argue the case for penpalships/epalships.

Although I do consider the anti-arguments largely misplaced, they serve as a useful springboard for the discussion and provide considerable food for thought. I divide them into *geographical/ontological, epistemological, psychological* and *social* arguments, respectively, and explore each in turn. Unfortunately, it is not always clear in this discourse whether it is about (a) persons who form and sustain friendships online (i.e. people who have never met face to face) or (b) persons who sustain friendships online but formed the friendship originally face to face (e.g. friends who met at university and now live in different parts of the world). To make my task of parrying the anti-arguments slightly more difficult, I assume (unless otherwise noted) that the crux of the debate is about (a).

The geographical/ontological argument(s). This argument is also known as the 'physicality objection' (see e.g. Elder, 2014). There are two ways to understand it: as a complaint about online friendships lacking the geographical proximity of two human persons in time and space, or as a deeper philosophical worry about the ontological distance between online friends, preventing the formation of friends as 'other selves' on Aristotle's (notably fairly ambiguous) understanding. This is why I use a double-barrelled designator for the argument in question. The valid empirical point that *most* online friendships still just complement or follow up on real-life ones (see e.g. Vallor, 2012, p. 186) does not blunt the force of this argument. If it is true that online friendships fail to make the grade as character friendships without such physical complementarity, that condition rules out of court examples of pure penpalships/epalships like the ones I draw upon in the following section. The geographical/ontological argument (esp. when eliciting the idea of 'multi-filtered communication', see below) often shades subtly into an epistemological argument, but I will try to prise the two apart in what follows.

The premise of the geographical argument is unambiguous. It relies on Aristotle's strict condition that character friends must 'live together' and 'share conversation and thought' (1985, p. 261 [1170b10–15]). The standard interpretation is to see this as requiring actual physical cohabitation and mutual participation in shared bodily activities. However, a couple of rejoinders have been made, or can be made. *First*, the standard ploy is to invoke Aristotle's own caveat that living together does not mean sharing the same pasture like grazing animals (1985, p. 261 [1170b13–15]; see e.g. Elder, 2014). Had Aristotle been aware of contemporary possibilities of sharing lives online, he might precisely have taken those as examples of mutual participation in activities that do not require 'grazing' in the same field. This truth has perhaps never been more obvious than during the recent coronavirus lockdown. As Elder (2014) observes, sharing a conversation about one's day with a friend online could well count as 'living together'. While Elder concedes that people might be badly off, friends-wise, if *none* of their friendships involved physical presence, this does not mean that particular friendships with merely online presence cannot count as (character) friendships.

Second, while examples of shared activities that Aristotle takes include gymnastics, hunting and playing dice, the fundamental activity that Aristotle considers character-building, and hence constitutive of character friendships, is engaging in philosophical conversation together. As Pangle notes, this is not so much because philosophy is 'grave and the others light-hearted, as because it is a deeper, more satisfying, more unmixed, and more lasting' pleasure-and-flow-yielding activity (2003, p. 195). Arguably, sharing thoughts stemming from contemplative activity (*theoria*) is something to which online media lend themselves well. Fröding and Peterson would object that friends spending time together in real life are 'more likely to face a wider spectrum of different situations, and consequently, encounter a wider range of topics meriting contemplation' (2012, p. 204). However, this is a dubious empirical claim. I would contend that I encounter more thought-provoking materials on Facebook, in all the exciting articles and news items posted by my philosophical friends, than I would be likely to come across playing dice with them—or even going hunting.

The more sophisticated rendering of this specific anti-argument is to focus on ontological rather than mere physical distance. McFall (2012, p. 224) offers an incisive consideration of this sort with his distinction between *multi-filtered* communication (where information about A's experiences is first filtered through A's [online, text-based] interpretation before being reflected to B) and *single-filtered* communication (where B has direct and simultaneous real-life access to A's experiences). McFall's assumption is that in single-filtered communication, 'nothing stands between A and B' and they can 'directly perceive each other' (2012, p. 224). One could read this assumption epistemologically, about the limits that online media place on knowledge transfer and how they can facilitate knowledge manipulation; I return to those concerns below. However, it is more instructive here to understand the assumption ontologically, about multi-filtered communication creating an ontological barrier between two people which makes it impossible for them to penetrate each other's selfhoods in the way that Aristotle's 'another-self' condition on character friendships requires. But interpreted in this way, the assumption reflects a strong positive bias towards the body (cf. Bülow & Felix, 2016, p. 31). Unfortunately, there are no immaculate perceptions of other people's selves available to us, no inherently un-warped mirrors that enable us to merge with them in a strong form of soulmateship simply by being placed next to them in time and space. If there is any such thing as the ontological sharing of selfhoods, it is not achieved through some sort of direct physical access to the innermost core of another person but rather by finding ways to navigate through the various filters that inevitably stand between any two persons, in order to co-create an extended self, or a self that is enlarged through emotional and intellectual attachments. We are constantly interpreting our own thoughts and actions to ourselves and to our friends, even when we are engaging in the most physically intimate acts of friendships with them, and who we think we are and how we self-interpret is partly constitutive of who we really are (Kristjánsson, 2010). Ontological extensions of selfhood—if there is any such thing—would surely be dependent upon many necessary variables, but actual physical cohabitation is, arguably, not one of them.

The epistemological argument. This argument (explored e.g. by Fröding & Peterson, 2012, Kaliarnta, 2016 and Bülow & Felix, 2016) can most helpfully be understood as being two-pronged. The first prong has to do with the limited information that online communication typically conveys about who we are, and a selection bias regarding the information that we typically choose to make available to the online receiver(s). This is not because we deliberately aim to deceive them but because we tend to disseminate this information with a particular purpose in mind and do not receive the ordinary prompts from face-to-face contact inducing us to explain and expand upon the information provided (see e.g. Sharp, 2012, on 'unintentional obfuscation', p. 233). There is not much that needs to be said about this argument here except that it is usually mounted in the context of discussions about social media (Facebook-type) friendships. However, to the best of my knowledge, no one has ever seriously argued that typical Facebook friendships constitute character friendships (although they may possibly complement already existing ones). Deeper and more multi-faceted online friendships, as I explore in the following section, seem immune to this first prong of the epistemological argument; hence it does not cast any serious chill over the idea of online character friendships.

A more explicit and in-your-face version of this argument is to frame it as a 'deceptiveness objection' (as elaborated upon and responded to by Elder, 2014). Online media allow people to engage in impression management and deliberately distorted self-representations that they would never get away with in the real world because people—at least their close friends—would see through such misrepresentations. At first glance, at least, it is difficult to deny that there are far more opportunities for deception when it comes to online relationships. There are, after all, far fewer opportunities in such cases to verify whether what the other person reports about her life (her habits, her relationships, her hobbies) is indeed true. If someone in my physical company falsely reports that they speak French fluently, or that they enjoyed reading a particular book, and I respond in French or respond by asking them whether they enjoyed a particular chapter, their fib is going to be quickly exposed because they have been put on the spot. It would be far easier to keep these sorts of lies going when one has adequate time to craft a response. Now, there may be various psychological mechanisms behind the intention to deceive, ranging from dissociative imagination to a more sinister moral disinhibition effect (Suler, 2004), but the upshot is the same: online self-representations are too easily amenable to manipulation to allow for the epistemic transparency that needs to be at issue between true character friends.

One response to this argument is to bite the bullet and acknowledge that it is, in principle, easier to engage in distorted and misleading identity construction online than face to face. However, perhaps there is less of a need to do so. The 'games' we play with people face to face, in projecting who we are, are often motivated by shyness and insecurity. The leisurely pace of some online communications, such as emails, may allow for more authenticity, candidness and deliberateness, as we are not put on the spot to reveal ourselves to the potential friend in a panicky way, without the necessary prior deliberation about how to express ourselves in the most appropriate manner (cf. Briggle, 2008). Another and quite different response is simply to reject empirically the claim that deceptions are easier to administer in online (text-based) communications. The assumption behind the epistemological argument may again reveal a positive bias towards the body as more revelatory (less 'filtered', recall above) of who we are than what we write. However, sociopaths and con artists are known to be particularly apt at using facial cues and bodily charm to mislead. In contrast, text correspondence leaves digital paper trails that can be revisited and 'deciphered' in an orderly and un-hasty fashion (Elder, 2014), not least in cases where various facts about the friends are common knowledge, as in the case of Voltaire and Catherine the Great that I explore presently. In any case, what seems at first glance obviously true—that the online world one-sidedly enhances opportunities for deception—may not seem true anymore if we study closely the features of actual deceptions.

The psychological argument. Recall that one of Aristotle's conditions for character friendships is that the friends—as soulmates—share joys and sorrows. However, a common complaint about online communication is that it waters down and degrades the expressions of 'being happy for' or 'empathising with' that human beings have learned to do so well in face-to-face encounters, through a long evolutionary process. While empirical evidence shows that empathy is often expressed online (see e.g. Morgan, Fowers & Kristjánsson, 2017), the worry would be that there is something about such expressions that makes them superficial, shallow and lacking in the intimacy that comes to the fore when we actually embrace a friend in the flesh. In that sense, online friendships would be inferior with respect to some of the virtues that *ex hypothesi* make character friendships 'complete' (by Aristotle's lights) and unique (see e.g. Vallor, 2012).

As Elder (2014) correctly notes, the psychological argument (which she refers to as the 'superficiality objection') is most often mounted against friendships forged on social media platforms, and it may leave other online-communication alternatives untouched. Rather than expanding on that point—although Section 7.4 obliquely does so—I propose to take a different tack here and focus on a specific feature of Aristotle's theory of virtue and virtue education that has rarely been elicited in the discourse on online character friendships. I am referring here to Aristotle's insistence on the *individualisation* of virtue and education for good character (be it formal education or education through encounters with character friends). Different people have different needs and tendencies, and hence the proper (medial) state of character is not the same for everyone and 'in the object' but rather 'relative to us', as I explained at the close of Chapter 4.

The upshot of these comments is that what counts as the proper sharing of joys and sorrows will depend essentially upon the individual constitution of the friends in question and how they exemplify the relevant virtues in their own personalised way. Contra McFall (2012, p. 222), there is arguably nothing in the nature of online means *per se* that diminishes the opportunity for robust moral reflection and the virtuous improvement of self and the friend *qua* 'another self'. To rely on a personal anecdote, I happen to be a person to whom acts of physical intimacy (embraces, hugs, high-fives) with close friends do not come easily. I even find myself inhibited from showing many of my deepest emotions to them face to face. However, I have engaged in lengthy email correspondence with a number of friends, including ones who have gone through serious trials and tribulations, and I am very proud of the feedback I have received from some of them, talking about the emotionally deep reflections in my emails as 'life-saving' and 'epiphanic'. Of course, some of this feedback might simply be polite gratitude talk. Be that as it may, I do identify with the character 'Pete' in Bülow and Felix's paper who referred to the online world as 'where I feel most myself' (2016, p. 27).

As a moral 'boxer'—to paraphrase Aristotle's example about different training regimes for different boxers (1985, p. 295 [1180b9–11])—my ideal 'way of fighting' is to exhibit my virtues via emails and texts. The psychological argument claims that there is something superficial and shallow about those means of communication. Dissenting, I would argue that I have found my virtue niche in exploiting those technological vehicles as conduits for who I am deep down, and how I convey to my closest friends the lessons that express my 'wishing them good for their own sake', as Aristotelian character friendship requires.

Objectors relying on the psychological argument may have one more trick up their sleeves, however. Character friendship requires intimate knowledge of local and individual circumstances, to secure the relevant insight and discernment.

It may be unclear whether online contexts, in general, allow for the development of such intimate knowledge and, more particularly, whether online forms of communication such as epalships allow for the expression of this knowledge unless the participants have, for example, unusually well- developed linguistic capacities that can make up for the lack of physical presence and the ability to convey meanings through facial expressions, gestures, etc. The example of a successful penpalship canvassed in the following section, between Voltaire and Catherine the Great, is already biased in the sense that both were unusually lucid and eloquent writers, with an exceptional command of the nuances of language. Could it not be that a lack of such command debars most people from becoming character friends through epalships only?

The answer to that question is yes. This is precisely why I suggest in what follows that in a modern friendship, Voltaire and Catherine would ideally complement their epalship with various technological advances in order not to have to rely on the written word only. The truth—although perhaps slightly exaggerated by Aristotle—is that true character friendships are not so easy to develop, and many people are debarred from forming them for a host of reasons, some of which have to do with the same lack of 'external necessities' that Aristotle considered to threaten flourishing in general (Kristjánsson, 2020). For example, bad health prevents many people from making close friends, as does extreme shyness. A lack of the linguistic tools to conceptualise and express particularist and individualist local knowledge is going to be a potential barrier to some forms of online character friendship and even make them rare. But conversely, for other people (such as myself) who find it easier to master and express clear thoughts in writing than in face-to-face communications, the online nature of a friendship may actually be a blessing rather than a burden.

The social argument. According to this argument, there is something socially faulty about the platforms on which online friendships take place. What is considered 'faulty' is usually the commercial nature of those platforms and how they represent ulterior motives for trying to sell us products (or even pitching certain political causes) at the same time as creating spaces for friendships; this is why Elder (2014) refers to this argument as the 'commercialization objection'. This concern is the one least potentially detrimental to the positive argument that I propose to make in the rest of the chapter. It suffices, therefore, to note here that the standard venues where close friendships have historically been pursued tend to be *commercial* in nature; consider tennis clubs, sport stadiums, pubs and restaurants. It seems implausible to think that just because someone has commercial interests in these venues, this undermines the quality of friendships pursued within them (although one might worry if *all* friendships were developed in environments of a commercial or profit-seeking nature).

To conclude this section, someone could argue that the whole discourse on the deepest and most profound friendships is cluttered with baggage from Aristotle's idiosyncratic concept of 'character friendships' and that we might be better off dispensing with the concept altogether. While I go on to reiterate some chinks in the armour of this concept in Section 7.5, the present section has failed to demonstrate the adequacy of the standard general arguments against the possibility of Aristotelian character friendships being pursued online. It is now time to turn from those 'negative' arguments to a 'positive' one about one form of online friendship that I do think can pass muster as true character friendship: a sophisticated and expanded form of epalship.

7.4 Penpalship as Character Friendship and How It Can Be Augmented as State-of-the-Art Epalship

Penpalship is a historically established form of communication and friendship which has now been mostly overtaken by email correspondence and other forms of epalship. It is a matter of some surprise and disappointment that neither old-fashioned penpalships nor contemporary epalships seem to have been subjected to sustained academic scrutiny as potential exemplifications of (Aristotelian) character friendship in the same way as general online friendships, especially on social media platforms, have been in recent times.

I happened to be an active participant in penpalships before the days of email, in particular with friends I had met at university and to whom the adage 'out of sight, out of mind' did not apply. More recently, I have engaged in extended epalships with a small group of people, including one person P. I have only fleetingly met P twice, as P happens to suffer from extreme anxiety caused by a borderline personality disorder, which makes ordinary face-to-face interactions extremely taxing. P happens to be highly intelligent, articulate and morally reflective, and I would argue that our correspondence has had a significant morally edifying influence on both of us. Whether the moral reform in question is at the level of character friendship, or of the sort of continence-enhancing utility friendship that I made a case for as also being morally valuable in Chapter 6, is open to debate. In any case, it is more instructive here to rely on a well historically documented form of penpalship that one would be loath to describe as anything but full-blown character friendship: that between Voltaire and Catherine the Great.

To be fair, it is not as if penpalship or epalship are never mentioned in the literatures on character friendship in general and (putative) online character friendship in particular. Barnard (2011, pp. 167–8) observes how letters between friends allow for the kind of 'fine-tuning, for carving out a space for your personality' that spontaneous face-to-face interactions rarely do. In addition to the possibility of reflective depth, many writers mention how email platforms become a helpful levelling field for people who suffer from physical or psychological impairments of various sorts—or simply shyness and social withdrawal—that prevent them from cultivating real-life friendships (see e.g. Kaliarnta, 2016; cf. also Schaubert's 2019 moving example of the deep online friendships of a severely disabled boy, to which I return later). However, the received wisdom seems to be, as suggested by Elder (2014), that because epalships are so remarkably like penpalships, they may not offer much that is distinctive enough for theorists engaging with emerging technologies to think about. I consider this suggestion misleading in two ways, both because, to the best of my knowledge, penpalships themselves have not been scrutinised systematically as forms of Aristotelian character friendships, and because epalships offer possibilities nowadays that go far above and beyond those of mere penpalships.

The great Enlightenment philosopher Voltaire (1694–1778) was a prolific letter writer, leaving behind at least 20,000 pieces of letter writing. His most well-known and sustained correspondence was with Catherine II (1729–1796), commonly referred to as 'Catherine the Great': empress of Russia 1762–1796. According to the close historical study by Reece Stuart (1914), on which most of the facts about this penpalship elicited here are drawn (apart from obvious general-knowledge sources such as Wikipedia), their correspondence began in 1763 with a letter from Catherine. The collection of letters includes seventy-four from Catherine to Voltaire and ninety-one the other way round. The liveliest period of their penpalship was between 1770 and 1771, when in all seventy-one letters were sent. The most conspicuous fact about this extensive correspondence is that the pair never met in real life. This marks their penpalship out from other famous historical examples, such as that between Harriet Taylor and John Stuart Mill, which also included face-to-face interactions and ended with their hooking up (although the eventual formal relationship continued, famously, to be more intellectually than romantically stimulated).

In the letters between Voltaire and Catherine all imaginable subjects of the day are touched upon, from philosophy, art, literature and politics to more practical and mundane matters. No visible signs of self-censorship or deliberate lack of self-transparency can be noted. The pair are incredibly forthright about all matters that arrest their attention, and although many of the issues they discuss are both politically and personally sensitive, they seem to speak about them as if the possibility of these letters ending up in the wrong hands had never occurred to them. If there ever were true soulmates, then Voltaire and Catherine seem to satisfy that description admirably. However, to establish that their soulmateship was genuinely a case of Aristotelian character friendship, it is helpful to revisit some of the criteria of such friendship from Section 1.1.

Shared activities. While establishing the precise conditions for an activity to be 'shared' in an Aristotelian sense is a tall order, as we saw above, there is no denying the fact that Voltaire and Catherine engaged in shared philosophical discussions about common topics. They also almost constantly exchanged gifts and favours, in a very balanced way. The 'favours' included 'books, translations, codes, nuts and plants from Siberia, advice, paintings, portraits, watches and other jewellery' as well as 'employment of friends' (Stuart, 1914, p. 66). Finally, they encouraged and closely followed each other's activities in various literary, political and humanitarian endeavours. To be sure, they never went hunting together or played dice, but given Aristotle's preoccupation with the shared activities of *theoria*, it is difficult to see why the activities of the pair in question should fail to count as 'shared'.

Sharing joys and sorrows. It may be difficult to realise this at first glance, because of the elaborate layers of feigned politeness and flattery that characterised all letter writing between learned people in the 18th century, but as Stuart (1914, p. 69) notes, when peeling these layers away, it becomes obvious how a 'very natural bond of sympathy' gradually developed and became sealed between these penpals. The utterances of mutual care and love are astoundingly personal, given codes of courtesy in letter writing of the day: for example, Catherine's genuine concerns about Voltaire's failing health and his concerns about her difficulties in putting some of her more ambitious philanthropic projects into action. Her eventual mourning for Voltaire's death comes straight from the heart: 'a great man who loved me so much' (Stuart, 1914, p. 87).

Loving the other qua that person's character. This is perhaps the most salient criterion of character friendship, as it determines precisely whether the two friends are mature enough, and brought up well enough characterologically, to count as either budding *phronimoi* or full-fledged *phronimoi*, capable of loving and learning from each other's virtues. Now, without being able to penetrate into the hearts of either Voltaire or Catherine, it would seem churlish in the extreme to deny them the status of at least developing *phronimoi*. The tenor of the discussion in their letters is not about how to help each other to force themselves, against the thrust of incontinence, to become good through self-control or continence, let alone to avoid vice, but rather how to make themselves more virtuous and the world a better place. It could even be argued that if any famous 18th-century historical figures deserve to be placed at the level above ordinary *phronimoi* in Aristotle's system, namely the level of *megalopsychoi*, Voltaire and Catherine should occupy those places. The *megalopsychoi*—or great-minded persons—possess all the same virtues as the *phronimoi* but at an advanced level of attainment and exhibition because of their access to resources that enable them to become public benefactors and engage in great deeds of philanthropy. While not an unmixed blessing, to be a *megalopsychos* gives a person unusual powers of social reform and public grandeur (see Kristjánsson, 2020, chap. 4).

It is clear that both Voltaire and Catherine saw their roles as public benefactors—witness for example the empress's commitment to modern medicine and public health by allowing herself to be inoculated against smallpox as a 'guinea pig'. She also established a schoolhome for nearly 40,000 children who had been abandoned by their parents. Her eagerness for acting as a social entrepreneur is beyond doubt, although her practical endeavours were not always successful, especially during the latter part of her reign. She was also considered 'mannish' or 'masculine' in a sense similar to that which Aristotle seems to ascribe to his *megalopsychoi* with their deep voices and alpha-male comportment. Voltaire's main contribution to the advancement of humanity may have been intellectual, but he was also keenly interested in more practical aspirations, as witnessed by the watch factory he built at Ferney to give employment to refugees from Geneva. Not the greatest of salespersons, he had to rely on his friends, most notably Catherine herself, to buy most of the watches. Particularly during the last years of his life, Voltaire became increasingly concerned with the welfare of the region around him. All these activities by our two protagonists mutually inspired each one of them in ways that cannot be better described than having been conducive to the cultivation of virtue—and they loved each other for all these gestures and activities as representative of who they were deep down.

The character friend as another self. At least during the most intensive period of their letter-writing and soulmateship, Voltaire and Catherine seem to have seen their lives as inseparably intertwined, despite the geographical distance. Their individual projects, such as Voltaire's infamous watch factory, became 'their' joint projects. Their friendship was dynamic and reactive, and no feat was considered complete until it had been talked through with the other. This penpalship demonstrates the sort of joint affirmation of moral and aesthetic sensibilities that Aristotle seems to have been referring to with his 'another-self' thesis (cf. Brewer, 2005). If the notion of 'extended selfhood' has any meaning at all, beyond the metaphorical, then it seems to have been instantiated in this uniquely deep penpalship.

The friend as intrinsically valuable and irreplaceable. Voltaire had such a high opinion of Catherine that he called her several times 'empress Saint Catherine'. Similarly, Catherine referred to Voltaire with undivided attention as 'the man to whom I owe all that I know and all that I am' (Stuart, 1914, p. 88). She had in her library a bust of Voltaire. Conversely, he possessed a portrait of her which he called a shrine. Two related caveats may be entered here, however, about this condition of intrinsic value and irreplaceability. One is that a moral mentor/educator may also count as irreplaceable in Aristotle's system, not only an equal character friend, and there is no denying the fact that, in the first instance, Catherine approached Voltaire very much as her superior. She admired him as a mentor rather than loved him as an intrinsically valuable character friend of equal standing. However, those dynamics seem to have changed fairly quickly, and once the relationship between them was on a more equal footing, their value to one another became that of an irreplaceable friend than an irreplaceable mentor and mentee.

Secondly, Aristotle is very sensitive to the complex power relations that exist between character friends. Notably, despite their putative character friendship,

Catherine obviously remained more powerful than Voltaire politically, on the world stage, and he had more symbolic capital as an intellectual figure. For those, who like McFall (2012) and Bülow and Felix (2016) think that true character friendship can only obtain between equals, this might undermine the specific example of penpalship as character friendship that I have been exploring in this section. However, Aristotle does allow for true character friendships between unequals, both in terms of social status and virtue development, subject to his principle of proportionality, or 'equalising principle' (1985, p. 221 [1158b26–9]) that I introduced in Chapter 2. So while the weaker party gets 'more profit' (presumably in terms of character growth), the stronger party gets more honour and devotion (1985, pp. 236–7 [1163b1–15]).

I am not sure that we need this principle here in terms of *social status*, because the superiority of Voltaire on the intellectual stage and Catherine on the political stage may well have levelled each other out. However, even if we argued that Voltaire remained superior to Catherine in his attainment and display of reflective *virtue development* (which is the sort of inequality that seems to worry McFall, 2012, and Bülow & Felix, 2016, rather than the social status one), we could apply Aristotle's equalising principle to show that, as long as Catherine gained more morally from her correspondence with Voltaire, and she showed him more honour and deference in the letters (which actually seems to have been the case), their penpalship can still count as one of true character friendship, albeit unequal in a certain way. The gender issue (that theirs was a cross-sex friendship) complicates this conclusion somewhat, however, from an Aristotelian perspective, as I explain in Section 7.5.

Do any of the general misgivings about character friendships between people who do not meet in real life (rehearsed in Section 7.3) threaten to undermine this conclusion? The *social argument* is not relevant here, but let me offer brief comments about the other three. According to the *geographical/ontological argument(s)*, distance in space creates barriers to full self-disclosure and the merging of selves. It is very difficult to detect any such barriers in the penpalship between Voltaire and Catherine. Indeed, a comment about another penpalship would seem to apply here: through 'absence, geographical distance, and the written word', yet 'somehow these two people created out of words a nearness we today do not entirely grasp' (Vernon, 2010, p. 116). The *epistemological argument* focuses on the limiting or intentionally deceiving nature of the information channelled between friends who do not meet in real life. The unerring mark of the correspondence between Voltaire and Catherine—despite the socially expected flattery—is, however, their 'sincerity' and apparent lack of 'some ulterior motive' (Stuart, 1914, p. 86). The necessary bluntness of correcting each other's perceived misconceptions is also there, although sometimes well concealed as 'a drop of acid in a bonbon' (Stuart, 1914, p. 68). What is so charming about the whole collection of these letters is precisely their unmitigated authenticity. There are no half-hearted evasions, no half-measures. Finally, I would challenge anyone to identify an aura of shallowness and superficiality in this correspondence, as suggested by the *psychological argument*. The trajectory of the letters shows increasing levels of personal intimacy (Stuart, 1914, p. 69). There is no fickleness or inconstancy, and the occasional gaiety of phrases is representative of the deep spiritual bonds that existed between this unlikely pair of people, even including a shared sense of humour.

All this extended and multi-faceted argument about the penpalship between Voltaire and Catherine as (Aristotelian) character friendship notwithstanding, I can still envisage misgivings to the effect that although *some* measure of character friendship had been reached in this penpalship (and others of a similar ilk), there was still something missing to perfect it and make it fully 'complete' in the Aristotelian sense. Would it not have been even better had they been able to meet and communicate more directly?

Those misgivings give me the opportunity to return more explicitly to the theme of this chapter, about contemporary online friendships as potential character friendships, by suggesting ways in which modern technologies would have made the penpalship between Voltaire and Catherine even more edifying and gratifying. Obviously, their correspondence was hampered by a slow postal service and the impossibility of immediate feedback. However, modern-day epalships allow for a number of extensions that would augment historic penpalships: rendering it even more plausible to consider them passing as true character friendships.

- Contra Barnard (2011, p. 164), email correspondence can function exactly like old-fashioned penpalship if the parties so wish. There is thus nothing in the nature of email correspondence *per se* that automatically causes cognitive shallowing by foreclosing the option of a leisurely pace of corresponding, deep reflection, forethought and finessing before the correspondence is sent. However, emails are received earlier than letters and can also be responded to immediately if that is deemed necessary. Given the immediacy of many of the projects in which Voltaire and Catherine were engaged, I am sure they would have loved the option of spontaneous responses and also of reverting to messaging platforms like Whatsapp for shorter and quicker forms of communication. They would most certainly have become Facebook friends and joined special interest groups on Facebook.
- For those who still believe facial cues are vital to decipher the mind of the friend *qua* 'another self' (cf. Turp. 2020), video-based platforms like Skype or Zoom are an ideal substitute for real-life meets. I conjecture that Voltaire and Catherine would have Skyped each other quite often.
- I am also sure that both Voltaire and Catherine would have relished the chance to blog and give TED talks, and then to correspond or Skype about them.

- Both Voltaire and Catherine were avid lovers of art. Modern technologies allow people to visit virtual museums on the web and even do so simultaneously, exchanging views in real time on what they see and experience. This would have been a heaven-sent option for our two famous penpals.

- Multiplayer games or, more specifically, MMORPGs (where people interact through avatars in virtual worlds) provide means of 'shared activities' in the literal sense. Many of those games test the participants' moral fibre in various ways and help them identify automatic emotional responses that they may not even be aware of themselves. Such games thus afford various opportunities by which to enhance both self-knowledge and other-knowledge. There is a cogent argument in Munn's 2012 paper for why MMORPGs satisfy Aristotle's criteria for shared activities, goods and interests more so than other online platforms. Munn argues that such games obliterate a clear distinction between the physical and virtual worlds and that they facilitate stronger social bonds between participants than most, if not all, other online activities. For a particularly striking and moving illustration of putative character friendships pursued in MMORPGs, I recommend Schaubert's 2019 account of Duchenne- muscular-dystrophy sufferer Mats Steen (aka Lord Ibelin Redmoore) who spent up to 20,000 hours (equivalent to more than ten years' full-time employment) in World of Warcraft (WoW) and made many close friends there, before his untimely death.

    Given Voltaire's and Catherine's common interest in the development of virtuous character, they would arguably have benefited from, and made use of, multiplayer games to get to know each other even better and to help each other grow in virtue. There is another reason why I have kept this point as the last, and perhaps best, example of how Voltaire and Cartherine could have augmented their penpalship if they were living today. Many MMORPGs, such as WoW, involve warfare, and both Catherine and Voltaire were deeply interested in questions of war and peace and how wars should ideally be justified and conducted. WoW would have been an ideal venue for them to cultivate those shared interests in an interactive way.

These are just a few scattered examples which show how contemporary forms of epalship can be extended to turn the psycho-moral mechanisms behind old-fashioned penpalships into even more productive vehicles for character friendships. Should any of the misgivings from Section 7.3 still remain with respect to mere penpalships, I think they will melt away once we consider the possible modern augmentations. Moreover, and as importantly, all these new technological options would have resonated well with the lively and curiosity-driven Enlightenment spirit of Voltaire and Catherine the Great.

7.5 Concluding Remarks

The early onslaught on the idea of online friendships as (Aristotelian) character friendships provoked an eruption of helpful responses, as already noted. My sympathies with those responses notwithstanding, I hope to have added to the argumentative arsenal by showing how the fairly simple and time-honoured form of friendship called penpalship could, even before the days of technological wonders, pass muster as character friendship, and how that categorisation is even more apt today as penpalships have shaded into contemporary epalships. I would thus conclude, to cite Barnard (2011, p. 118), that 'contrary to all the nay-sayers and doom-mongers, technological developments are injecting a new dynamism into [character] friendship'. Some of the sceptical writings about online friendships as character friendships smack of a nostalgic elegy on the disappearance of a world in which human relations were deeper and character friendships easier to establish. The example of Voltaire and Catherine shows, however, in my view, that their character friendship thrived *in spite of*, but not *because of*, the low-tech means of communication that were available to them. Modern technology would have made it so much easier to cultivate, maintain and deepen.

All that said, I do not want to be seen to be replacing an elegy with a panegyric on how emancipatory technological innovations have taken character friendships to a new higher qualitative level. I have not been arguing that online friendships have some unique qualities that make them stand above the fray. For example, for every successful penpalship/epalship that migrates easily into real-life encounters, there are probably just as many that break down once the two friends actually meet—witness well-known historical examples of Groucho Marx and T. S. Eliot, on the one hand, and Rousseau and David Hume, on the other. I have simply been making the more modest claim that epalships *can* satisfy the conditions of Aristotelian character friendship and that standard misgivings about online friendships as character friendships *do not necessarily* undermine them.

In Chapter 2, I lamented that Aristotle's exploration of character friendships is strangely devoid of examples of conditions that threaten such friendships. I revisit two of those threats below that I think might be even more difficult to deal with or remedy in even the most advanced forms of epalships than in ordinary real-life character friendships.

The first is possible eros–*philia* conflict. It is difficult to untangle the extent to which the friendship between Voltaire and Catherine may have had romantic undertones. At the time their correspondence began, Voltaire was already a relatively old man (although never too old to fall in love!). It is sometimes hard to distinguish between flattery and flirtations in their correspondence

(Stuart, 1914, p. 70). We do not know whether one or both of the parties were romantically motivated. However, eros can be potentially detrimental to character friendships and create ineliminable tensions, especially when one of the parties is not keen on anything beyond *philia*. One might think that such eros–*philia* conflicts would be far less likely to arise in this case (or indeed, in any case of penpalship where the parties do not ever meet or expect to meet in person). But mutual uncertainty can be particularly damaging here. Human beings have evolved such as to be able to pick up signs of sexual interest in the other person's bodily movements and facial expressions—features which may not reveal themselves as well even in video calls as they would in face-to-face encounters. Perhaps there was no real sexual chemistry at work between Voltaire and Catherine, as they would have found out had they met. But it is not unlikely that the fact that they never met made one or both of them misinterpret the other's feelings and intentions.

It could be argued that the reason Aristotle does not address eros–*philia* conflicts is that his discussion of *philia* is exclusively about friendships between male (budding or fully fledged) *phronimoi*. This would then also make my long-drawn-out example of Voltaire and Catherine the Great rather ill-suited to the purpose of illustrating specifically (online) *Aristotelian* character friendship. Although Aristotle leaves open the possibility of character friendships between husbands and wives, it is quite true that the intended readership of the *Nicomachean Ethics* comprises well brought-up *men*. However, eros–*philia* conflicts between older and younger men was a well-known theme in Aristotle's time (witness e.g. Plato's *Symposium*), so this does not explain Aristotle's conspicuous silence on the matter. I chose the example of the penpalship between Voltaire and Catherine because of how well-known and well-documented it is, although it does invite complications as an 'Aristotelian' example. There is a more 'Aristotelian sounding' example of penpalship, which appears to pass muster as character friendship, in Briggle's paper (2008, pp. 73–4), concerning the friendship between a soldier in the Civil War and a male Boston school teacher, whom he has never met—but the problem with that example is that it is fictitious and hence easier to 'manipulate' to serve the purpose of the argument.

The second problem I want to address in this final section is that of our strong need for self-verification. People tend to be in the business of 'seeking to confirm their own view of themselves' (Aristotle, 1985, p. 222 [1159a21–4]). Since one of the fundamental roles of character friendships is the mutual correction of evaluative outlooks and virtuous make-up, in order to help one another on the way to *phronetic* virtue, this may require considerable doses of nudging and even admonition. However, people—even true character friends—may not always take well to having their view of themselves challenged. In face-to-face encounters, human beings have evolved intricate strategies to do this in measured ways, through constant feedback from the other party, in order to gauge whether the criticism is too 'soft' or too 'hard'. This will be more difficult to decipher, in a measured way, in text-based communication, even when complemented with the odd video call.

So there may, after all, be specific problems that stand in the way of epalships instantiating true character friendships. However, the two issues mentioned here are just intensified versions of problems that already exist in ordinary real-life character friendships, and they do not impugn the overall diagnosis offered in this chapter of advanced epalships as potential forms of character friendships.

8

Concluding Remarks

Some Retrospective Reflections on Friendships

8.1 Introduction: The Four Aims Revisited

Neither of two important books about friendship that came out in 2016, by
Nehamas and Digeser, has a concluding or summarising final chapter. After com-
pleting the first seven chapters of this book, I have realised what the reason might
be. Friendship is such a capacious topic, with so many ramifications and complications, that it does not yield itself easily to a concise, integrative overview. For
example, even though Aristotle's three types of 'true' friendship—as distinct from
friendliness or acquaintanceship—can be braided into a single skein for certain
argumentative purposes, such as showing why any true friend is loved for her
own sake, they manifest themselves differently across specific domains of life and
carry with them diverging aspirations, expectations and obligations. I have almost
said nothing important, let alone new, in this book about friendships for pleasure,
for example; I have mainly focused on character friendship and a proposed higher
level of utility friendships. Civic friendship is another salient topic that I have
mostly eschewed. Given these omissions, I cannot pretend to be able to offer a
concluding chapter with pithy general lessons about friendship as such.

Nevertheless, in the first section of this final chapter about friendship*s* (notice
the plural), I will rehearse some themes that have emerged from this study, and
I begin by revisiting the four aims that I set out with in Chapter 1. Sections 8.2–8.4,
on the other hand, take the shape of some additional retrospective reflections on
issues that occupied my mind while I was writing the first seven chapters but
somehow did not fit into any of them. Those relate to the friendship theme in literature and lessons to be learned from it (Section 8.2), potential practical applications of the educational resources that friendship has to offer (Section 8.3), and
topics relating to friendship within the family (Section 8.4). I close with a gloss on
a possible research agenda (Section 8.5): on where I would ideally like to see
friendship research head next—at least research of the kind conducted in
this book.

My *first professed aim* was to give the virtue of friendship the pride of place it
deserves in contemporary Aristotle-inspired virtue ethics. I have shown throughout that, while friendship cannot be understood as either a master virtue or a

Friendship for Virtue. Kristján Kristjánsson, Oxford University Press. © Kristján Kristjánsson 2022.
DOI: 10.1093/oso/9780192864260.003.0008

meta-virtue within such virtue ethics, it constitutes a significant moral virtue with important axiological, developmental and educational reverberations. The role that character friendships (and arguably some utility friendships also) play in the development of *phronesis* can hardly be overestimated, for example. This needs to be foregrounded because friendship tends to be either subtly neglected in recent virtue ethical literatures of the non-exegetical kind or put on a pedestal as being somehow shielded, within a virtue ethical system, from the difficult decision procedures to which friendship needs to succumb within other ethical systems. From a neo-Aristotelian perspective, the vices of overestimating and underestimating the value, power and scope of friendship are both equally pernicious.

It almost beggars belief how all philosophical writings on friendship to the present day tend to be studded with references to Aristotle, if not always beholden to him theoretically. However, by considering this in an historical light, some of the mystery as to why this is the case disappears. If nobody had written a book about cooking before, and an articulate and competent chef were given the chance to write the first one, there is a high chance that her work would be seen as canonical from then on and most subsequent cookbooks would take their cue from, and respond to, the original exemplar. This is exactly what happened with Aristotle on friendship. To be sure, Plato wrote quite a lot about friendship, especially in the dialogue *Lysis*, but *Lysis* is one of those early dialogues that is characterised by irony and paradoxes and ends in *aporia*. Aristotle's is therefore truly the first systematic account of friendship ever given and, as a prescient text presaging much of the subsequent literature, a pretty solid one, although not above criticism as I have demonstrated repeatedly. There is good reason to take Aristotle's account as the *first word* on friendship, although certainly never as the *last word*.

The *second aim* of the present work was to delve into the social-science (especially psychological) literature and explore to what extent it can augment and update Aristotle's theory. Whole sections of this book have been devoted to empirical findings, and elsewhere I referred to those at regular junctures. In my previous books (e.g. Kristjánsson, 2018), I have devoted considerable space to showing why academics pursuing virtue ethics and/or its educational incarnation as character education had better learn to wriggle themselves out of academic pigeon-holes and combine insights from philosophy, psychology and education (and possibly other social sciences). At the same time, I have also highlighted the challenges of such transdisciplinary work and the frustrations that academics, on both sides of the barbed wire typically separating the disciplines, may encounter when trying to cross it.

The same lessons have emerged from this book. I have explained how scholarly approaches to friendship are rooted in different methodological, epistemological and axiological paradigms. Yet efforts at crossover work are unavoidable if one aspires to get the 'big picture'. For instance, in order to avoid special pleading with respect to Aristotle's taxonomy, it has helped to notice that, for most argumentative purposes, the difference between what he calls 'character friendship' and what psychologists simply refer to as 'close' or 'best friendship' can be ignored with impunity. Another example is the issue of potential conflicts between eros and *philia*, say in cross-sex friendships. It so happens that Aristotle did not address this issue except very indirectly, by noting possible misunderstandings between friends about the type of friendship in which they are engaged. However, even if he had addressed this topic, it is difficult to see how it can be resolved from a pure philosophical position without significant empirical evidence on whether cross-sex friendships are, in fact, characterised by more potential friction (and then of what kind) than same-sex ones.

The *third aim* of the present work was to repair the lack of attention paid by Aristotle and most Aristotelians to the actual difficulties affecting close (character) friendship: explore to what extent they threaten the viability of Aristotelian friendship theory and to what extent they can be ameliorated. Here, for once, I do agree with Nehamas when he says that friendship is 'more fraught with risk' than Aristotle imagined (2016, p. 25). Here, furthermore, input from contemporary psychology is an invaluable complement to any conceptual or theoretical work. Psychologists tend to be more sensitive than philosophers to how friendships are ripe for conflict and a breeding ground for hurtful transgressions and disappointments, for example because of mismatched expectations (Perlman, 2017). Although friendship experts within psychology also complain about the 'comparatively few articles on transgressions and provocations' (Hojjat, Boon & Lozano, 2017, p. 196), the situation is much more dire in philosophy, especially within Aristotelian accounts of friendships where Aristotle's own rosy-eyed view still prevails. All that said, I would want to distance myself from Trujillo's recent (2020) cynical and pessimistic view that friendship is too risky and potentially toxic to be necessary for flourishing at all.

I devoted a whole chapter to potential threats to Aristotelian character friendship, beyond those identified by Aristotle himself, and then returned to those with further examples later. While many of the relevant threats and examples were speculative and sometimes based on my own experiences only—simply because of a shortage of salient case studies in the empirical literature—I hope they did resonate with readers, at least serving as food for further reflection.

The fourth and final aim of the book was to retrieve friendship as a moral educational concept: to explain how moral educational goals ground and sustain close friendships, and how common friendship terminations are associated with the depletion of the friendship's relevant educational rationale. Practically speaking, this aim was perhaps the most important one of the four because of the current mismatch between the crucial role that friendship plays in Aristotle's character educational theory and the lack of attention devoted to it in current accounts of character education for pupils or for budding professionals. We need to be reminded from time to time of Aristotle's edict that the aim of good ethical theorising is not to understand what virtue is but to become good (1985, p. 35 [1103b27–9]). Virtue ethics without a robust account of character cultivation is like *Hamlet* without the Prince. I have not said much about practical educational applications yet but will briefly touch upon those in Section 8.3. However, I have written more explicitly educational works previously, with practical advice about (Aristotelian) character education and education towards (Aristotelian) flourishing (Kristjánsson, 2015; 2020), although I now feel slightly embarrassed now about not having given friendship a higher profile in those writings.

In addition to fleshing out arguments relating to the four above-mentioned themes, various sub-themes have emerged over the course of this work. Some of those have been mostly concerned with polishing and supplementing insights harking back to previous theorists, from Aristotle onwards, while others can make claim to a stronger novelty factor. Among the latter, I would for example single out (in no particular order), arguments relating to (a) the typically overlooked moral and educational value of (some) utility friendships, (b) online friendships, in general, and penpalships, in particular, as potential character friendships, (c) the specific educational dynamics and processes of the friendship relation, (d) the possibility of incorporating insights from an aestheticised view of friendship within a moralised view, by taking account of the individualisation of virtue and (e) the relationship between friendship and *phronesis*. However, I leave it to readers to judge what they find original and appealing in this work and what not. My experience with previous works is that what happens to grab readers' attention is often what I least expected.

I hope I have fulfilled my promise not to produce a self-help book on friendship in any sense of that term, pejorative or not. Nevertheless, I have allowed myself academic licence to draw on my personal experiences, for instance relating to my sudden-hearing-loss event. Moreover, I would be dishonest if I did not admit that researching about friendship has made me reflect upon my own merits and demerits as a friend. Indeed, given Aristotle's practical edict for works of this kind, I would say that it would count in its disfavour, rather than its favour, if it did not evoke personal reflections in the writer and in readers. Without wanting to engage in any soppy self-disclosures, I would like to share with readers the main personal lesson that I derived from my writing journey. I have often been puzzled by the discrepancy between my sense of myself as an incomplete character friend, whose friendships tend to be fairly short-lived and vicissitudinous, and the positive feedback I often get back from friends about having had a positive influence on their lives. I have now come to understand that I am probably good at what I called in Chapter 6 Level-2 character-like utility friendships, where I help friends in urgent need or receive help from them, but bad at sustaining character friendship through the mundane periods in life in which nothing much dramatic is happening.

This personal insight is academically relevant because it helps explain my sense of disbelief in Chapter 1 at the claim that novels and poems about friendship typically fail to capture its essence. The reason proffered there, that those forms of art are inferior to films and plays in describing the leisurely non-dramatic everyday interactions between friends who simply enjoy each other's company, failed to cut ice with me precisely because I tend to equate close friendships with spectacular, even grandiose, heroic and *megalopsychia*-like, acts of mutual benefits and support. I am not very good at small talk and meaningful silences. This is why the friendship literature I favour—and I give some examples in the following section—describes friendships that are in various senses radical and edgy.

If one really takes seriously Aristotle's message about the individualisation of virtue, and how it may steer our choice of friends and the sort of friendships in which we wind up engaging, it is important to gain self-knowledge about where one's potential strengths and weaknesses as a friend lie so that, even if one is not necessarily able psychologically to fix the shortcomings, one is at least better equipped to maximise the strengths, in order to make one's friendships as reward-ing and virtue-cultivating for one's friends—and oneself—as possible. Virtue ethics without the personal touch is a sterile form of virtue ethics, or at least a very un-Aristotelian form. Just as, in Aristotle's often-cited example, the boxing instructor does not impose the same training regime on all the boxers, one would be foolish to try to mould one's friendships in a way that does not take account of one's unique characterological make-up and developmental capacities.

8.2 Some Further Insights from Literature

I first thought seriously about friendship when, as a secondary-school student, I was introduced to the Viking poem *Hávamál*, enshrining the ethical code of what MacIntyre (1981) calls 'heroic society' in settlement-time Iceland (and probably reflective of the rest of the Norse cultural region at the time). When writing the present book, my mind was cast back repeatedly to *Hávamál*'s primary theme on the role of friendship: notably, as a relationship between individuals in a kinship-and-friendship driven society without centralised executive powers. Some similarities with an Aristotelian take on friendship obviously stand out—not necessarily so much because of the convergence that MacIntyre identifies between ancient Greek and medieval Icelandic heroic societies, but simply because any normative claims about friendship are bound to have some com-monalities woven into them, for conceptual reasons. Otherwise we would not understand them as claims about 'friendship'.

For example, *Hávamál* (2020, No. 41) tells us:

> Friends should provide their friends
> with weapons and clothing;
> this kind of generosity shows.
> Generous mutual giving
> is the key
> to lifelong friendship.

Anyone who understands what friendship is about will agree that it involves mutual generosity. Whether the generosity is represented through giving 'weapons and clothing' or something else is a contextual matter; we are almost dealing with platitudes here.

But there are other, slightly more controversial, topics on the agenda also:

> Be a friend
> to your friend
> and also to his friend,
> but never be a friend
> to the enemy
> of your friend (No. 43).

Aristotle does not talk about relationships with one's friend's friends and foes. However, whether or not we agree unconditionally with the strict injunction not to befriend one's friends' enemies, this piece of 'advice' at least reminds us of the intricate net of moral obligations and expectations that being a friend involves, just as with any moral roles that we take on. This is why friendship cannot be divorced from *phronesis*—unless we want to settle for the 'the low-hanging fruit' only.

Hávamál talks about friendship terminations:

> The friendship
> among false friends
> burns warmly for five days,
> but then it's extinguished
> by the sixth day,
> and the friendship is over (No. 51).

This is very much in line with Aristotle's message about the break-up of mismatched friendships. However, *Hávamál* does not address the topic of the vicissitudes of true friendships. Its picture of the nature of friendships is, in most ways, as one-sidedly positive as Aristotle's. That said, Hávamál emphasises the role of a critical friend:

> Men become friends
> when they can share
> their minds with one another.
> Anything is better
> than being lied to:
> a real friend will disagree with you openly (No. 124).

Those who approach *Hávamál* in the hope of finding ammunition for MacIntyre's claim about the uniqueness of heroic societies will be disappointed. Those who are non-relativists about friendship (and perhaps other virtues) will find in this poem, however, considerable grist for the mill of moral universalism. *Hávamál* is not a source of quirky insights about friendship. Rather, it dresses up proverbial truths in stylistically beautiful poetic trappings in classic Icelandic—much more so than comes across in the fairly flat English translations above.

Hávamál's conception of friendship is very much geared towards friendship among equals. That is understandable, given the sort of highly stratified society in which the author(s) lived and the literary focus there on relationships between great-minded (*megalopsychia*-like) heroes. I took the friendship between the equals Egill and Arinbjörn as an example in the Preface of a friendship within Saga morality. Mentorships are frequently seen in the Sagas but they are usually between a heroic mentor and a mentee (e.g. a farmer occupying the hero's land) so low in the social hierarchy that even what Aristotle would call 'unequal friend-ship' is out of place. So the benefactor in the relationship is a mentor without being a friend. Another reason for the lack of unequal friendships in Saga litera-tures could be that an Aristotelian character type that is frequently most in need of such friendship to ameliorate her sense of inferiority, the 'pusillanimous' (in today's jargon, the person with high self-respect but low self-esteem), is almost completely missing from the Sagas. They are full of the great-minded (high self-respect and high self-esteem), the small-minded (low self-respect and low self-esteem) and the vain (high self-esteem and low self-respect) but the pusil-lanimous are conspicuous by their absence, the reason for which can only, at best, be the object of educated guesses (Kristjánsson, 1998).

When I was writing about unequal friendships, for instance in Chapters 2 and 5, my mind thus turned to completely different kinds of literature from different eras. Aristotle speaks as if the inequality with respect to psycho-social roles is pretty obvious, and it often is in the cases which he seems to have in mind (parent–child; teacher–student, etc.). But there are interesting cases where the power relations, and hence the friendship dynamics, are much more treacherous and blurred.

Take Don Quixote and Sancho Panza, for example. Generally speaking, friendship and role-modelling are major themes in Cervantes's masterpiece. The narrator uses various literary tricks to lure the reader into 'befriending him', gaining his trust. In the story, Don Quixote is driven by his motivation to emulate chivalric lives but he cannot do so, in practice, without the help of his sidekick Sancho. Don Quixote conceives of himself as Sancho's virtue teacher: unequal benefactor-friend, if you like. Sancho pretends, at least, to occupy the role of a beneficiary, but in reality he is as much the benefactor in the relationship as Don Quixote is. To avail myself of a much abused word, Cervantes 'problematises' the unequal friendship relationship between mentor and mentee by showing how one or both can be deceived about who is in fact the stronger party.

This problematisation is brought to a grand finale in the highly condescending letter that Don Quixote sends Sancho after the latter is installed as the governor of the island of Barataria. The 'mentor' writes as if he is a paragon of virtue and world-wisdom and Sancho an immature simpleton:

> Dress well; a stick dressed up does not look like a stick; I do not say thou shouldst wear trinkets or fine raiment, or that being a judge thou shouldst dress like a soldier, but that thou shouldst array thyself in the apparel thy office requires, and that at the same time it be neat and handsome. To win the good-will of the people thou governest there are two things, among others, that thou must do; one is to be civil to all (this, however, I told thee before), and the other to take care that food be abundant, for there is nothing that vexes the heart of the poor more than hunger and high prices.   (Cervantes, 2020)

Don Quixote goes on to list various virtues that Sancho had better adopt. However, most of these happen to be about capacities at which the teacher is much worse than the pupil (as the reader already knows). This novel is obviously a parody at many levels of engagement; one of the things caricatured is friendship between apparent unequals but where the inequality is not all what it seems, especially not what it seems to the protagonists themselves.

Another famous literary relationship which complicates the notion of unequal friendships is that between Sherlock Holmes and Doctor Watson. Conan Doyle was clearly writing a series of stories about friendship (indeed creating one of the most iconic friendships in history) as much as about meticulous detective work. Two things stand out that make these stories highly relevant as illustrations of some aspects of Aristotle's friendship theory. Firstly, Holmes and Watson are engaging in a sort of friendship that is doubly unequal or differentially unequal in two areas. There is a vague similarity here to the case of Voltaire and Catherine the Great, explored in Chapter 7, where Voltaire was (perhaps) her superior in terms of intellectual capital but she his superior in terms of political power.

In the case of Holmes and Watson, the imbalance is between the professional and personal. Holmes is clearly Watson's superior in terms of professional expertise in solving crimes; but his lack of sensitivity and emotional intelligence makes him increasingly reliant on Watson's friendship simply in order to thrive in everyday life. Both are aware of their enormous debt to each other and acknowledge it frequently.

However, there are complex interactions between the two fields of expertise. For example, Watson remarks in *The Hound of the Baskervilles* that 'some people who aren't geniuses have an amazing ability to stimulate it in others'. More specifically, Holmes's intellect needs the stimulation that comes from Watson's often fairly mundane comments and questions in order to remain active and alert. In *A Study in Scarlet*, Holmes describes Watson's role in this regard as that of 'a conductor of light'. On the other hand, Holmes is of course unable ever to be friends with Moriarty, despite their intellectual similarities and mutual psychopathic tendencies. Moriarty is incapable of mutual goodwill, let alone virtue; hence cannot be a friend (Sherlock Cares Web, 2020). So, to recall Chapter 4, a plus there for Aristotle and a minus for Nehamas! The question remains whether the doubly unequal friendship between Holmes and Watson satisfies Aristotle's 'equalising principle'— in the sense that the two different superiorities somehow level each other out—or simply makes this principle redundant. In any case, this principle constitutes one of the oddest aspects of Aristotle's friendship theory, as noted in Chapter 2, although it is certainly worthwhile reflecting on the nature of the benefits that either of the two parties receives from an unequal friendship.

The second distinctly Aristotle-relevant aspect of the Sherlock Holmes stories is the development of his friendship with Watson through, so to speak, the three Aristotelian types of friendship: from utility, to pleasure, to mutual character-appreciation-and-cultivation. At the beginning, in *A Study in Scarlet*, Watson sees his friendship with Holmes as strictly a utility-based one. It is simply about sharing lodgings with someone in an affordable way in a city with expensive rents. Holmes seems motivated by the same concerns although he is not as articulate about them. After all, he is not the narrator in the stories. In 'The Adventure of the Speckled Band', however, utility concerns have been superseded by pure pleasure: 'I have no keener pleasure than in following Holmes in his professional investigations, and in admiring the rapid deductions, as swift as intuitions, and yet always founded on a logical basis.' Similarly, Holmes garners more and more hedonic satisfaction from having Watson follow him and write about him. But the trajectory does not end there. Gradually, Watson and Holmes develop intimate affections and true soulmateship. In 'The Adventure of the Devil's Foot', Watson derives 'sanity' and 'strength' in a time of need by contemplating his friend's facial features, and in 'The Empty House', Watson describes the joy of simply being with his friend, doing nothing except sharing his company: 'I found myself seated beside him in a hansom, my revolver in my pocket, and the thrill of adventure in my heart' (Sherlock Cares Web, 2020).

All in all, the Sherlock Holmes stories illuminate a relationship that epitomises true friendship in the Aristotelian sense, not only through highlighting its nature but also its development towards the 'complete' type. The recent obsession with the potential homosexual features of this friendship demonstrate little more than pervasive prejudices against the possibility of close same-sex friendships without sexual undertones. A whole book about Aristotelian friendships could be written just by studying the Sherlock Holmes novels and short stories in more detail than I have had space to do here.

The aim of this section has been to demonstrate how literature can serve as a rich resource for nuancing, and adding colour, to the friendship dynamics that academics try to analyse. By focusing, as literature often does, on the marginal and extreme, it directs our attention away from the stereotypes in which philosophers' armchair examples often trade and also away from the average persons in whom psychologists are most interested. Some philosophers make ample use of literary examples in their writings—Martha Nussbaum offers a modern case in point—while others avoid them like the plague. Literary references are becoming more difficult to apply in our fragmented times when we cannot anymore rely on all 'well educated' people being familiar with the same literary canons. This necessitates long-winded rehearsals of background facts about persons and plots that readers need to know before the examples begin to resonate with them: witness my extensive use of a specific Meg Wolitzer novel in Chapter 5 that I suppose few readers had prior familiarity with. On the other hand, constant references to the same few stock novels that most people can still be expected to have read (or at least have read about) can appear hackneyed and soporific. This is the main reason why I have been fairly parsimonious in my use of literary examples in this book until the present brief section; it is certainly not on the grounds of sharing the view of Nehamas and C. S. Lewis about the unsuitability of works of fiction and poetry to illuminate the intricacies of real-world friendships. Indeed, the effectiveness of literary friendships is dependent on their consonance with the real world: it underpins the characterisation process, which is the literary effect of readers combining their knowledge of the real world (top-down) with textual cues (bottom-up).

8.3 Friendships as a 'Method' of Moral Education

I argued in Chapter 5 that the *raison d'être* of character friendship is mutual character development. 'Good people's life together allows the cultivation of virtue' (Aristotle, 1985, p. 259 [1170a11–13]). My argument was conducted, however, at a fairly high level of abstraction without much attention paid to practical applications, except by providing brief examples of teacher–student friendships. Here, as we come to the close of this book, I want to be more forthright and allow myself to make the provocative suggestion that character friendship be seen as an apt *method of moral education*. This book is not a teaching manual, so I will not be offering a set of exercises and interventions. However, I want to open this topic up in a more explicit way than I did in Chapter 5 as one ripe for further thought and development.

My above suggestion is provocative for two reasons. One is that nowhere does Aristotle himself refer to his highest type of friendship, namely 'character friendship' (nor indeed any lower type), as a 'method'. However, bear in mind once again that there is a strong educational thread running through the *Nicomachean Ethics*, not to mention the *Politics*. Aristotle wrote his works before the time of explicit theories of educational methods. However, only plodding docility before these ancient texts would debar us from giving his account of friendship a more direct educational spin by couching it in the current language of educational methods. The second reason why my suggestion will seem provocative is that whereas the standard view of friendship—dating back to no other than Aristotle himself—is that friendship has intrinsic value, talk of it as a 'method' smacks of instrumentalisation: the reduction of its value to extrinsic benefits. However, here is a helpful analogy. It is well known that Aristotle mentions *music* as a method of moral education (or, more precisely, of emotion regulation which is a foundation of balanced character development) in his *Politics*. It could well be that music only carries those benefits for people who, antecedently, appreciate the intrinsic worth of music. There is thus no incoherence in supposing that the same thing can have both non-instrumental and instrumental value (take *health* as another telling example).

To be sure, my provocative suggestion may need to be modified and reframed if we choose to understand 'method' in a formal and operationalisable sense, such as a rigorous teacher-led Kohlbergian discussion about a moral dilemma in a classroom. However, if we understand 'method' here as a strategy that can be encouraged and nourished systematically by an educator, for example through subtle hints and nudges, to help students grow morally, then I see nothing speaking against character friendships being referred to as a 'method', at least in this more permissive sense. Notably, this meaning of 'method' is different from that of using friendships as a 'method' to elicit important information from respondents (see e.g. Heron, 2020). I am talking about friendship as a method of cultivating virtue, not as a method to unearth data about such cultivation, however useful that may be.

In Section 5.3, I identified three educational mechanisms unique to character friendship. To demonstrate that these mechanisms carry traction outside of the hermetically sealed hothouse of Aristotelian scholarship, it suffices to mention that they correspond substantially to the three 'fruits of friendship' that

Francis Bacon identified much later: 'peace in the affections', 'support of the judgement' and the bringing together of the 'many kernels' that friendship has, 'like a pomegranate', into a coherent whole (Bacon, 1910–14, p. 59). It bears repeating that identifying these mechanisms is not the same as instrumentalising friendship. The person who forms character friendships just in order to gain self-knowledge, for example, has not so much misunderstood what character friendship is *for* as what such friendship really *is*. The following analogy from C. S. Lewis says all there is to say about instrumentalisation: 'Say your prayers in a garden early, ignoring steadfastly the dew, the birds and the flowers, and you will come away overwhelmed by its freshness and joy; go there in order to be overwhelmed and [...] nothing will happen you' (1960, p. 39).

Nothing that I said in Chapter 5 undermines the educational value of standard role-model education, activated through admiration and emulation. Such education may be particularly apt for projecting on our mental screens visions of the good life, for the sake of either adoption or consolidation. It may even, contra Aristotle, inspire us towards radical (epiphanic) self-change—although, again contra Aristotle, attraction to abstract ideals may be even better at leveraging such change (Kristjánsson, 2020, chap. 6). However, for the everyday 'plank by plank' (Hursthouse, 1999, p. 165) revision and refining of our moral character traits, I think Aristotle was right: nothing beats the critical collaboration with close character friends who, *qua* soulmates, are psychologically intimate enough with us to know where the shoe pinches.

The most obvious educational implication of this view is that teachers should encourage the formation of close friendships between their students, young or old, and help enlighten them on the merits of turning those into true character friendships. To be sure, best-friendship dissolutions are often profoundly painful, and one may thus have some sympathy with the head teacher, reported upon in Chapter 5, who discouraged pupils from forming best friendships so as to avoid the pain and upset caused by fallings out. However, for those who believe schools have any role to play in moral education—a view shared by the vast majority of teachers and parents—a no-best-friends policy in schools seems to be not only unduly paternalistic but, indeed, profoundly inimical to the moral development of the child (Healy, 2017a). The idea that rather than have a best friend, children should be 'friends with everyone' bespeaks an inadequate grasp of moral psychology and a conflation of the concepts of friendliness on the one hand and (true) friendship, on the other (cf. Healy, 2015).

Taken to the other extreme, a strict consequentialist demand to maximise overall utility at every turn would put a positive non-supererogatory obligation on teachers to play 'friendship matchmakers', in order to enhance the flourishing of the greatest number of children in their care (cf. Collins, 2013). While one may grumble that the strict utilitarian demand is counter-productive in the long run from the utilitarian perspective itself because of its extreme burn-out-threatening demandingness, in this case the excess of playing friendship matchmaker seems closer to the golden mean of appropriate teacher intervention than the deficiency of ignoring or discouraging the role of student friendships.

Should teachers take the extra step of offering themselves as unequal character friends (mentors) to students? Patricia White probably echoes the voices of many teachers when she argues that 'norms of impartiality' and the dangers of 'ethical complexities' rule out intimate friendships with individual students (1990, pp. 88–9). Contrast that view, however, with the Montessori approach to teacher–pupil relationships, according to which it is incumbent on every teacher to act *in loco parentis* and offer pupils domestic affection through frequent hugs and gestures towards close personal friendships (Martin, 1992, esp. pp. 16–19, 39). One could retort, first, that the *Casa dei Bambini* was a school type for a special kind of deprived children and, second, that more serious worries obtrude about potential abuse in the present age than in Montessori's time. However, nowadays no less than in decades past, there are children who—being shy, withdrawn or deprived of domestic affection—crave that special attention from a significant adult, and by resisting friendships with such students, teachers are closing down spaces that would enhance their flourishing. Moreover, teacher attention is not necessarily a zero-sum game. Showing a needy child special attention does not automatically mean than other, less needy, children are being neglected, from the point of view of impartiality. At any rate, viewing students as friends seems to be a healthier attitude than viewing them as clients or customers, as seems to be demanded by a neo-liberal agenda of schooling (cf. Noddings, 2005, esp. p. 102).

Notice here as an aside that Pangle offers some thoughts about the nature of the best teacher–student friendships that speak against Aristotle's 'equalising principle':

> The clear-sighted teacher knows that his position is more choiceworthy than that of his student because he is the wiser of the two. He may love more than he is loved, but he will find that actively loving, when it involves sharing what gives one joy, really is more satisfying than merely being loved. He may benefit more than he is benefited, but here, too, he will feel no deprivation, since his teaching allows him a fuller array of activity than solitary thought is likely to do. If indeed the benefactor loves more than the beneficiary, he will not find his friendship equalized by greater affection from the inferior in the way that Aristotle proposed […] but neither will he feel a need for such equalization.
>
> (Pangle, 2003, p. 167)

These are wise words, indeed, which will resonate with most people who have derived satisfaction from teaching (cf. Davids & Waghid, 2020, chap. 2). Perhaps the time has come to be more explicit than I allowed myself to be in Chapter 2 and add the 'equalising principle' to those aspects of Aristotle's theory that need to be consigned to the academic scrapheap.

Her scepticism about teacher–student friendships notwithstanding, White (1990, p. 87) does agree at least that teachers should encourage student friendships by taking them seriously and reinforcing them. How to do so obviously depends on the nature of the friendship in question (e.g. if it can be considered character friendship) and the age-related mode of the friendship, as it typically shifts from concerns with equality and reciprocity in children aged 8–12, to mutuality and understanding for those aged 9–14 (Rawlins, 2008, pp. 39–40). Encouraging student friendship does not mean introducing 'friendship lessons' in schools or placing friendship explicitly on the school curriculum as a discrete subject matter (as noted by Healy, 2017b), although a recent UK governmental document seems to recommend just that (Department for Education, 2019). Nevertheless, it does mean incorporating discussions of friendship in any curriculum that is geared towards the moral education of the child, however it is conceptualised and labelled. What must be avoided at the same time is the unnecessary institutionalising of something that is deeply personal in nature; the sense of non-instrumentalism and voluntariness must be retained (cf. Enslin & Hedge, 2019, on academic friendships). Ruehl's (2018) clarion call for a whole new educational framework grounded in a philosophy of friendship may sound like a menacingly radical idea. Yet, given the links between friendship and mutual trust, delineated in Section 5.3—not to mention the flow-like qualities, conducive to positive learning outcomes (Csikszentmihalyi, 1990) supervening upon the actualisation of true friendship—the idea of turning the classroom into a community of character friendships may be less radical and far-fetched than it appears at first sight.

There is a further complication here, however, that Aristotle would have been wise to pay heed to. Given that the *raison d'être* of character friendship is supposed to be mutual character education, and given how interested Aristotle is in unequal but 'complete' character friendships between mentors and mentees, it is again odd that he does not consider the possibility that those friendships can get out of hand. To be sure, Aristotle's times and today's Me-Too times diverge in many ways, socially and legally; yet the possibility of inappropriate erotic relations between teachers and students, perverting the nature of the educational process, surely should not have been alien to the ancient mindset. Indeed, it is arguably already a theme in Plato's *Symposium*. One way to foreclose those relations as much as possible is to avoid teachers and students becoming character friends in the first place (e.g. by characterising such friendships as ethically untenable) and trying to keep the educational relationship at as impartial and emotionally neutral a level as possible through some sort of professional detachment. Although this is a goal that many contemporary professors and teachers ascribe to in principle, as noted above, it is in many ways inimical to the very ideal of an educational relationship, at least when understood along broadly Aristotelian lines, that close friendships cannot be formed between mentors and mentees—and, in practice, such friendships are often formed for reasons that seem perfectly respectable (Shuffelton, 2012; Weithman, 2015).

A recent special issue of the *Journal of Philosophy of Education* (vol. 53, 3, 2019) sheds an interesting light on the question of eros in education by pointing out how the potential problem of the strong bond between teachers and students being disrupted through erotic attraction is further compounded by the intimacy of the educational impulse itself. At least on a Platonic understanding, what drives the quest for knowledge is a specifically intimate kind of intellectual love of the previously unknown, often aroused in the student by a specific teacher through a 'courtship of sensibility' (Hogan, 2010, p. 57). However, when this intimate desire for knowledge of the previously unknown becomes intermingled with the psychological intimacy of friendship *and* the potentially inhibited desire for physical intimacy between the teacher and the student, this can become a lethal blend, leading to pedagogical excesses (Aldridge, 2019; Williams, 2019).

Hooks (1996, p. 50) argues that pedagogical passion 'is likely to spark erotic energy. It cannot be policed or outlawed'. However, 'the erotic energy can be used in constructive ways both in individual relationships and in the classroom setting'. This short quotation from Hooks would merit a book-length study in itself. It may well be that the energy Hooks is referring to cannot be policed or outlawed in the strict sense; yet it does not mean that teachers and students cannot learn to 'respect boundaries', as Williams (2019) puts it. That said, the educational process, at its most passionate, flow-like and intrinsically motivated, is in many ways disruptive and subversive by its very nature. This process is precisely about violating boundaries and experiencing or grasping something radically new. Can one aspect of it be tamed while others are allowed to run amok? This is a question that is at once ethical, psychological and educational: hence, right up Aristotle's street. It is a great loss to the historical literature on eros, friendship and education that Aristotle chose not to pay attention to it.

8.4 Friendships within the Family

Aristotle discusses friendships within families in some detail (1985, pp. 229–32 [1161b11–1162a33]): between parents and children, husbands and wives and siblings. I will offer a few comments about the first of those two sorts of friendship below because they are relevant to many of the topics that have occupied previous chapters.

When Aristotle talks about friendship (*philia*) within the family, the direction of argument and illustration is at once striking and surprising. He does not argue, as one might perhaps have expected, that character friendships can, in their most advanced forms, aspire to the same levels of intimacy and love as, say, the love between parents and children, but rather he argues the other way round: that in the best of family affections, those can aspire to emulating or representing character friendships. This is one more indication of the high premium that Aristotle places on character friendships as the deepest and most enduring affectionate bonds that one can imagine between human beings.

Aristotle takes the example of parent–child associations as a paradigmatic case of unequal friendships, and he is clearly referring to character friendships there because he says that this sort of friendship 'also' includes pleasure and utility (1985, p. 231 [1162a4–9]). A 'parent is fond of his children because he regards them as part of himself; and children are fond of a parent because they regard themselves as coming from him'. Furthermore, a parent 'loves his children as [he loves] himself [...] Children love a parent because they regard themselves as coming from him' (1985, p. 230 [1161b16–29]). Despite this textual evidence, the standard view is that Aristotle did not consider children capable of character friendship. The apparently clear references to parent–child friendships ('being fond of' and 'loving' are renderings of *philia* and its grammatical derivatives) are then typically written off on grounds of the fact that the word *philia* in ancient Greek could also cover parental love.

I provided some Aristotle-derived argument in Chapter 5.2 to challenge the view that friendships between parents and children must be excluded for moral developmental reasons. At all events, no good reasons emerged there for ruling out such friendships. Since not even Aristotle's strict criteria seemed to exclude them, it is difficult to imagine what else in the area of moral development would. Children will, on a plausible Aristotelian account, not benefit from friendship with their parents by simply replicating the parental virtues, but rather by critically enlarging their knowledge of life's options and gradually shaping their own evaluative outlooks. Similarly, parents will reshape and reinvigorate their evaluative outlooks by attending to the guilelessness and sincerity of their children. To the extent that the benefits of this collaboration enter the texture of conduct and thought of *both* parties—the parents and their children—character friendship between them has, arguably, been instantiated and actualised.

We are not out of the woods yet, however, for although standard moral developmental concerns may leave the possibility of parent–child friendships intact, there are other potential barriers in the way. In a much-cited article, Joseph Kupfer (1990) argues that parents and their children are incapable of mutual friendships for various psycho-structural and socio-structural reasons, even after the children have reached adulthood. Although Kupfer's article is not couched in the poststructuralist language of ubiquitous power relations, readers versed in that language may detect hints of Nietzschean or Foucauldian themes in his argument.

Kupfer offers a whole smorgasbord of arguments, large and small, to bolster his case, and I have previously tried to rebut them specifically one by one (Kristjánsson, 2007, chap. 8). Since this discussion is highly relevant for the present section and indeed for my overall argument, I will rehearse some of my old writings below. However, rather than delving into every argument individually, as I did before, I aim for more of a general synthesis here of, and a response to, Kupfer's critical stance.

It is one thing to argue that children lack moral developmental maturity to form friendships with parents. Kupfer does not aim to do so. His arguments take us rather, as already noted, into the structural psychology and sociology of close human relationships. He partly assumes and partly argues for a certain conception of human selfhood—its nature and genealogy—that makes it unamenable to parent–child friendships. Part of the delight in friendship, Kupfer says, turns upon the way in which two people discover each other and gradually get to know each other as distinct individuals. However, the relationship between parents and their children cannot progress in this way because their lives have already been entwined since the child's beginning. Hence, they will never be able to encounter and discover each other as beings with independent histories: as true 'others'. The parents are too 'naturally familiar' to the child, and vice versa, for them to become friends (1990, pp. 20–1).

To rephrase this *psycho-structural* argument in the language of selfhood, friends have distinct selves at the beginning. When they meet and start to get to know each other, one of the delights—if they happen to be kindred spirits—is to familiarise oneself with the selfhood of the other and gradually to become entwined in it. If one buys into Aristotle's 'another-self' metaphor, one can even accept the notion that the distinction between the selves of friends gradually becomes obliterated, psychologically, morally and epistemologically (if not strictly speaking ontologically or biologically). However, this developmental process cannot take place in the case of parents and children because their selves have been intertwined from the outset. The parents see the child as an extension of their own selves and the children see themselves, originally at least, as an outgrowth of their parents' selves, even viewing themselves and the outside world through the eyes of the parents.

One way to respond to this developmental story about a trajectory from independence of selfhood to interdependence in the case of friends (as opposed to parents and children) would be to try to rebut the whole interdependent-selves developmental thesis. However, the natural Aristotelian response is exactly the opposite one: namely, to bite the bullet and deny that anyone has a fully independent self *vis-à-vis* friends in the first place. The first thing to note here is that, as I have explained before, although Aristotle believed that selfhood is objectively identifiable and not reducible to mere self-concept, he also subscribed to the 'soft realist' credo that self-concept forms part of actual underlying selfhood. Aristotle thus considered it of paramount interest, for instance in terms of potential character growth, that our views about who we are correspond to who we really are 'deep down'. However, he realised that we are lacking in self-transparency (as we possess no fully independent self-mirror) and need someone who knows us well to correct our self-conceptions. So the epistemological implication to be drawn from Aristotle's self-theory is, as we have seen before, that character friends are invaluable for self-knowledge in the sense that they (often) know us better than we do ourselves. In this sense, Aristotle's 'another-self' metaphor is not about two fully independent selves who happen to meet and gradually become interdependent. It is about my own self being incomplete and inaccessible to introspection until I interlock it with that of a character friend.

The bottom line here is that, according to the Aristotelian conception, there is no human self that is formed and sustained independent of the selves of others and that exists prior to all its contingent ends. Our lives as human beings are, by necessity, intertwined and shackled with the heavy chains of social and psycho-logical interdependence, not only at the beginning but throughout our lives. Therefore, if we accept that my self-concept requires me to seek recognition and self-information from others, and my social existence and social relations are essential rather than contingent parts of my selfhood, it is unreasonable to insist that because someone else has helped shape my self-concept from the outset, I cannot be a friend of that person.

The Aristotelian response to Kupfer's psycho-structural argument is then basically this: you are right in that the psychological structure of the child's self is dependent upon his or her parental relationships. But, far from signalling a departure from the relationship with a friend, this is exactly what characterises (complete) friendships also. And because there is no essential difference between these two kinds of relationships in terms of self-knowledge or self-constitution, there are no good psycho-structural reasons to conclude that a parent cannot also be a friend.

The second main strand of Kupfer's argument relates to *socio-structural* bar-riers that have to do with unequal power relations. While the underlying idea very much mirrors the one motivating the psycho-structural argument, the focus here turns from independent versus interdependent selves or selfhoods to unequal capacities for autonomous decision making *vis-à-vis* the other party. According to Kupfer's unequal-autonomy argument, friendship requires that the parties enjoy equal autonomy; otherwise unequal influence and power will lead to unequal dependency and to one party's disproportionate reliance on the other. Because children are less autonomous than parents in their relationship, then (that is, according to Kupfer's understanding of autonomy, less self-determining, less able to choose for themselves on the basis of their own values) such a rela-tionship cannot constitute friendship. Kupfer seeks indirect support in a parallel thesis, which he ascribes to Aristotle, about the need for equal virtue in friend-ships: 'Only if the friends are equally virtuous will they mutually strive for the other's good for his own sake' (1990, p. 16). Recall from previous chapters, how-ever, that although Aristotle thinks friendship is ideally a relationship between persons of equal virtue, he does not exclude relationships based on superiority from the category of friendship. Quite the contrary, Aristotle states explicitly that within each of the three types of friendship are some that rest on equality and others on superiority: 'For equally good people can be friends, but also a better and worse person; and the same is true of friends for pleasure or utility' (1985, pp. 232–3 [1162a34–b4]).

We must avoid an *argumentum ad verecundiam* here, however. Aristotle might simply be wrong about the possibility of friendship between unequal parties, and, after all, Kupfer concentrates on the problem of unequal autonomy rather than that of unequal virtue, which could be a different and less surmountable problem. Aristotle aside, Kupfer can nevertheless be criticised for proposing too restrictive a conception of friendship. If friendship is possible only between persons of equal autonomy (in Kupfer's sense), then various relationships that seem to constitute standard examples of friendship, such as the relationship between a mentor and mentee, are excluded from the reckoning. Kupfer's deliberations about the impossibility of the parent–child relationship ever growing fully out of the social dependency relationship that characterises its beginnings seem equally applicable to the mentor–mentee relationship. However enlightened mentees eventually become—one would have to argue by analogy—they may never able to interact with their old mentors on a completely equal footing. Yet—and here is the rub—it would be counter-intuitive to suppose that mentors and their mentees cannot be friends.

Both the psycho-structural and socio-structural arguments may seem to be built upon a *deficit model* of parent–child relationships: namely, about inadequacies that bar them from making the grade as friendships. However, I deem both to fall short of being persuasive.

Another way to explore parent-child relationships is through the concept of flourishing (*eudaimonia*). That concept, grounded in Aristotelian or quasi-Aristotelian assumptions, has recently become the hottest ticket in town in educational theory (Kristjánsson, 2020). According to Aristotle, having good friends is an indispensable constituent of a flourishing life—but so is having good parents and good children (Wolbert, de Ruyter & Schinkel, 2018). The question is whether these essential goods are somehow related or not. Although I have tried to rebut moral developmental, psycho-structural and socio-structural arguments that speak against the possibility of parents and their children being friends, I do not claim to have come up with a definitive answer to that relatedness question. There may still be a sneaking intuition lurking in the background that something in the nature of parent–child relationships, however crucial for flourishing, debars them from passing muster as true friendships.

Parenting is obviously an educational enterprise, so a question which may suggest itself is whether the 'sneaking intuition' has something to do with contrasting educational affordances and challenges related to friendship, on the one hand, and parenting, on the other. Perhaps learning to hone one's character through interactions with parents follows a different psycho-moral trajectory from learning the same through interactions with friends. However, even if that were the case, we would not be compelled to provide a negative answer to the question of whether parents and children can be friends. The same persons can wear different hats at the same time and occupy distinct roles. So for a parent to count as a friend also it is not necessary that the former role be reducible to the latter. There could be special parental obligations and bonds that go beyond even the closest of friendships; yet the parent could also at the same time assume the responsibilities of a friend and act as one.

There is nothing more common in everyday life than hearing people refer to a parent as their best friend. Now, ordinary language may sometimes need to be departed from for the sake of conceptual clarity and economy. However, such departures must be well motivated. In this section, no compelling reasons for a departure from the common-sense idea of parents as potential friends of their children have emerged. Indeed, I think Aristotle would most likely have endorsed the observation made by one of Gabriel Garcia Marquez's characters that 'one does not love one's children just because they are one's children but because of the friendship formed while raising them' (1988, p. 211).

I skirted the issue of character friendships between husbands and wives in Chapter 2 for reasons of space, simply citing Aristotle's point that such friend-ships, while characterised by inequality, are natural and possible, as long as both parties are 'decent'; for each 'has a proper virtue' (1985, p. 232 [1162a25–6]). In Section 2.4, I noted how both Plato and Aristotle rejected what I called there Assumption (2), that the best partnership/marriage is between a couple who are both character friends and erotic lovers. I explained how this rejection was motiv-ated by Plato's unfortunate sublimation and elevation of eros, on the one hand, and Aristotle's equally unfortunate deprioritisation of it, on the other. But even if the ancients had been right and the ideals of friendship and erotic love were somehow incommensurable, incommensurability does not imply incompatibility. As Klaasen has argued with respect to those two ideals, while 'we cannot square a circle, because squares and circles are incommensurable, we can inscribe a circle within a square, or a square within a circle' (2004, p. 414).

Going beyond Aristotle, there are many reasons, in my own view, which would make it plausible to argue that a stable marriage provides the ideal soil in which true character friendship can grow (cf. Friedman, 2021). Marriage forms a trad-itional institution with many inbuilt buffers against the problems identified in Chapter 2. It presents a form of life with levels of intimacy and the existence of common tasks (such as child-rearing and mutual financial provision) that seem to offer unprecedented opportunities for mutual self-affirmations and for avoid-ing problems of paternalism, divergent developmental paths, and so forth. Yet the fact that so many apparently stable marriages eventually break down may, by parity of reasoning, offer a testament to the fragility of character friendships.

We humans are weak-willed beings, constantly facing moral and developmental challenges that do not always admit of any happy denouement.

Voltaire says in his *Philosophical Dictionary* that friendship 'is the marriage of the soul; and this marriage is subject to divorce' (cited in Grayling, 2013, p. 102). Now, I hesitate to make the strong claim for marriage that I did for character friendships that its *raison d'être* is mutual character education. Obviously, marriage has many other salient functions: procreative, socio-political, legal, etc. Nonetheless, experience tells me that the reason why marriages break down often has to do with the exhaustion of educational resources: namely, the couple feel they have nothing more to learn from one another. In that sense, one could say that divorce is but the formal external recognition of the rupture of a character friendship. In other words, once Voltaire's 'marriage of the soul' loses its rationale, the ideal bond that Aristotle describes between a husband and wife as character friends goes into decline, and then a formal rupture is likely to follow in its wake—although many people stay married for pragmatic reasons beyond the gradual dissolution of the relevant soulmateship.

Speaking of divorce, Hursthouse's (2007) short but punchy piece about 'women who love too much' has always intrigued me. One of the puzzles she addresses in this paper is why women commonly find it incomprehensible how men can appear to love them so much non-instrumentally but then just decide to leave them one day, often for another woman. She tries to explain to them how 'did (lots and lots) of things for my sake' and 'loved me for myself alone' do not always go together (2007, p. 333). It was not until I had written Chapter 6 that I realised how the distinction I made there between instrumental and extrinsic valuing can help us reformulate Hursthouse's explanation in even more felicitous terms. It is possible to love a partner non-instrumentally, and see her as non-fungible, but without seeing her as intrinsically valuable in the sense of being completely non-expendable. Just as this distinction helps make sense of higher level, character-friendship-like utility friendships, it helps make sense of what happens in many marriages and partnerships that ultimately break down because, though neither party instrumentalised the other while it lasted, the love had not advanced from the extrinsic to the fully intrinsic state that typifies the most mature and long-lasting character friendships.

8.5 Future Research Directions

In the concluding chapter of the 2017 OUP volume on the *Psychology of Friendship*, Perlman helpfully draws together from the previous chapters and his own reflections some recommendations for future research. Those recommendations have a lot to recommend them. Among the topics that Perlman mentions are the examination of more diverse populations (given that women and psychology students tend to be over-represented in studied cohorts); a closer look at technology-aided friendships; more causal as distinct from correlational studies of how friendship is associated with psycho-social and health-related variables; more carefully scrutinised friendship interventions; more qualitative research; and more research on mentors as friends (2017, p. 293).

I would second all those items, and in particular his suggestion that more *interdisciplinary research* be conducted. As I hope to have demonstrated in previous chapters, philosophy and the social sciences, when properly integrated, draw symbiosis from one another. A study of friendship without input from psychology risks obscurity and triviality; a study of friendship without input from philosophy risks conceptual bloating and barrenness. Good fences do not always make good neighbours. However, Perlman obviously wrote his recommendations from the perspective of psychology. There is ample work for philosophers to do themselves also, or in collaboration with psychologists. Here are just a few scattered suggestions (in no particular order) that came to my mind over the course of writing this book, especially when ruing the various lacunae that I encountered in the theoretical literature:

- A closer conceptual analysis of civic friendship and how it is connected to the other Aristotelian types. Also a study of the potential political relevance of civic friendships in today's, increasingly fragmented, liberal democracies.
- Explorations of friendship in non-Western traditions, for example Confucianism, and how it relates to Aristotelian friendship (cf. Yuanguo, 2007; Yu, 2007).
- Closer studies of friendship as depicted in literature, films and painting. What exactly can those sources tell us beyond lessons from philosophical and social scientific research?
- Research on the effects of current and emergent technologies on friendship (see e.g. a list of challenges in Curzer, 2018)—including explorations of potential friendships with robots (Danaher, 2019).
- Research, in collaboration with psychologists, following up on Anderson and Fowers's (2020) study of the differential empirical correlates of Aristotle's three friendship types.
- More research into the developmental trajectory of character friendships, from childhood into old age, and how it relates or fails to relate to Aristotelian developmental theory. Particular attention needs to be paid here to the initial developmental pathways of friendship in early childhood (e.g. as depicted in Adams & Quinones's 2020 book).
- Research, from the perspective of educational philosophy, on the educative role of classroom friendships and how those can be stimulated, directly or indirectly (building on Healy 2011; 2015; 2017ab), with a special emphasis on online friendships among young people (Harrison, 2021; Healy, 2021).

- More work also needs to be done on friendships among academics and how those have been affected by recent managerial reconceptualisations of the very idea of a university (Enslin & Hedge, 2019; Clack, 2020). It would be particularly intriguing to study the effects that the 2020–2022 pandemic has had on research collaborations across borders: collaborations that are often motivated by or lead to close academic friendships. (A spoiler: this effect may not always have been negative, see Metcalfe & Blanco, 2021.)
- Research into the contribution of friendship to the development of *phronesis*. Would it be likely, for example, as a student has suggested to me, that friendship is most useful in cultivating the emotion-regulation component of *phronesis*, while role-modelling is more conducive to the development of the blueprint component (recall Chapter 3)? And then what about the moral sensitivity and moral adjudication components? Research of this kind is becoming even more relevant now that wisdom research in psychology has taken a distinct, if somewhat unexpected, turn towards a reunion with *phronesis* research (Grossmann et al., 2020; Kristjánsson et al., 2021; Darnell et al., 2022).
- Research, along with social scientists and possibly neuroscientists, into how people actually prioritise friendship in relation to other values and virtues, and how *phronesis* is applied to adjudicate value conflicts involving friendship.
- Studies of real-life friendship terminations and how those exemplify (or add further items to the list of) the reasons delineated in Chapter 2.

I could have made this list much longer. It shows that there is no shortage of future work in this area for dedicated philosophers and theoretically minded educationists. There are PhDs waiting to be researched and more monographs waiting to be written…

I always find it difficult to end books. In a way, it is like leaving a friend, not so much in the sense of dissolving the friendship—because the book, just as the friend, can be revisited and the relationship rejuvenated—but rather in the sense of saying goodbye to a friend who is leaving for some far-away place. I hope I have not conveyed the impression that friendships are ticking time bombs. At best, they 'fling wide the doors of existence' (Lunsford, 2017, p. 141, citing Emerson) and open up vistas that would otherwise be hidden to us. However, they are very complex relationships with both sunny and shadowy sides.

'Friendship is something that won't be boxed. It wriggles' (Barnard, 2011, p. 55). Aristotle did his best to 'box' friendship conceptually into different types and he advanced the discourse considerably by doing so. However, when attempting to box character friendship as the complete type and to put an educational spin on it, he tried to control and contain a phenomenon that, like all education, has an inherent tendency to wriggle and get out of hand. It is not so much that Aristotle was wrong about the value of close friendships; indeed, I think his insights were *fundamentally right*. The best friendship is, as the title of this book indicates, *friendship for virtue*. It is rather that Aristotle underestimated the extent to which even potentially educationally rewarding friendships are fraught with risk and remain, for various reasons, liable to conflicts and disruptions.

References

Adams, M. & Quinones, G. (2020). *Collaborative pathways to friendship in early childhood: A cultural-historical perspective.* London: Routledge.

Afshordi, N. & Liberman, Z. (2021). Keeping friends in mind: Development of friendship concepts in early childhood. *Social Development, 30*(2), 331–42.

Ahedo, J. (2016). Educating in friendship based on Aristotle's ethics. Unpublished conference paper. Retrieved May 24, 2020, from https://www.philosophy-of-education.org/dotAsset/3e910fa5-16db-44b4-887c-bc40390c92dd.pdf

Aldridge, D. (2019). Education's love triangle. *Journal of Philosophy of Education, 53*(3), 531–46.

Allport, G. W. (1937). *Personality: A psychological interpretation.* New York: Holt.

Alpern, K. D. (1983). Aristotle on the friendships of utility and pleasure. *Journal of the History of Philosophy, 21*(3), 303–15.

Anderson, A. R. & Fowers, B. J. (2020). An exploratory study of friendship characteristics and their relations with hedonic and eudaimonic well-being. *Journal of Social and Personal Relationships, 37*(1), 260–80.

Andrew, K., Richards, R. & Fletcher, T. (2020). Learning to work together: Conceptualizing doctoral supervision as a critical friendship. *Sport, Education, and Society, 25*(1), 98–110.

Annas, J. (2011). *Intelligent virtue.* Oxford: Oxford University Press.

Anscombe, G. E. M. (1958). Modern moral philosophy. *Philosophy, 33*(1), 1–19.

Arendt, H. (1978). *The Jew as pariah: Jewish identity and politics in the modern age.* New York: Grove Press.

Aristotle (1915). *Magna moralia*, trans. St. George Stock. Oxford: Clarendon.

Aristotle (1935). *The Athenian constitution, The eudemian ethics, On virtues and vices*, trans. H. Rackham. London: William Heinemann.

Aristotle (1941). *Categories*, trans. E. M. Edghill. In R. McKeon (Ed.), *The basic works of Aristotle*. New York: Random House.

Aristotle (1985). *Nicomachean ethics*, trans. T. Irwin. Indianapolis: Hackett Publishing.

Aristotle. (2007). *On rhetoric*, trans. G. A. Kennedy. Oxford: Oxford University Press.

Arthur, J., Kristjánsson, K. & Vogler, C. (2021). Seeking the common good in education through a positive conception of social justice. *British Journal of Educational Studies, 69*(1), 101–17.

Asexuality Visibility and Education Network (2020). Welcome. Retrieved March 1, 2020, from https://www.asexuality.org/

Bacon, F. (1910–14). *Essays: Vol. 3.* Cambridge, MA: Harvard University Press.

Badhwar, Kapur N. (1987). Friends as ends in themselves. *Philosophy and Phenomenological Research, 48*(1), 1–23.

Badhwar, Kapur N. (1991). Why it is wrong to be always guided by the best: Consequentialism and friendship. *Ethics, 101*(3), 483–504.

Bagwell, C. L., Bender, S. E., Andreassi, C. L., Kinoshite, T. L., Montarello, S. A. & Muller, J. G. (2005). Friendship quality and perceived relationship changes predict psychosocial adjustment in early adulthood. *Journal of Social and Personal Relationships, 22*(2), 235–54.

Barnard, J. (2011). *The book of friendship.* London: Virago Press.

Baron, M. W. (1995). *Kantian ethics almost without apology*. Ithaca: Cornell University Press.

Beard, A. (2020). True friends at work. *Harvard Business Review* (July–August). Retrieved September 1, 2020, from https://hbr.org/2020/07/true-friends-at-work

Bernstein, M. (2007). Friends without favouritism. *Journal of Value Inquiry*, *41*(1), 59–76.

Blum, L. A. (1980). *Friendship, altruism and morality*. London: Routledge.

Bowker, A. (2004). Predicting friendship stability during adolescence. *Journal of Early Adolescence*, *23*(2), 85–112.

Bowker, A. (2011). Examining two types of best friendship dissolution during early adolescence. *Journal of Early Adolescence*, *31*(5), 656–70.

Brewer, T. (2005). Virtues we can share: Friendship and Aristotelian ethical theory. *Ethics*, *115*(4), 721–58.

Brienza, J. P., Kung, F. Y. H., Santos, H. C., Bobocel, D. R. & Grossmann, I. (2018). Wisdom, bias, and balance: Toward a process-sensitive measurement of wisdom-related cognition. *Journal of Personality and Social Psychology*, *115*(6), 1093–126.

Briggle, A. (2008). Real friends: How the internet can foster friendship. *Ethics and Information Technology*, *10*(1), 71–9.

Broad, J. (2009). Mary Astell on virtuous friendship. *Parergon: Journal of the Australian and New Zealand Association for Medieval and Early Modern Studies*, *26*(2), 65–86.

Brogaard-Clausen, S. & Robson, S. (2019). Friendship for wellbeing? Parents' and practitioners' positioning of young children's friendships in the evaluation of wellbeing factors. *International Journal of Early Years Education*, *27*(4), 345–59.

Brooks, D. (2015). *The road to character*. London: Allen Lane.

Bryan, K. S., Puckett, Y. N. & Newman, M. L. (2013). Peer relationships and health: From childhood through adulthood. In M. L. Newman et al. (Eds.), *Health and social relationships: The good, the bad, and the complicated* (pp. 167–88). Washington: APA.

Bukowski, W. M. & Sippola, L. K. (1996). Friendship and morality: (How) are they related? In W. M. Bukowski, A. F. Newcomb & W. W. Hartup (Eds.), *Cambridge studies in social and emotional development. The company they keep: Friendship in childhood and adolescence* (pp. 238–61). Cambridge: Cambridge University Press.

Bülow, W. & Felix, C. (2016). On friendship between online equals. *Philosophy and Technology*, *29*(1), 21–34.

Burnett, A. (Ed.) (2007). *The letters of A. E. Housman*. Oxford: Clarendon Press.

Burnyeat, M. F. (1980). Aristotle on learning to be good. In A. O. Rorty (Ed.), *Essays on Aristotle's ethics* (pp. 69–92). Berkeley: University of California Press.

Campodonico, A., Croce, M. & Vaccarezza, M. S. (2019). Moral exemplarism and character education: Guest editors' preface. *Journal of Moral Education*, *48*(3), 275–9.

Card, R. F. (2004). Consequentialism, teleology, and the new friendship critique. *Pacific Philosophical Quarterly*, *85*(2), 149–72.

Carnegie, D. (1936). *How to win friends and influence people*. New York: Simon and Schuster.

Carr, D. (2009). Virtue, mixed emotions and moral ambivalence. *Philosophy*, *84*(1), 31–46.

Cervantes, M. de (2020). *The history of Don Quixote*. Retrieved April 18, 2020, from http://www.gutenberg.org/files/996/996-h/996-h.htm

Cheng, E. (2019). Aristotelian realism: Political friendship and the problem of stability. *The Review of Politics*, *81*(4), 549–71.

Cicero (2018). *How to be a friend: An ancient guide to true friendship*, trans. P. Freeman. Princeton: Princeton University Press.

Clack, B. (2020). Wisdom, friendship and the practice of philosophy. *Angelaki*, *25*(1–2), 141–55.

Cocking, D. & Kennett, J. (1998). Friendship and the self. *Ethics*, *108*(3), 502–527.

Cocking, D. & Kennett, J. (2000). Friendship and moral danger. *Journal of Philosophy*, *97*(5), 278–96.

Cocking, D. & Matthews, S. (2000). Unreal friends. *Ethics and Information Technology*, *2*(4), 223–31).

Cocking, D. & Oakley, J. (1995). Indirect consequentialism, friendship, and the problem of alienation. *Ethics*, *106*(1), 86–111.

Collins, S. (2013). Duties to make friends. *Ethical Theory and Moral Practice*, *16*(5), 907–21.

Conee, E. (2001). Friendship and consequentialism. *Australasian Journal of Philosophy*, *79*(2), 161–79.

Cooper, J. M. (1977). Aristotle on the forms of friendship. *Review of Metaphysics*, *30*(4), 619–48.

Csikszentmihalyi, M. (1990). *Flow: The psychology of optimal experience*. New York: Harper Perennial.

Curren, R. (2000). *Aristotle on the necessity of public education*. Lanham: Rowman and Littlefield.

Curzer, H. J. (2005). How good people do bad things: Aristotle on the misdeeds of the virtuous. *Oxford Studies in Ancient Philosophy*, *28*(1): 233–56.

Curzer, H. J. (2012). *Aristotle and the virtues*. Oxford: Oxford University Press.

Curzer, H. J. (2017). Against idealisation in virtue ethics. In D. Carr, J. Arthur & K. Kristjánsson (Eds.), *Varieties of virtue ethics* (pp. 52–73). London: Palgrave-Macmillan.

Curzer, H. J. (2018). Yesterday's virtue ethicists meet tomorrow's high tech: A critical response to *Technology and the Virtues* by Shannon Vallor. *Philosophy and Technology*, *31*(2), 283–92.

Damon, W. & Colby, A. (2015). *The power of ideals: The real story of moral choice*. Oxford: Oxford University Press.

Danaher, J. (2019). The philosophical case for robot friendship. *Journal of Posthuman Studies*, *3*(1), 5–24.

Darnell, C., Gulliford, L., Kristjánsson, K. & Paris, P. (2019). *Phronesis* and the knowledge-action gap in moral psychology and moral education: A new synthesis? *Human Development*, *62*(3), 101–29.

Darnell, C., Fowers, B. & Kristjánsson, K. (2023). A multifunction approach to assessing Aristotelian *phronesis* (practical wisdom). *Personality and Individual Differences*, in press.

Davids, N. & Waghid, Y. (2020). *Teaching, friendship and humanity*. Singapore: Springer.

Demir, M. & Weitekamp, L. A. (2007). I am so happy cause today I found my friend: Friendship and personality as predictors of happiness. *Journal of Happiness Studies*, *8*(2), 181–211.

Department for Education (2019). *Relationships: Education, relationships and sex education (RSE) and health education*. London: Crown Publishers.

Deresiewicz, W. (2009). Faux friendship. *The Chronicle of Higher Education*. Retrieved September 5, 2019, from https://www.chronicle.com/article/Faux-Friendship/49308

Derrida, J. (1997). *The politics of friendship*. London: Verso.

Digeser, P. E. (2016). *Friendship reconsidered: What is means and how it matters to politics*. New York: Columbia University Press.

Dineen, K. (2019). Kant, emotion and autism: Towards an inclusive approach to character education. *Ethics and Education*, *14*(1), 1–14.

Dunne, J. (1993). *Back to the rough ground: 'Phronesis' and 'technē' in modern philosophy and in Aristotle*. Notre Dame: University of Notre Dame Press.

Elder, A. M. (2013). *Metaphysics of friendship*. Unpublished doctoral dissertation. University of Connecticut. Retrieved March 22, 2020, from https://opencommons.

uconn.edu/cgi/viewcontent.cgi?referer=https://www.google.com/&httpsredir=1&articl e=6478&context=dissertations

Elder, A. M. (2014). Excellent online friendships: An Aristotelian defense of social media. *Ethics and Information Technology*, 16(4), 287–97.

Elder, A. M. (2018). *Friendship, robots, and social media: False friends and second selves.* London: Routledge.

Emerson, R. W. (2020). Friendship. Retrieved April 7, 2020, from https://archive.vcu.edu/ english/engweb/transcendentalism/authors/emerson/essays/friendship.html

Enslin, P. & Hedge, N. (2019). Academic friendship in dark times. *Ethics and Education*, 14(4), 383–98.

Ephron, N. & Reiner, R. (1989). *When Harry met Sally*. Motion Picture. Hollywood: Castle Rock Entertainment.

Erdley, C. A. & Day, H. J. (2017). Friendship in childhood and adolescence. In M. Hojjat & A. Moyer (Eds.), *The psychology of friendship* (pp. 3–19). Oxford: Oxford University Press.

Flanagan, O. (1991). *Varieties of moral personality: Ethics and psychological realism.* Cambridge, MA: Harvard University Press.

Flanagan, O. (2017). *The geography of morals: Varieties of moral possibility.* Oxford: Oxford University Press.

Fowers, B. J. (2010). Instrumentalism and psychology: Beyond using and being used. *Theory & Psychology*, 20(1), 102–24.

Fowers, B. J. (2019). Is there a plausible moral psychology for civic friendship? In J. Arthur (Ed.) *Virtues in the public sphere* (pp. 79–91). London: Routledge.

Fowers, B. J. & Anderson, A. R. (2018). Aristotelian *philia*, contemporary friendship, and some resources for studying close relationships. In T. Harrison & D. I. Walker (Eds.), *The theory and practice of virtue education* (pp. 184–96). London: Routledge.

Fowers, B. J., Carroll, J. S., Leonhardt, N. D. & Cokelet, B. (2021). The emerging science of virtue. *Perspectives on Psychological Science*, 16(1), 118–47.

Friedman, M. (1993). *What are friends for? Feminist perspectives on moral relationships and moral theory.* Ithaca, N.Y.: Cornell University Press.

Friedman, R. Z. (2021). Friendship as a non-relative virtue. *Journal of Ethics and Social Philosophy*, 20(1), 30–45.

Fröding, B. & Peterson, M. (2012). Why virtual friendship is no genuine friendship. *Ethics and Information Technology*, 14(3), 201–7.

Gallie, W. B. (1955–1956). Essentially contestable concepts. *Proceedings of the Aristotelian Society*, 56, 167–98.

George, D., Adalikwu-Obisike, J., Boyko, J., Johnson, J. & Boscanin, A. (2014). Harry and Sally revisited: The influence of spirituality and education on sexual tension in cross-sex friendships in secular and Christian universities. *Journal of Research on Christian Education*, 23(1), 70–94.

Gergen, K. J. (1991). *The saturated self: Dilemmas of identity in contemporary life.* New York: Basic Books.

Gibbs, P. & Angelides, P. (2008). Understanding friendship between critical friends. *Improving Schools*, 11(3), 213–25.

Gottlieb, P. (2020). Aristotle on self-knowledge. In F. Leigh (Ed.), *Self-knowledge in ancient philosophy* (pp. 130–44). Oxford: Oxford University Press.

Grayling, A. C. (2013). *Friendship*. New Haven: Yale University Press.

Grossmann, I. (2017). Wisdom in context. *Perspectives on Psychological Science*, 12(2), 233–57.

Grossmann, I., Weststrate, N. M., Ardelt, M., Brienza, J. P., Dong, M., Ferrari, M., Fournier, M. A., Hu, C. S., Nusbaum, H. C. & Vervaeke, J. (2020). The science of wisdom in a polarized world: Knowns and unknowns. *Psychological Inquiry*, 31(2), 103–33.

Grunebaum, J. O. (2005). Fair-weather friendships. *Journal of Value Inquiry, 39*(2), 203–14.

Gulliford, L. & Roberts, R. C. (2018). Exploring the 'unity' of the virtues: The case of an allocentric quintet. *Theory and Psychology, 28*(2) 208–26.

Haidt, J. (2001). The emotional dog and its rational tail: A social intuitionist approach to moral judgment. *Psychological Review, 108*(4), 814–34.

Hardy, S. & Carlo, G. (2011). Moral identity. In S. Schwartz, K. Luyckx & V. Vignoles (Eds.), *Handbook of identity theory and research* (pp. 495–513). New York: Springer.

Harrison, T. (2021). *Thrive: Character, cyber-wisdom and how children can flourish online.* London: Robinson.

Harvey, D. (1991). *The condition of postmodernity: An enquiry into the origins of cultural change.* Oxford: Wiley-Blackwell.

Hávamál (2020). Retrieved April 18, 2020, from https://viskumal.tumblr.com/post/163054625762/h%C3%A1vam%C3%A1l-friends-and-friendship

Healy, M. (2011). Should we take the friendship of children seriously? *Journal of Moral Education, 40*(4), 441–56.

Healy, M. (2015). 'We are just not friends anymore': Self-knowledge and friendship endings. *Ethics and Education, 10*(2), 186–97.

Healy, M. (2017a). Should children have best friends? *Studies in Philosophy and Education, 36*(2), 183–95.

Healy, M. (2017b). After friendship. *Journal of Philosophy of Education, 51*(1), 161–76.

Healy, M. (2021). Keeping company: Educating for online friendship. *British Educational Research Journal, 47*(2), 484–99.

Heinrich, J., Heine, S. J. & Norenzayan, A. (2010). Most people are not WEIRD. *Nature, 466*, 29.

Heron, E. (2020). Friendship as method: Reflections on a new approach to understanding student experiences in higher education. *Journal of Further and Higher Education, 44*(3), 393–407.

Hitz, Z. (2011). Aristotle on self-knowledge and friendship. *Philosophers' Imprint, 11*(12), 1–28.

Hogan, P. (2010). *The new significance of learning: Imagination's heartwork.* London: Routledge.

Hojjat, M., Boon S. D. & Lozano, E. B. (2017). Transgression, forgiveness, and revenge in friendship. In M. Hojjat & A. Moyer (Eds.), *The psychology of friendship* (pp. 195–211). Oxford: Oxford University Press.

Holt-Lundstad, J. (2017). Friendship and health. In M. Hojjat & A. Moyer (Eds.), *The psychology of friendship* (pp. 233–48). Oxford: Oxford University Press.

Hooks, B. (1996). Passionate pedagogy; erotic student/faculty relationships. *Z Magazine*, March, 45–51.

Houston, J. (2020). Divinity, *noēsis*, and Aristotelian friendship. *Journal of Ancient Philosophy, 14*(1), 1–29.

Howard, C. (2019). Fitting love and reasons for loving. *Oxford Studies in Normative Ethics, 6*(1), 116–37.

Hoyos-Valdés, D. (2018). The notion of character friendship and the cultivation of virtue. *Journal for the Theory of Social Behaviour, 48*(1), 66–82.

Hursthouse, R. (1999). *On virtue ethics.* Oxford: Oxford University Press.

Hursthouse, R. (2007). Aristotle for women who love too much. *Ethics, 117*(1), 327–34.

Irrera, E. (2005). Between advantage and virtue: Aristotle's theory of political friendship. *History of Political Thought, 26*(4), 565–85.

Irwin, T. H. (1975). Aristotle on reason, desire, and virtue. *Journal of Philosophy, 72*(17), 567–78.

Irwin, T. H. (2010). The sense and reference of *kalon* in Aristotle. *Classical Philology*, *105*(4), 381–96.

Isserow, J. (2018). On having bad persons as friends. *Philosophical Studies, 175*(12), 3099–116.

Jacquette, D. (2001). Aristotle on the value of friendship as a motivation for morality. *Journal of Value Inquiry, 35*(3), 371–89.

Jarvie, S. (2019). 'O my friends, there is no friend'. Friendship and risking relational (im)possibilities in the classroom. *Review of Education, Pedagogy, and Cultural Studies, 41*(2), 115–38.

Jerome, L. & Kisby, B. (2019). *The rise of character education in Britain: Heroes, dragons and the myths of character.* London: Palgrave-Macmillan.

Jeske, D. (2019). *Friendship and social media: A philosophical exploration.* London: Routledge.

Jordan, K. & Kristjánsson, K. (2017). Sustainability, virtue ethics, and the virtue of harmony with nature. *Environmental Education Research, 23*(9), 1205–29.

Juričková, M. (2021). Frodo and Sam's relationship in the light of Aristotle's philia. *Journal of Tolkien Research, 12*(1). Retrieved May 20, 2021, from https://scholar.valpo.edu/cgi/viewcontent.cgi?article=1217&context=journaloftolkienresearch

Kakkori, L. & Huttunen, R. (2007). Aristotle and pedagogical ethics. *Paideusis, 16*(1) 17–28.

Kaliarnta, S. (2016). Using Aristotle's theory of friendship to classify online friendships: A critical counterview. *Ethics and Information Technology, 18*(2), 65–79.

Karches, K. (2019). Temperance, moral friendship, and smoking cessation. *Journal of Medicine and Philosophy, 44*(3), 299–313.

Kaspar, D. (2015). How we decide in moral situations. *Philosophy, 90*(1), 59–81.

Kierkegaard, S. (1991). You shall love your neighbour. In M. Pakaluk (Ed.), *Other selves: Philosophers on friendship* (pp. 233–47). Indianapolis: Hackett.

Kim, B. J.-H. (2021). Aristotle on friendship and the loveable. *Journal of the History of Philosophy, 59*(2), 221–45.

Kim, B. J.-H. (2022). Is Aristotelian friendship disinterested? Aristotle on loving the other for himself and wishing goods for the other's sake. *European Journal of Philosophy, 30*(1), 32–44.

King, A. R., Russell, T. D. & Veith, A. C. (2017). Friendship and mental health functioning. In M. Hojjat & A. Moyer (Eds.), *The psychology of friendship* (pp. 249–66). Oxford: Oxford University Press.

Klaasen J. (2004). Friends and lovers. *Journal of Social Philosophy, 35*(3): 413–19.

Koltonski, D. (2016). A good friend will help you move a body: Friendship and the problem of moral disagreement. *Philosophical Review, 125*(4), 473–507.

Konstan, D. (1997). *Friendship in the classical world.* Cambridge: Cambridge University Press.

Konstan, D. (2006). *The emotions of the ancient Greeks: Studies in Aristotle and classical literature.* Toronto: University of Toronto Press.

Kraut, R. (1989). *Aristotle on the human good.* Princeton: Princeton University Press.

Kraut, R. (2006). Doing without morality: Reflections on *Dein* in Aristotle's *Nicomachean Ethics. Oxford Studies in Ancient Philosophy, 30*(1), 159–200.

Kreft, N. (2019). Aristotle on friendship and being human. In G. Keil & N. Kreft (Eds.), *Aristotle's moral anthropology* (pp. 182–99). Cambridge: Cambridge University Press.

Kristjánsson, K. (1996). *Social freedom: The responsibility view.* Cambridge: Cambridge University Press.

Kristjánsson, K. (1998). Liberating moral traditions: Saga morality and Aristotle's *megalopsychia. Ethical Theory and Moral Practice, 1*(1), 397–422.

Kristjánsson, K. (2006). *Justice and desert-based emotions*. Aldershot: Ashgate/Routledge.

Kristjánsson, K. (2007). *Aristotle, emotions and education*. Aldershot: Ashgate/Routledge.

Kristjánsson, K. (2010). *The self and its emotions*. Cambridge: Cambridge University Press.

Kristjánsson, K. (2013). *Virtues and vices in positive psychology: A philosophical critique.* Cambridge: Cambridge University Press.

Kristjánsson, K. (2015). *Aristotelian character education*. London: Routledge.

Kristjánsson, K. (2018). *Virtuous emotions*. Oxford: Oxford University Press.

Kristjánsson, K. (2019). Is the virtue of integrity redundant in Aristotelian virtue ethics? *Apeiron, 53*(1), 93–115.

Kristjánsson, K. (2020). *Flourishing as the aim of education: A neo-Aristotelian view.* London: Routledge.

Kristjánsson, K., Darnell, C., Fowers, B., Moller, F., Pollard, D. & Thoma, S. (2020). *Phronesis: Developing a conception and an instrument.* Research Report. Birmingham: Jubilee Centre for Character and Virtues. Retrieved April 12, 2020, from https://www. jubileecentre.ac.uk//userfiles/jubileecentre/pdf/Research%20Reports/Phronesis_ Report.pdf

Kristjánsson, K., Fowers, B., Darnell, C. & Pollard, D. (2021). *Phronesis* (practical wisdom) as a type of contextual integrative thinking. *Review of General Psychology, 25*(3) 239–57.

Kristjánsson, K. (2022). Reason and intuition in Aristotle's moral psychology: Why he was not a two-system dualist. *Philosophical Explorations, 25*(1), 42–57.

Kupfer, J. (1990). Can parents and children be friends? *American Philosophical Quarterly, 27*(1), 15–26.

Lapsley, D. (2019). Phronesis, virtues and the developmental science of character, *Human Development, 62*(3), 130–41.

Lewis, C. S. (1960). *The four loves*. London: G. Bles.

Ludwig, P. W. (2020). *Rediscovering political friendship: Aristotle's theory and modern identity, community, and equality*. Cambridge: Cambridge University Press.

Lunsford, L. G. (2017). Mentors as friends. In M. Hojjat & A. Moyer (Eds.), *The psychology of friendship* (pp. 141–56). Oxford: Oxford University Press.

Lynch, S. (2005). *Philosophy and friendship*. Edinburgh: Edinburgh University Press.

Lyons, D. (1965). *Forms and limits of utilitarianism*. Oxford: Oxford University Press.

McAleer, S. (2015). Caught in *eutrapelia*: Kraut on Aristotle on wit. *Journal of Philosophical Research, 40*, 297–312.

McCoy, M. B. (2013). *Wounded heroes: Vulnerability as a virtue in ancient Greek literature and philosophy*. Oxford: Oxford University Press.

McFall, M. T. (2012). Real character-friends: Aristotelian friendship, living together, and technology. *Ethics and Information Technology, 14*(3) 221–30.

MacIntyre, A. (1981). *After virtue*. Notre Dame: University of Notre Dame Press.

Majors, K. (2012) Friendship: The power of positive alliance. In S. Roffey (Ed.), *Positive relationships: Evidence-based practice across the world* (pp. 127–44). Dordrecht: Springer.

Marquez, G. G. (1988). *Love in the time of cholera*. London: Jonathan Cape.

Martin, J. R. (1992). *The schoolhome: Rethinking schools for changing families*. Cambridge, MA: Harvard University Press.

Martínez-Priego, C. & Romero-Iribas, A. (2021). The emotions behind character friendship: From other-oriented emotions to the 'bonding feeling'. *Journal for the Theory of Social Behaviour, 51*(3), 468–88.

Meilaender, G. (1993). Men and women: Can we be friends? *First Things*. Retrieved March 1, 2020, from https://www.firstthings.com/article/1993/06/001-men-and-women-can-we-be-friends

Metcalfe, A. S. & Blanco, G. L. (2021). 'Love is calling': Academic friendship and international research collaboration amid a global pandemic. *Emotion, Space and Society*, *38*(1), 1–4.

Mill, J. S. (1998). *Utilitarianism*. Oxford: Oxford University Press.

Millgram, E. (1987). Aristotle on making other selves. *Canadian Journal of Philosophy*, *17*(2), 361–76.

Mitias, M. H. (2012). *Friendship: A central moral value*. Amsterdam: Rodopi.

Monsour, M. (2017). The hackneyed notions of adult 'same-sex' and 'opposite-sex' friendships. In M. Hojjat & A. Moyer (Eds.), *The psychology of friendship* (pp. 59–74). Oxford: Oxford University Press.

Montaigne, M. de (2015). Of friendship. Retrieved March 25, 2020 from https://toleratedindividuality.files.wordpress.com/2015/11/montaigne_essays.pdf

Moremen, R. D. (2008). Best friends: The role of confidantes in older women's health. *Journal of Women and Aging*, *20*(1–2), 149–67.

Morgan, B., Fowers, B. & Kristjánsson, K. (2017). Empathy and authenticity online. Research paper. Retrieved April 5, 2020, from https://www.jubileecentre.ac.uk/userfiles/jubileecentre/pdf/Research%20Reports/ParentsandMedia_EmpathyOnline.pdf

Morrison, R. L. & Cooper-Thomas, H. D. (2017). Friendship among coworkers. In M. Hojjat & A. Moyer (Eds.), *The psychology of friendship* (pp. 123–39). Oxford: Oxford University Press.

Müller, A. W. (2004). Aristotle's conception of ethical and natural virtue. In J. Szaif & M. Lutz-Bachmann (Eds.), *Was ist das für den Menschen Gute?/What is good for a human being?* (pp. 18–53). Berlin: De Gruyter.

Munn, N. J. (2012). The reality of friendship within immersive virtual worlds. *Ethics and Information Technology*, *14*(1), 1–10.

Murdoch, I. (2001). *The sovereignty of good*. London: Routledge.

Murstein, B. & Spitz, L. (1974). Aristotle and friendship: A factor analytic study. *Interpersonal Development*, *4*(1), 21–34.

Nehamas, A. (2016). *On friendship*. New York: Basic Books.

Nietzsche, F. (2020). Human, all too human. Retrieved April 7, 2020, from https://digital-assets.lib.berkeley.edu/main/b20790001_v_1_B000773557.pdf

Noddings, N. (1999). Two concepts of caring. In R. Curren (Ed.), *Philosophy of education 1999* (pp. 36–9). Urbana: Philosophy of Education Society.

Noddings, N. (2005). *Critical lessons: What our schools should teach*. Cambridge: Cambridge University Press.

Nussbaum, M. C. (1986). *The fragility of goodness: Luck and ethics in Greek tragedy and philosophy*. Cambridge: Cambridge University Press.

O'Connor, D. K. (1990). Two ideals of friendship. *History of Philosophy Quarterly*, *7*(2), 109–22.

O'Meara, J. D. (1989). Cross-sex friendship: Four basic challenges of an ignored relationship. *Sex Roles*, *21*(7/8), 525–43.

Oswald, D. L. (2017). Maintaining long-lasting friendships. In M. Hojjat & A. Moyer (Eds.), *The psychology of friendship* (pp. 267–82). Oxford: Oxford University Press.

Pangle, L. S. (2003). *Aristotle and the philosophy of friendship*. Cambridge: Cambridge University Press.

Paris, P. (2019). Moral beauty and education. *Journal of Moral Education*, *48*(4), 395–411.

Perlman, D. (2017). Conclusion. Friendship: An echo, a hurrah, and other reflections. In M. Hojjat & A. Moyer (Eds.), *The psychology of friendship* (pp. 283–300). Oxford: Oxford University Press.

Peterson, A. (2020). Character education, the individual and the political. *Journal of Moral Education*, 49(2), 143–57.

Peterson, C. & Seligman, M. E. P. (2004). *Character strengths and virtues: A handbook and classification*. Oxford: Oxford University Press.

Pettigrove, G. (2023). What virtue adds to value, *Australasian Philosophical Review*, in press.

Pinsent, A. (2023). Commentary on Glen Pettigrove's 'What virtue adds to value', *Australasian Philosophical Review*, in press.

Poulin, F. & Chan, A. (2010). Friendship stability and change in childhood and adolescence. *Developmental Review*, 30(3), 257–72.

Railton, P. (1984). Alienation, consequentialism, and the demands of morality. *Philosophy and Public Affairs*, 13(2), 134–71.

Railton, P. (2016). Intuitive guidance: Emotion, information and experience. In M. E. P. Seligman, P. Railton, R. F. Baumeister & C. Sripade (Eds.), *Homo prospectus* (pp. 33–85). Oxford: Oxford University Press.

Rawlins, W. K. (2008). *Friendship matters: Communication, dialectics, and the life course*. London: Aldine.

Reeder, H. M. (2000). 'I like you … as a friend': The role of attraction in cross-sex friendship. *Journal of Social and Personal Relationships*, 17(3), 329–48.

Reiner, P. (1991). Aristotle on personality and some implications for friendship. *Ancient Philosophy*, 11(1), 67–84.

Robertson, D. (2010). *The philosophy of cognitive-behavioural therapy (CBT): Stoic philosophy as rational and cognitive psychotherapy*. London: Karnac Books.

Romero-Iribas, A. & Smith, G. M. (2018). Friendship without reciprocation? Aristotle, Nietzsche, and Blanchot. *The Good Society*, 27(1–2), 1–28.

Rorty, A. O. (1993). The historicity of psychological attitudes: Love is not love which alters not when it alteration finds. In N. K. Badhwar (Ed.), *Friendship: A philosophical reader* (pp. 73–88). Ithaca, NY: Cornell University Press.

Ruehl, R. M. (2018). The value of friendship for education. *Philosophy Now*, 126(June/July), 14–17.

Salim, E. (2006). Embracing the half: Aristotle's revision of Platonic *erôs* and *philia*. Unpublished thesis, Texas A&M University. Retrieved March 1, 2020, from http://oaktrust.library.tamu.edu/bitstream/handle/1969.1/5775/etd-tamu-2006A-PHIL-Salim.pdf?sequence=1

Salkever, S. (2005). Aristotle's social science. In R. Kraut & S. Skultety (Eds.), *Aristotle's Politics: Critical essays* (pp. 27–64). Lanham: Rowman and Littlefield.

Salkever, S. (2008). Taking friendship seriously: Aristotle on the place(s) of *philia* in human life. In J. v. Heyking & R. Avramenko (Eds.), *Friendship and politics: Essays in political thought* (pp. 53–81). Notre Dame: University of Notre Dame Press.

Schaubert, V. (2019). My disabled son's amazing gaming life in the World of Warcraft. Retrieved September 5, 2019, from https://www.bbc.co.uk/news/disability-47064773

Schoeman, F. (1985). Aristotle on the good of friendship. *Australasian Journal of Philosophy*, 63(3), 269–82.

Schudder, J. R. & Bishop, A. H. (2001). *Beyond friendship and eros: Unrecognized relationships between men and women*. Albany: State University of New York Press.

Schuh, G. (2020). Friendship and Aristotle's defense of psychological eudaimonism. *Review of Metaphysics*, 73(4), 681–714.

Seligman, M. E. P. (2011). *Flourish: A visionary new understanding of happiness and well-being*. New York: Free Press.

Sharp, R. (2012). The obstacles against reaching the highest level of Aristotelian friendship online. *Ethics and Information Technology, 14*(3), 231–9.

Sherlock Cares Web (2020). Holmes and Watson: The adventure of the iconic relationship. Retrieved April 18, 2020, from http://sherlockcares.com/holmes-watson-adventure-iconic-relationship/

Sherman, N. (1987). Aristotle on friendship and the shared life. *Philosophy and Phenomenological Research, 47*(4), 589–613.

Sherman, N. (1989). *The fabric of character: Aristotle's theory of virtue.* Oxford: Oxford University Press.

Sherman, N. (2021). *Stoic wisdom: Ancient lessons for modern resilience.* Oxford: Oxford University Press.

Shuffelton, A. N. (2012). *Philia* and pedagogy 'side by side': The perils and promise of teacher–student friendships. *Ethics and Education, 7*(3), 211–23.

Slomp, G. (2019). As thick as thieves: Exploring Thomas Hobbes' critique of ancient friendship and its contemporary relevance. *Political Studies, 67*(1), 191–206.

Smetana, J., Jambon, M. & Ball, C. (2014). The social domain approach to children's moral and social judgments. In M. Killen & J. Smetana (Eds.), *Handbook of moral development* (pp. 23–45). New York: Psychology Press.

Smith, G. M. (2019). Friendship as a political concept: A groundwork for analysis. *Political Studies Review, 17*(1), 81–92.

Smith, M. E. & Smith, M. K. (2002). Friendship and informal education. *The encyclopedia of informal education.* Retrieved April 6, 2020, from http://infed.org/mobi/friendship-and-education/

Stangl, R. (2023). Commentary on Glen Pettigrove's 'What virtue adds to value', *Australasian Philosophical Review,* in press.

Stern-Gillet, S. (1995). *Aristotle's philosophy of friendship.* Albany: State University of New York Press.

Steutel, J. (1999). The virtues of will-power: Self-control and deliberation. In D. Carr & J. Steutel (Eds.), *Virtue ethics and moral education* (pp. 125–37). London: Routledge.

Stocker, M. (1976). The schizophrenia of modern ethical theories. *Journal of Philosophy, 73*(14), 453–66.

Stroud, S. (2006). Epistemic partiality in friendship. *Ethics, 116*(3), 498–524.

Stuart, R. (1914). Voltaire's correspondence with Catherine II. Unpublished thesis. Retrieved March 5, 2020, from https://ir.uiowa.edu/cgi/viewcontent.cgi?article=3904&context=etd

Suler, J. (2004). The online disinhibition effect. *Cyberpsychology & Behaviour, 7*(3), 321–6.

Swann, W. B., Jr. (1996). *Self-traps: The elusive quest for higher self-esteem.* New York: W. H. Freeman & Co.

Talisse, R. B. (2019). *Overdoing democracy: Why we must put politics in its place.* Oxford: Oxford University Press

Telfer, E. (1970–1971). Friendship. *Proceedings of the Aristotelian Society, 71,* 223–41.

Thomas, L. (1987). Friendship. *Synthese, 72*(198), 217–36.

Toner, J. (2003). *Love and friendship.* Milwaukee: Marquette University Press.

Trujillo, G. M. (2020). Friendship for the flawed. *Southwest Philosophy Review, 36*(1), 199–209.

Turp, M.-J. (2020). Social media, interpersonal relations and the objective attitude. *Ethics and Information Technology, 22*(3), 269–79.

Um, S. (2021a). What is a relational virtue? *Philosophical Studies, 178*(1), 95–111.

Um, S. (2021b). Solving the puzzle of partiality. *Journal of Social Philosophy, 52*(3), 362–76.

Vakirtzis, A. (2014). *Character friendship and moral development in Aristotle's ethics.* Unpublished PhD thesis, University of Birmingham. Retrieved September 22, 2020, from https://www.researchgate.net/publication/308611789_Character_Friendship_and_Moral_Development_in_Aristotle's_Ethics

Vallor, S. (2010). Social networking technology and the virtues. *Ethics and Information Technology, 12*(2), 157–70.

Vallor, S. (2012). Flourishing on Facebook: Virtue friendship and the new social media. *Ethics and Information Technology, 14*(3), 185–99.

Vallor, S. (2016). *Technology and the virtues: A philosophical guide to a future worth wanting.* Oxford: Oxford University Press.

Veltman, A. (2004). Aristotle and Kant on self-disclosure in friendship. *Journal of Value Inquiry, 38*(2), 225–39.

Verkerk, W. (2019). *Nietzsche and friendship.* London: Bloomsbury.

Vernon, M. (2010). *The meaning of friendship.* London: Palgrave-Macmillan.

Vernon, M. (2017). Pity poor Prince George—discouraged from having a best friend at school. *Guardian*, Sep. 8. Retrieved May 28, 2020, from https://www.theguardian.com/commentisfree/2017/sep/08/prince-george-school-best-friend

Vlastos, G. (1981). The individual and an object of love in Plato. In G. Fine (Ed.), *Platonic Studies* (pp. 3–42). Princeton: Princeton University Press.

Vos, P. H. (2018). Learning from exemplars: Emulation, character formation and the complexities of ordinary life. *Journal of Beliefs & Values, 39*(1), 17–28.

Wagner, L. (2019). Good character is what we look for in a friend: Character strengths are positively related to peer acceptance and friendship quality in early adolescents. *Journal of Early Adolescence, 39*(6), 864–903.

Walker, D. I., Curren, R. & Jones, C. (2016). Good friendships among children: A theoretical and empirical investigation. *Journal for the Theory of Social Behaviour, 46*(3), 286–309.

Weithman, P. (2015). Academic friendship. In H. Brighouse & M. McPherson (Eds.), *The aims of higher education: Problems of morality and justice* (pp. 52–73). Chicago, IL: University of Chicago Press.

Werking, K. (1997). *We're just good friends: Women and men in nonromantic relationships.* New York: Guilford Press.

White, P. (1990). Friendship and education. *Journal of Philosophy of Education, 24*(1), 81–91.

Whiting, J. E. (1991). Impersonal friends. *Monist, 74*(1), 3–29.

Whiting, J. E. (2006). The Nicomachean account of *philia*. In Richard Kraut (Ed.), *The Blackwell guide to Aristotle's Nicomachean ethics* (pp. 276–304). Oxford: Blackwell.

Williams, B. (1981). *Moral luck: Philosophical papers 1973–1980.* Cambridge: Cambridge University Press.

Williams, K. (2019). 'How can we know the dancer from the dance?' Personal concern and sexual desire in the educational relationship. *Journal of Philosophy of Education, 53*(3), 560–73.

Wojtyla, K. (Pope John Paul II) (2013). *Love and responsibility.* Boston, MA: Pauline Books and Media.

Wolbert, L. S., de Ruyter, D. J., & Schinkel, A. (2018). What attitudes should parents have towards their children's future flourishing? *Theory and Research in Education, 16*(1), 82–97.

Wolf, S. (2012). 'One thought too many': Love, morality, and the ordering of commitment. In U. Heuer & G. Lang (Eds.), *Luck, value, and commitment: Themes from the ethics of Bernard Williams* (pp. 71–92). Oxford: Oxford University Press.

Wolitzer, M. (2014). *The Interestings.* London: Vintage.

Woodcock, S. (2010). Moral schizophrenia and the paradox of friendship. *Utilitas, 22*(1), 1–25.

Wright, J., Warren, M. & Snow, N. (2021). *Understanding virtue: Theory and measurement.* Oxford: Oxford University Press.

Wrzus, C., Zimmermann, J., Mund, M. & Neyer, F. J. (2017). Friendship in young and middle adulthood. In M. Hojjat & A. Moyer (Eds.), *The psychology of friendship* (pp. 21–38). Oxford: Oxford University Press.

Yaugn, E. & Norwicki, S. (1999). Close relationships and complementary interpersonal styles among men and women. *Journal of Social Psychology, 139*(4), 473–8.

Yeste, C. G., Mar, J. Joanpere, Rios-Gonzalez, O. & Morla-Folch, T. (2020). Creative friendship and political diversity in Catalonia. *Journal of Social and Personal Relationships, 37*(7), 2035–52.

Yu, J. (2007). *The ethics of Confucius and Aristotle: Mirrors of virtue.* London: Routledge.

Yuanguo, H. E. (2007). Confucius and Aristotle on friendship: A comparative study. *Frontiers of Philosophy in China, 2*(2), 291–307.

Zagzebski, L. (2017). *Exemplarist moral theory.* Oxford: Oxford University Press.

Index

Note: Figures and tables are indicated by an italic '*f*' and '*t*' following the page numbers.

For the benefit of digital users, indexed terms that span two pages (e.g., 52–53) may, on occasion, appear on only one of those pages.